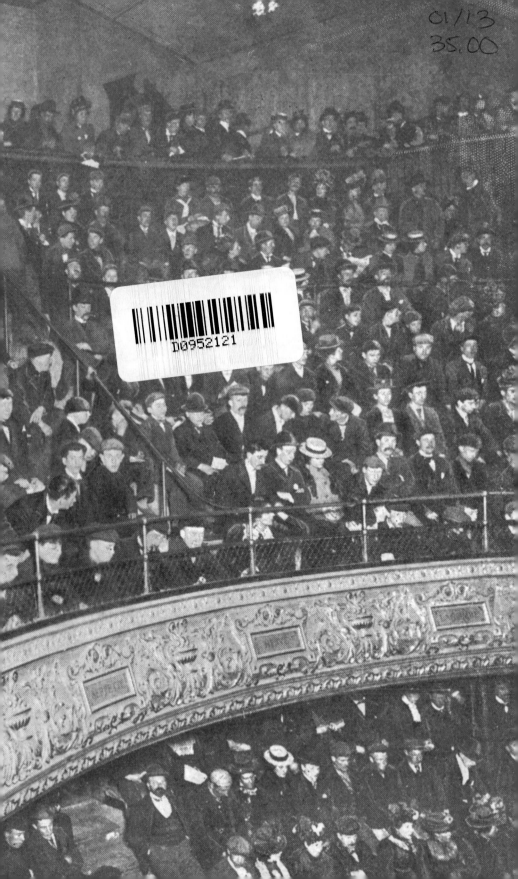

01/13
35.00

MY OLD MAN

MY
OLD MAN

*A Personal
History of Music Hall*

JOHN MAJOR

Harper
Press

HarperPress
An imprint of HarperCollins*Publishers*
77–85 Fulham Palace Road,
Hammersmith, London W6 8JB

www.harpercollins.co.uk

Published by HarperPress in 2012

1

Endpaper illustration: Mary Evans Picture Library

The author asserts the moral right to
be identified as the author of this work

A catalogue record for this book is
available from the British Library

ISBN 978-0-00-745013-8

Set in Minion with Janson and Castellar display
by G&M Designs Limited, Raunds, Northamptonshire
Printed and bound in Great Britain by
Clays Ltd, St Ives plc

MIX
Paper from
responsible sources
FSC
www.fsc.org   FSC® C007454

FSC™ is a non-profit international organisation established to promote
the responsible management of the world's forests. Products carrying the
FSC label are independently certified to assure consumers that they come
from forests that are managed to meet the social, economic and
ecological needs of present and future generations,
and other controlled sources.

Find out more about HarperCollins and the environment at
www.harpercollins.co.uk/green

In loving memory of Tom, Gwen and Kitty,
and of my brother Terry, whose ambition in life
was to see this book written

Contents

Illustrations

The rotunda at Ranelagh Gardens, by Canaletto, 1754. (*Getty Images/Leemage*)

The Old Drury, Brydges Street, London, c.1830. (*Getty Images*)

Evans' song and supper rooms (aka Joy's Hotel, aka Evans' Late Joy's) in the 1850s, by Gustav Doré. (*Museum of London*)

W.G. Ross achieved huge success with his 'Ballad of Sam Hall'. (*©The Trustees of the British Museum*)

Sheet music for 'The Ratcatcher's Daughter', composed and sung by early music hall star Sam Cowell. (*Victoria and Albert Museum, London*)

The Eagle in City Road, Shoreditch. It achieved immortality with its inclusion in the song 'Pop Goes the Weasel'. (*Victoria and Albert Museum, London*)

Wilton's Music Hall, opened in 1859. (*Image by Andrea Marchi, courtesy of Wilton's Music Hall*)

Charles Morton, 'the Father of the Halls'. (*Mary Evans Picture Library*)

The sumptuous interior of Morton's Canterbury Music Hall. (*Reproduced by permission of London Borough of Lambeth, Archives Department Ref.#10150*)

Ticket for the Canterbury, 1874. (*Victoria and Albert Museum, London*)

George Leybourne, a great favourite at the Canterbury. (*Victoria and Albert Museum, London*)

Acrobats often performed just above the heads of the audience. *(Getty Images)*

George Ware, one of the first music hall agents and Marie Lloyd's long-time mentor, friend and manager. *(Mary Evans Picture Library)*

Jenny Hill, one of the earliest and greatest 'serio-comediennes'. *(Victoria and Albert Museum, London)*

Gus Elen, one of the most popular 'coster' comedians. *(Mary Evans Picture Library)*

Sheet music for Elen's 'The Coster's Mansion'. *(Victoria and Albert Museum, London)*

The Great Farini, acrobat and tightrope walker, with his adopted son Sam Westgate, who performed as 'El Nino' Farini. *(Victoria and Albert Museum, London)*

Vesta Tilley, the best-known and best-loved of music hall's male impersonators. *(Mary Evans Picture Library)*

Bessie Bellwood could hold her own with the toughest of audiences. *(Victoria and Albert Museum, London)*

Lottie Collins made her name with 'Ta-ra-ra Boom-de-ay' and its catchy chorus. *(Getty Images)*

Dan Leno as the pantomime dame in *Mother Goose* at Drury Lane in 1902. *(Mary Evans Picture Library)*

Sheet music for Leno's 'The Grass Widower'. *(Victoria and Albert Museum, London)*

Little Tich in his famous big boots. *(Mary Evans Picture Library)*

Marie Lloyd, the unchallenged 'Queen of the Halls'. *(Getty Images)*

George Robey, 'the Prime Minister of Mirth'. *(Mary Evans Picture Library)*

Harry Lauder, the archetypal professional Scot. *(Getty Images)*

Tom and Kitty Major in an undated photograph, probably taken before the First World War. *(Author's collection)*

Tom and Kitty top the bill at the Leeds City Varieties in 1915. *(Author's collection)*

Tom in character, with a cast member from one of his shows. *(Author's collection)*

Tom and Kitty, c.1915–16, in a promotional photograph for the sketch 'After the Overture'. *(Author's collection)*

Tom, Kitty and the cast of his revue *Special Edition* in the 1920s. *(Author's collection)*

Tom – probably in his mid-forties – enjoying an anecdote. *(Author's collection)*

Black-face minstrel Eugene Stratton. *(Victoria and Albert Museum, London)*

Sheet music for Stratton's 'Little Dolly Daydream'. *(Victoria and Albert Museum, London)*

G.H. Chirgwin, the multi-instrumentalist black-face comedian, in typically eccentric stage attire. *(Victoria and Albert Museum, London)*

Vesta Victoria built a very successful career out of playing the superficially innocent girl next door. *(Getty Images)*

Sheet music for Victoria's 'Daddy Wouldn't Buy Me a Bow-Wow', a big hit for her on both sides of the Atlantic. *(Mary Evans Picture Library)*

1893 programme for the Oxford Music Hall. *(Mary Evans Picture Library)*

Sheet music for 'Daisy Bell', made famous by Katie Lawrence. *(Mary Evans Picture Library)*

Oswald Stoll, impresario and co-founder of the Stoll Moss theatre empire. *(Mary Evans Picture Library)*

Noctes Ambrosianae by Walter Sickert. © Estate of Walter R. Sickert. *(All rights reserved, DACS 2012. Nottingham City Museums and Galleries/The Bridgeman Art Library)*

Sickert's controversial *Katie Lawrence, Gatti's Hungerford Palace of Varieties* (1903). © Estate of Walter R. Sickert. *(All rights reserved, DACS 2012. Art Gallery of New South Wales, Sydney, Australia/Watson Bequest Fund 1946/The Bridgeman Art Library)*

A leaflet from the 'music hall war' of 1907, which pitted
   performers against owners and managers. *(Victoria and Albert
   Museum, London)*
Sheet music for Florrie Forde's 'Oh Flo! Did You But Know!'
   (Victoria and Albert Museum, London)
'Mr Memory' in Alfred Hitchcock's 1935 film *The Thirty-Nine
   Steps*. The character was based on the music hall artiste John
   Bottle, otherwise known as 'Datas'. *(ITV Global/THE KOBAL
   COLLECTION)*
Leeds City Varieties, originally Thornton's Music Hall, from which
   the BBC televised *The Good Old Days* for thirty-two years from
   1953. *(Tony O'Connell, Courtesy of Leeds City Varieties)*

Author's Note

This book is the story of music hall. It is not a full history, which – even if it could be written – would fill many volumes.

For me, it has been a labour of love, although on occasion rather frustrating: Victorian music hall was often chaotic. The source material that exists – and much is now lost – is elusive, and often contradictory.

Wherever there is uncertainty, I have made a judgement based on what I regard as the most reliable sources, although I am aware that some may disagree with my assumptions.

Whatever debates there may be over dates, places and the names of theatres, none affect the overall direction of the story itself, and it is the telling of that story that has been my overall priority.

Acknowledgements

This book has been written in the margins of many conflicting priorities, and would not have been finished without the significant help and advice I have received from many quarters. My thanks are heartfelt and widespread.

Music hall is a huge subject, and as word spread that I was writing on it, many unexpected gems came to light. Mark Jones wrote from Malta, with welcome tales of my father on tour; and Mrs Hilda Sayers, with first-hand reports of my father's professional partner and first wife, Kitty. Bryan Forbes provided some hugely helpful literature; John Goulstone provided useful census records; and encouragement and other material came from Sir Brian Harrison. I received many letters – far too numerous to mention – that were both illuminating and entertaining. The contents of some of them were fascinating, but went far beyond the scope of this book. The canon of music hall books is vast, and many of them helped point to original reviews, putting flesh on the lives of artistes long gone and – in too many instances – long forgotten. I owe a particular debt to Stuart Turner, who was enormously generous in his loan of many rare and otherwise unavailable books, together with various items of family memorabilia, all of which proved invaluable.

The staff of the Reading Room – and most especially in Rare Books and Music – at the British Library were consistently helpful throughout this entire project; and the newspaper archive at

Colindale, although buried in microfiche records, reopened the past as seen through contemporary eyes. The British Music Hall Society was a rich source of information, and has done a remarkable job in preserving a rapidly disappearing world. Specifically, I would like to thank its historian, Max Tyler, and Geoff Bowden, editor of its wonderful in-house journal, *The Call Boy*. Notebooks, song sheets, posters, recordings and ephemera came from many different sources, all sent to me with the open-heartedness so typical of those who love theatre. John MacGregor – Lord MacGregor, himself a magician as well as a legislator – provided me with valuable information about his music hall predecessors.

Last, but by no means least, I would like to thank the artistes who continue to keep the music hall genre alive, specifically Roy Hudd, President of the British Music Hall Society, and Elizabeth Mansfield, whose portrayal of Marie Lloyd is a delight to behold.

The research for this book has been long, arduous – and often deeply frustrating due to conflicting and contradictory records – and I simply would not have had the time or the energy to tackle it alone. During the past few years Piers Warburton has buried himself in this world, hunting down original sources with great tenacity and skill. Where, as was often the case, the information was incomplete, we have tried to assemble the jigsaw in order to tell the story as accurately as possible. Piers's role has been invaluable, and is appreciated enormously.

In my office, both Anne Stenson and Vanessa Burgess have translated my handwritten scrawl, and typed and amended chapters time and again as they were altered and updated. I am hugely grateful for their patience and good humour throughout. Towards the end of the exercise, my Chief of Staff, Arabella Warburton, read through the final manuscript in sequence, proposing alterations which greatly improved the narrative.

My wife, Norma, has endured early-morning writing, late-night writing, lost weekends and lost holidays with perfect equanimity. Herself the author of two books, she has contributed massively to this one, both with research and advice on narrative. Piers, Arabella and Norma have all left their stamp on this book, although responsibility for any error or misjudgement is entirely mine.

At HarperCollins, Martin Redfern was unfailingly encouraging, and Robert Lacey suggested reorderings, additions and omissions in his determination to produce a tight, readable narrative. Just as Robert is a prince among editors, Helen Ellis is a princess among publicists, and although Helen's work only really begins once the book is finally put to bed, I would not wish her to be omitted from my roll call of thanks. This is a tried and tested team, and one which I still have the good fortune to have around me.

I hope that – between us all – we have succeeded in bringing alive a remarkable phenomenon. For me, it has been something of a personal pilgrimage and a voyage of discovery. For you, the reader, I hope it will make for an informative – but most of all entertaining – read.

John Major
London, August 2012

Leaving the Stage

'Who is to write the history of music hall?
What a splendid theme ...'

JOHN ROBERTSON, HISTORIAN (1856–1933)

In March 1962, I sat with an old man as he lay dying. He was barely conscious, with familiar half-smiles dancing across his well-worn and gentle face, but I knew where he was in his imagination – where he wanted to be. The lights were bright. A boisterous audience was cheering. Aged eighty-two, and over thirty years since he had left it, he was back on the stage. In life he had few possessions, but he died a richer man than most, with a song in his heart and joy in his soul.

He was my father, Tom.

The men and women who entertained so royally are all dead. They are gone, but not quite forgotten. We know some of their names, and some of their songs, but there is no one living who saw them onstage. Their magic is now the stuff of myth and legend.

But then, music hall has always been an elusive concept. What exactly is it? Is it a style of singing comic ballads? That is certainly the principal ingredient, but it is far from the whole. Is it a theatre, hosting a mixture of variety? Up to a point, yes – but it is so much more than that.

1

Even the name is misleading. 'Music' hall was never simply music, but encompassed everything from the sublime to the surreal. A typical evening's fare might include opera and ballet, popular singers and comedians, speciality acts, animal acts, acrobats, monologists and any other performer who might, however loosely, 'entertain'. Nor was the setting necessarily a hall. Elements of music hall were widespread in pleasure gardens, taverns, streets and markets long before the nineteenth century. Its growth was organic: often haphazard, ramshackle – more the product of events than rational planning. And always, always it was a reflection of the lives and tastes of its audience.

The term 'music hall' was invented by the early entrepreneurs who built theatres to exploit widely popular forms of entertainment. These entrepreneurs have a role to play in the history of music hall, but it is sentimental myth to claim they invented it. It had its heart in the East End of London, yet it was not purely a southern phenomenon. It was centred on the capital because that was where the biggest audiences were to be found, but from the outset it was popular in towns and cities across the length and breadth of Great Britain. Lancashire, in particular, provided music hall talent almost on a level to rival London.

Music hall was able to thrive because of a fortunate combination of circumstances. In Victorian Britain, wages rose and working hours fell. The nineteenth century was an intensely musical era that saw a huge growth in choral societies, brass bands and religious music. Street entertainers earned a few pennies playing zithers, piccolos, banjos, concertinas or fiddles. Opera companies toured the provinces. Popular music embraced minstrel songs and the ballads of Tin Pan Alley. Popular operetta arrived as the gift of Gilbert and Sullivan. The development of railways enabled performers to tour the whole country. Demand for their work saw the publication of inexpensive sheet music. There was a huge growth in the sale of musical instruments. Amidst all this, music hall was shaped and defined as one of the glories of the Victorian era. Sentimental, vulgar, class-conscious, insular – but always patriotic, and on the side of the underdog. It held up a mirror to people's hopes and fears, joys and heartbreaks, and the general absurdity of life.

The strands of music hall began to come together in the early nineteenth century, but had comprehensively disentangled by the mid-twentieth. Like a shooting star, it flared brightly into orbit, then fizzled out; but its heyday was brilliant, and its lifespan encompassed the story of a world changed beyond recognition.

In its formative years, the vulgarity and sentimentality of music hall attracted a largely working-class audience, but its appeal was far wider. It took root in England only a few years after there had been a real fear of revolution, and helped to turn sour resentment into a patriotic roar of joy. It was low-born but irresistible. Its songs have become the folk songs of a nation. As Kipling observed, they filled a gap in our history. Music hall attracted the magic brush-strokes of Sickert, Degas and Toulouse-Lautrec. Long after its heyday, entertainers such as Max Miller, Tommy Cooper, Frankie Howerd and Morecambe and Wise had an empathy with their audience reminiscent of music hall in its prime. Bruce Forsyth and Roy Hudd have it to this day.

Popular artistes from music hall shaped the attitudes of our nation: Harry Lauder's nightly jokes about Scottish miserliness fed a public perception that turned a myth into an accepted truth. Charlie Chaplin, Stan Laurel and Dan Leno personified the 'little man', put upon by life. Other stereotypes entered folklore. Music hall eulogised courtship and motherhood, yet ridiculed marriage as a comic disaster. It mocked single women for being unmarried, but made 'the missus' the butt of jokes. It was never politically correct, and in a less sensitive age 'nigger minstrels' and 'coon' acts were part of its staple diet. At times of war it could be fiercely jingoistic – indeed, the word was popularised in 'By Jingo', a music hall song, during the Baltic crisis of 1877–78. Even after its demise, music hall continued to have an impact. In 1942, the pro-nudist magazine *Health & Efficiency* denounced 'music hall comedians and their imbecilic jokes' for the reluctance of the public to join nudist camps. More positively, the demand for entertainment without alcohol led to the foundation in 1880 of the 'Old Vic' theatre in south London.

Once scorned, music hall would come to be seen as epitomising a past age of success, and as an art form that gave pleasure to millions. It had some powerful advocates. In 1978, James Callaghan, then Prime Minister, used a music hall song at a TUC congress to announce that he would not be holding an expected general election: 'There was I, waiting at the church ...' he sang, echoing Vesta Victoria three-quarters of a century earlier. The country was praying for an election – but it was not to be. Nor was this an isolated acknowledgement of Callaghan's affection for music hall. At another trades union gathering he charmed his dinner companions by singing, 'I'm the man, the very fat man, who waters the workers' beer.' It is an irony that he used a music hall song to draw grumpy trades unionists closer to the government, since over seventy years earlier disputes over music hall had bitterly divided the Puritan and non-Puritan elements of the embryonic Labour movement.

Tories were susceptible too. Lord Randolph Churchill had 'an almost music hall style of public speaking', claimed his biographer, while his son Winston, a great admirer of the music hall artiste Dan Leno, was apt to sing 'old world cockney songs with teddy bear gestures'. Churchill, like the Labour movement, will enter our story again.

Music hall reached its zenith in the 1890s. Vast auditoriums were packed each night in nearly every British town and city, and fourteen million tickets were sold each year. The most popular performers were among the highest-paid and most celebrated figures in the land. 'I earn more than the Prime Minister,' noted Little Tich, 'but I do so much less harm.' Owners of theatres became rich, and their money and fame gave them an entrée to the Establishment elite. But even as music hall stood unchallenged in its supremacy, the forces that would destroy it were taking shape.

On 28 December 1895, in the dimmed artificial light of Le Grand Café, avenue des Capucines, Paris, a small group of thirty-three individuals were viewing the first public screening of commercial cinema. On the bill were ten one-minute films, the brainchild of two brothers, Auguste and Louis Lumière.

Five years later, at the turn of the century, my father Tom, then twenty-one, entered the profession. For nearly thirty years – the prime of his working life – he earned his living in music hall and variety. His fortunes fluctuated, but in old age, when his health and prosperity were gone, these were the years he remembered with the greatest affection.

In 1902, Tom met Kitty Grant, a vivacious and attractive brunette five years older than him, and they formed a double act, Drum + Major.* When Kitty's husband, David, died in 1910, she and Tom legalised a relationship that had long been stable. They wrote their own songs, sketches and monologues, and as they became more popular they formed their own revues, with which for over twenty years they toured the country, as well as North and South America. In February 1906, they became founder members of the Variety Artists' Federation. Playbills reveal that they performed with the greats: Marie Lloyd, George Robey, Florrie Forde, Vesta Tilley and Harry Champion.

These great and happy times ended in tragedy when Kitty died following an onstage accident. My father carried on alone, although not for long. In Tom and Kitty's show there were two young special-ity dancers, 'Glade and Glen'. 'Glen', whose real name was Gwen Coates, a slender imp of a girl, had been asked by the dying Kitty to 'look after Tom'. And so she did for the next forty years. She was at his side when he died, caring for him as she had done for so long. My mother, the eternal, uncrushable optimist, knew the show must go on, but her smile was never again so bright. When she herself died ten years later, in the dark of a long night, she was in hospital, alone for once, for her death was unexpected. Did she think of Tom? I am sure she did, for she had done so all her life.

* My father was born Thomas Ball. 'Major' was a stage name. Had he not changed it, I would have been John Ball, and thus have shared the name of one of the leaders of the Peasants' Revolt in 1381.

When I was born my father was sixty-four, my mother thirty-eight. I was Tom and Gwen's late child, a just-in-time baby – the one she had hoped for, but feared she would never have. It was not an easy birth: my mother, never robust in health, nearly died, and I became dangerously ill. But we both survived. Most of my mother's hopes for the future were invested in me, but whatever gifts my parents passed on to their children, the talent to entertain was not among them. My eldest brother, Thomas, had died within hours of his birth. My sister Pat, a fine dancer as a child, was eccentric enough for a stage career, but had no interest in joining the profession. My brother Terry and I were devoid of artistic talent, although I often reflected that my chosen career was akin to show business. Certainly, Prime Minister's Questions often resembled my father's description of a raucous night at the Glasgow Empire.

There may have been a good reason for our parents' lack of disappointment that we failed to follow them onto the stage – at least in my father's case. At the age of twenty-two he had had a brief liaison with Mary Moss, the wife of a young musician, and in 1901 their son, another Tom, was born. Like his father – *our* father – Tom became a music hall performer. He had a beautiful tenor voice, but also, I fear, a horrible temper – particularly after a night's carousing.

Tom Junior appeared onstage in many guises – as 'Signor Meneghini', 'Tom Moss' or 'Signor Bassani'. Physically, he was about as unlike my muscular father as it was possible to be: medium height, with a small van Dyke beard, and the plump body of the archetypal tenor. Even when he was past fifty, when I first came to know him, he could sing, and when he did (which was rare), I would listen enraptured as, unaccompanied by music, his voice soared effortlessly to the higher notes. If it had not been for his rebellious, anti-authoritarian nature, his career might have progressed from the shadows into the spotlight. He had the talent, but not the discipline. As my mother put it, 'Tom doesn't like being told what to do.' Truly, Tom was my father's son.

My parents lived life on a rollercoaster. Alternately well-off and hard-up, in work or out, on top or in difficulty, they inhabited a

Micawberish world in which – somehow, sometime – all would be well. But, of course, it hardly ever was. And when the problems piled up, my mother – who had never even heard of Voltaire, let alone read him – echoed Dr Pangloss in *Candide* in believing that, as disaster followed disaster, it was, no doubt, 'all for the best in the best of all possible worlds'. She had learned to expect hardship, and when it came knocking at her door she was ready to confront it.

One day, at around the age of nine, I remember rushing home for tea and, in my hurry, throwing open the kitchen door. My father, who was fitting a lightbulb, fell from the stool he was standing on and cracked his head on the tiled floor. Clearly dazed, he was taken off to bed. Although I did not know it at the time, his sight had been fading for many months, as cataracts dimmed his vision; but as it worsened, I was certain that his failing sight was as a direct result of my childhood exuberance. No one ever suggested anything of the kind, but since my feelings of guilt were never known, I was never disabused.

This was but one of many family misfortunes: business failure, debt, bankruptcy, failing health, the loss of our home. The two rented rooms in Brixton in which we found sanctuary were in a house owned by my half-brother Tom, who until then I had never met. My parents had not told me who he really was. My father was too lofty to explain, and my mother would have moved heaven and earth to protect me from 'that sort of thing'. My father's health and sight continued to worsen while my mother shielded him from as much as she could, particularly her worries over debt. Her world centred on him, and he accepted her care as his right. In this, if in little else in life, he was a very lucky man. Throughout their travails, my parents had always accepted setbacks with equanimity. Misfortune was nothing new. Shows opened, shows closed. You were top of the bill, or bottom. But tomorrow always held glittering possibilities. That was their philosophy of life.

My father's health deteriorated further, and he became bedridden. An active man all his life, he now had nothing to do, and nowhere to go. Nor did he have an audience to bring him alive.

Here, at least, I could make amends for my nine-year-old clumsiness. I became his audience. He sang the songs he'd known, and recited the monologues he and Kitty had written. 'The girl I love is up in the gallery,' he would sing – quietly changing the gender of the lover – and as his eyes watered I'd wonder if he was thinking of Kitty. But when he spoke of his life in the theatre, a smile was never far away. I learned that although Marie Lloyd had a saucy tongue, she had a heart of gold. That Dan Leno and Little Tich were giants of the profession. That Nellie Wallace was 'ugly but funny', and Gertie Gitana was lovely in every way. That Nosmo King, in haste to create a stage name for himself, glimpsed the 'No Smoking' sign on the carriage windows of a train he was boarding, and never looked back. That Vesta Tilley was the finest cross-dresser of them all – 'And what's more,' said my father, clearly impressed with titles, 'she became a Lady.' And so she did.

Somehow, word of my father's plight spread. Strangers, often eccentric men and women, would arrive at our door. Careworn, often shabbily dressed, they were all of my father's vintage, or near to it. Prosperity, if it had ever touched them, had long since fled. Some were talented, some loveable; some both, some neither. But all had the urge to entertain. Often vulnerable, they were intensely human in their wish to give pleasure, in their thirst for applause and in the love they had for their profession.

They sat at my father's bedside drinking whisky until supplies ran out, and then called for tea. If their conversation was stilted at first, it soon became intimate. Memories were stirred, emotions flowed. Old stories were told, old times remembered – no doubt, as Shakespeare put it, with advantages. Sometimes, these reunions became uproarious, and tears of mirth rolled down their and my father's cheeks. Sometimes emotion overcame them, and tears of a different kind were wiped away.

I can see and hear them still. I saw how cheers and applause had filled their lives, and for a short time they were back there, in the good old days, positively aglow with their reminiscences, a fierce joy in their hearts. They were full of generous impulse. They treasured their remembered triumphs, but had not forgotten the flops, the rejections, the let-downs, the days without work, the lash of critical opinion. It was not until years later, with the political critics poised, invective flowing and the national audience restive, that I fully understood all the emotions that had been so familiar to them.

I listened avidly as they talked of their shared past. They were born to perform. Onstage they had come alive. The career they chose was one in which fame and fortune was elusive, but heartbreak was not. Few had enjoyed great material rewards, although they talked with affection and without envy of those who had been successful. Once, several guests around my father's bed argued over whose songs had the most memorable choruses. Was it Florrie Forde or Harry Champion? An impromptu concert ensued, in which 'Pack Up Your Troubles' and 'Down at the Old Bull and Bush' competed with 'Any Old Iron' and 'I'm Henery the Eighth, I am' before a draw was declared. At the time it seemed there was an unending flow of guests, but memory plays tricks. There were perhaps fifteen in all. But the pleasure their presence gave to my father was disproportionate to their number.

Many years later, when I became a public figure, some commentators wrote disparagingly of my parents and their profession. My parents may not have had much in the way of possessions or money, but as human beings, in their kindness and goodness, they were richer than most. And, most important of all to them, they had standing amongst their peers, and careers that had not only given personal joy to themselves, but pleasure to others. As my father, with whisky in hand and philosophy in flow, once observed: 'Entertainers exist to brighten people's lives – critics are their antidote.'

The lives of many music hall performers were poignant. Each act was individual, and most had no support structure. The glad hand proffered to the multitude often hid a lonely soul. Some had only modest talent. Many fell upon hard times, and even the successful often found it hard to cope with fame. The artistes' interests often fared badly in a commercial world. And, stripped of its glamour, music hall was, first and last, a commercially driven business. Its leading entrepreneurs – Charles Morton, Edward Moss, Oswald Stoll, Richard Thornton and their colleagues – were quintessentially Victorian figures, vigorous believers in profit who were always on the lookout for market opportunities. They were not in *show* business; they were in *business*. Understanding market forces as well as any modern businessman, they found that the music hall model worked, and so they cashed in. They brought together the talent that wished to perform, and a public that wished to be entertained.

Performers were in a poor position to negotiate. They started off being paid a share of the venue's profit – essentially from drink sales – and thereafter their salary was linked to their popularity. It was brilliantly straightforward: the bigger the house they attracted, the more they were paid to perform. If their popularity waned, their wages went down – they had no illusions about that. If they didn't work, they weren't paid. As a result, many worked too hard, and died too young.

In the early days of music hall the public demanded affordable entertainment, and they got it: a drink, a seat, a song, the chance to place a bet, a show to watch, something to eat – all for sixpence. There was nothing novel about the entertainment concept – all the artistic forms that featured in the music halls were already in existence – but the business model *was* new: pub, choral society, restaurant, theatre, comedy venue, betting shop all brought together under one roof. It was imaginative, and for many years it was to prove irresistible.

By 1901, as the Victorian Age ended, music hall faced a new world as rival attractions multiplied: first non-catered variety shows, then radio and recorded music, began to crowd in on the music hall monopoly of mass entertainment. The death blow came with the flickering images first seen in Paris courtesy of the Lumière brothers. Cinema was on its way. Audiences still enjoyed intimate theatres, comic songs, patter, magic tricks – as they do today – but

bigger sets and new technology were needed to create more extravagant productions.

Music hall was born of no fixed abode. It was one strand of an
impulse to entertain that, throughout the centuries, faced down
religious prejudice, social and political hostility, attempts at licensing and censorship. It was the child of many parents, raised in many
guises and even more places. But always, it was an art for individuals. And when the individual began to be subsumed beneath a
demand for greater spectacle, the pulse of music hall began to slow.
There were other changes too. As transport improved, audiences
were able to travel more easily, and their entertainment options
widened. The success of music hall had come from the people, and
as the people tired of it, its allure faded.

This book is not an attempt at a definitive history of music hall –
that would fill many volumes. But it is the story of the rise and fall
of a unique form of entertainment. Whilst I was writing it, figures
who were at first simply names on playbills took shape and came to
life. I hope I have painted them faithfully. They were, like all of us,
shaped by time and circumstance; fighting – at first for survival,
and then for success – in a tough and ruthless profession. Some
dreamed but failed. Some succeeded gloriously. Some could not
cope with fame. Some were stalked by heartbreak and failure. But
they are all part of the story.

The great days of music hall are now gone forever. But its story
is glamorous, its impact widespread and its legacy enduring. The
art form that was once derided for moral degeneracy has, over time,
assumed the iconic status of a world we have lost, and values that
have been misplaced. At its core stood the entertainers. Their echo
still resounds. This is their story.

It is the final encore for my parents, Tom and Gwen.

1

The Road to Music Hall

'Beer flowed freely … occasionally there were big
banquets … where there would be heavy
drinking, and sometimes a row.'

EDWARD YATES, WRITER, DRAMATIST AND JOURNALIST,
RECALLING CREMORNE GARDENS IN THE 1840S IN
RECOLLECTIONS AND EXPERIENCES (1865)

All the components of music hall derive from earlier forms of
theatrical entertainment: music, dance, comedy, variety, mime,
clowning, costume; rapport with the audience; the marriage of food
and drink and entertainment; and affordable tickets to attract a
mass audience. By the end of the Restoration period all of these
were understood, but the full recipe for music hall was not yet in
place: some disparate ingredients were still needed before, in John
Betjeman's memorable phrase, it became 'the poetry and song of
the people'. Throughout the eighteenth century the seeds were
germinating in pleasure gardens, saloon theatres and catch and glee
clubs, and they would soon blossom in song and supper rooms,
taverns and music houses.

Pleasure gardens had a long history. The concept had existed
since Ancient Rome, when gardens acquired by the Emperor
Tiberius were opened to the public. These were free of charge, but
their English successors were commercial operations, offering

refreshment in an attractive setting. It is easy to see why they became popular. They were a refreshing contrast to rival amusements such as bear-baiting, dog fights and public executions. In an age when travel was too expensive for most, they offered relaxation at weekends and the gentle leisure of walking, playing, eating and drinking at modest cost in pleasant surroundings.

The most fashionable gardens were magnets for refined patrons seeking a genteel mixture of concerts, masquerades, quality dining and, often, fireworks to enliven the evening. Vauxhall Gardens, now the network of streets to the north of The Oval cricket ground, was perhaps the most famous. Cupers Gardens, on the site of the present-day National Theatre, Marylebone Gardens, between Marylebone High Street and Harley Street, and Ranelagh Gardens, broadly on the site of the Royal Hospital, Chelsea, were also popular venues. Each garden had its own charm and special attractions. Concerts and novelty acts rubbed shoulders with skittles and bowls. Some gardens featured defined walks punctuated by ornate plantations, water fountains, grottos and follies lured quieter souls, while others offered more raffish customers the wilder delights of gambling.

When Vauxhall Gardens opened around 1660, admission was free but charges were levied for refreshments. It rose to pre-eminence under the management of Jonathan Tyers, who having enlarged the gardens to about sixteen acres, began to charge an admission fee. Orchestras played nightly, and concerts were held in a rotunda where patrons could dine and dance. The energetic Tyers dotted the grounds with architectural attractions and fake gothic ruins. Vauxhall was widely copied at home and overseas. Whales in Bayswater, Highbury Barn in Clerkenwell, Bagnigge Wells in King's Cross and St Helene Gardens in Rotherhithe all borrowed ideas from Vauxhall, So too did Tivoli Gardens in Copenhagen.

Cupers Gardens, the principal London rival to Vauxhall, specialised in firework displays and boasted an ornamental lake, bowling greens, arbours and attractive walks. Each night, at the height of its popularity an orchestra and band played nightly. But it also became a haunt for prostitutes, card sharps and general villainy, which in due course undermined its appeal to more sober citizens. In 1753, its licence was revoked on the grounds that it was 'a haunt of vice', and after a brief interlude as a tea garden, Cupers closed in 1760.

The larger gardens built promenade platforms and elaborate music rooms to present the most popular performers of the day. In 1765, the nine-year-old Mozart performed in the rotunda at Ranelagh. This was the birth of saloon theatre, a hybrid of theatre and tavern standing in its own gardens.

The admission charge for the pleasure gardens varied from half a crown for the best-appointed and most fashionable to sixpence for semi-rural tea-house gardens in places like Highbury, Hornsey and White Conduit House in Pentonville, where the entrance fee included a token to be redeemed for refreshment. Tea had only been introduced to England in 1652, but swiftly replaced ale as the national drink. Every strata of society patronised the tea houses, and their new 'exotic' import was considered to be a cure for all ills, from headaches to syphilis.

Apart from the efficacious powers of tea, the gardens offering benefits to health were generally spas, whose waters were widely believed to have healing properties. They also provided entertainment, no doubt in the belief that it would soothe their customers and make them less likely to question the effectiveness of the health treatment. But fashions changed, and the spas began to lose custom. Bermondsey Spa is typical: in 1795 a visitor noted: 'the once famed place was most rapidly on the decline … three idle waiters were clumped for want of a call … As we reached the orchestra, the singer curtsied to us, for we were the only persons in the gardens.' Nine years later, Bermondsey closed.

The pleasure gardens too fell out of favour. Cupers Gardens closed in 1753, Marylebone in 1778 and Ranelagh in 1803. Vauxhall struggled on, but became an irresistible attraction for vice. One customer commented acidly that it would be better 'if there were more nightingales and fewer strumpets'. In 1813, in an attempt to boost its fortunes, Vauxhall staged a fête to celebrate Wellington's victory at the Battle of Vitoria, and in the 1820s it introduced sword-swallowers, military re-enactments, shadow pantomimes and performances of comic songs. Crowds flocked to see the intrepid Madame Saqui walk down a tightrope to the ground from a height of sixty feet amid bursting fireworks. In 1827, a thousand soldiers re-enacted the Battle of Waterloo, and in the 1830s the gardens were illuminated by 15,000 glass lamps for 19,000 visitors on a single evening. As the spectacles grew, the price of admission fell from its peak of four shillings and sixpence to one shilling. But economic times were tough, and shillings were hard to come by: the demise of Vauxhall was inevitable.

As Vauxhall declined, it tried to cash in on the growing popularity of comic singers. Novelties were tried: Herr von Joel, an eccentric German comic entertainer, would jump out from behind bushes to entertain passers-by, but unsurprisingly, this often caused more alarm than amusement. In 1840 the owners went bankrupt and the gardens closed. They attempted a relaunch two years later, but even the novelty of balloon ascents and the appearance of popular vocalists like Sam Cowell, Jack Sharp and W.G. Ross could not save them. Fashion had moved on, and in 1859 the gardens closed for ever. By 1832 the roots of music hall were being firmly established in pubs and clubs across England. Yet that year a new pleasure garden opened: Royal Cremorne in Chelsea, which would provide a platform for music hall pioneers, as well as an extraordinary variety of entertainment: balloonists, orchestras, a theatre, archery and a gypsy tent.

The Spa at Sadler's Wells provides an illustration of the early forces that drove the creation of music hall. A local businessman, Richard Sadler, owned a 'Musick House' near the site of the present-day theatre. In 1683 he excavated his land for minerals and discovered an ancient well, and with the skill of a snake-oil salesman, he saw a marketing opportunity.

Sadler promoted the waters as able to cure 'dropsy, jaundice, scurvy, green sickness and other distempers to which females are liable [he knew his clientèle] – ulcers, fits of the mother, virgin's fever and hydrochondriacal distemper'. He obtained endorsements from 'eminent' physicians, and hundreds of fashionable Londoners were sufficiently convinced to become patrons. Sadler added pipe, tabor and dulcimer musicians to sweeten the experience. 'Sadler's Wells' was soon staging operas.

As competition grew with the discovery of more wells, the genteel air gave way to less refined customers demanding a more earthy experience. Sadler provided it. The operas were replaced by such tasteless absurdities as 'the Hibernian Cannibal', who devoured a live cockerel, 'feather, feet and all', washed down with a pint of brandy.

William Wordsworth recorded seeing 'giants and dwarfs, clowns, conjurers, posture makers, harlequins/Amid the uproar of the rabblement, Perform their feats'. A noisy audience and a variety of acts was not yet music hall, but entertainment was being propelled in that direction. Managers were prepared to stage anything to find and hold an audience.

One of the ruses at Sadler's Wells was to brew very strong beer, and advertise it:

> Haste hither, then, and take your fill,
> Let parsons say whate'er they will,
> The ale that every ale excels
> Is only found at Sadler's Wells.

Sadler's Wells is relevant to the story of music hall because it shows how landlords, proprietors and managers relentlessly followed the market to maximise profitability. It was their job to give the public what it wanted and to 'talk it all up'. It was exactly this approach that would drive the development of music hall.

Other early influences on music hall were catch and glee songs. 'Catches' – so-called because they were catchy – were songs with simple harmonies composed almost exclusively for male voices. They were initially humorous and light-hearted in content, and intended for the convivial atmosphere of clubs and taverns. As they became identified with low humour and bawdy lyrics, their fan base widened and they became a staple of late-night entertainment.

The first collection of catches was published by Thomas Ravenscroft in 1609. Yet we know they existed by 1600. In Shakespeare's *Twelfth Night* (c.1601) Sir Toby Belch and Sir Andrew Aguecheek are rebuked by Malvolio, never one for mirth, for singing catches with Feste the clown: 'My masters, are you mad? Have you no wit ... but to gabble like tinkers? Do ye make an alehouse of my Lady's house, that ye squeak out your coziers' [tailors'] catches?' It is a revealing accusation, telling us that catches were considered plebeian, but were enjoyed by gentlemen as well as tradesmen. They were convivial and drink-related, probably very rude, and were disapproved of by the Puritan-minded.

Ironically, Puritan hostility may have actively promoted catch-singing. When the Puritan Parliament of 1642 passed legislation to close the theatres, it inadvertently moved the displaced musicians and singers to taverns and inns, where catch-singing took hold. Even worse, many of the organs the Puritans removed from churches also found their way into taverns. In 1657 Parliament responded by passing an ordinance banning 'idle, dissolute persons commonly called fiddlers and minstrels ... from making musick in any Inn, Tavern or Alehouse'. Singing was also banned, but enterprising tavern-owners either turned a blind eye to the law or deliberately misinterpreted it. A mere two years later, the Black Horse tavern in Aldersgate Street was operating as a 'Musick House' featuring catches.

The following year, the Puritan Commonwealth was gone and Charles II was on the throne. Music houses began to proliferate, and to move upmarket, as is shown by Samuel Pepys dedicating a book of catch lyrics to his friends at 'the late Musick Society and Meeting at the Old Jury, London'. Pepys and other contemporary commentators describe a tavern-based scene of music, ale or wine, enjoyed convivially, served by a landlord-in-attendance to a socially diverse group of singers. Henry Purcell was responsible for providing the music to some of the ripest lyrics, perhaps as light relief among the operas, anthems, Court odes and other works of this great British composer.

The most famous of the 'catch clubs' was founded by the 4th Earl of Sandwich at the Thatched House tavern in 1762, on a site that is now at the lower end of London's St James's Street. The Noblemen's and Gentlemen's Catch Club was a highly exclusive dining and drinking club for the cream of Georgian society, where dukes and earls mingled with generals and admirals. Its secretary, Edmund Warren, published collections of catches and left an exhaustive record of the club. The membership clearly shared a love of wine as well as music: in June 1771, 798 quart bottles of claret alone were purchased for only twenty-six members. Non-alcoholic drinks were frowned on, and members who requested them were asked, presumably tongue-in-cheek, to drink 'at a distant table', and to do so with 'a due sense of the society's indulgence'. Fines were levied for absence or lateness, and 'drinking fines' for talking about politics or religion – or singing out of tune. A donation to the club, in the guise of a fine, was expected from any member benefiting from a large inheritance. But the club was more than a bolt-hole for society drunkards. It supported the contemporary music scene, awarding medals and prizes to young performers, while profes-sional musicians such as the popular tenor John Beard and the composer Thomas Arne were among the honorary members.

The club medals bore the motto 'Let's drink and sing together', and they ate together too. The landlord of the Thatched House, William Almack,* served dinner at 4 p.m., and kept refreshment coming for the next nine hours. After dinner and Grace were concluded, fines were announced, the singing began and the drink flowed .

By 1800, catch-singing was a feature of autumn and winter evenings in taverns across the country. Such evenings took a form

* The rewards of hosting the catch club were significant – Almack became extremely wealthy; among his enterprises was a gambling club in Pall Mall which subsequently became Brooks's Club.

that would set a pattern for music hall. A chairman was appointed – usually the publican – who would preside over the entertainment, introduce guest singers and direct the club's affairs: he did, after all, have a pecuniary interest in its success. The evenings would grow increasingly raucous as the drinking proceeded, and thus the chairman would give events a continued focus. Membership was by subscription, and catch clubs attracted a wide social mix, from aristocrats to the working class, although the more staid middle classes were rarely there. As the evening wore on, the songs became more ribald, and vulgar and obscene lyrics were performed to enthusiastic applause.

The sheer vulgarity of catches helped encourage the popularity of glees. Musicians began to shy away from the crude nature of catches, preferring the more musically sophisticated glees. Glees were also more sentimental, and had wider appeal to both men and women. When a glee club was established at the Newcastle Coffee House in 1787, its founders were largely professional members of the existing catch club who were serious about their music and shied away from the bawdiness of taverns. Coffee houses became their favoured meeting places.

Thomas Lowe presented both catch and glee concerts at Ranelagh Gardens in 1765 in an attempt to boost its flagging fortunes. This, at least, was a success, and catch and glee songs – the catch lyrics being suitably sanitised for the mixed audiences – became a staple ingredient of the pleasure gardens' programme by the end of the eighteenth century. Drury Lane copied Lowe's initiative, followed by the Haymarket Theatre in 1770. Until well into the nineteenth century, catches and glees featured on the bill of any theatre or pleasure garden that wished to attract a popular crowd.

By the early nineteenth century, glees – with their sentimentality, inoffensive lyrics and more complex music – began to outstrip the popularity of catches, and the two genres went their separate ways. Catches – with their bawdy, single-sex conviviality and association with bibulous revelry – were to find a new home, and a wider audience, in song and supper clubs. As these began to attract the patronage of the well-heeled bohemian man-about-town, the taverns lost their social mix and became more of a working-class preserve. Glees went on to lay the basis for the songs that would delight audiences throughout and well beyond the era of music hall. Catch and glee singing, and their tavern roots, laid the foundations for the informal, accessible, and initially amateur, but later professional-led, sing-songs that were an important staging post to music hall.

2

The Basement and the Cellars

'A guinea a week and supper each night.'

TERMS OF EMPLOYMENT AT THE CYDER CELLARS

Song and supper rooms, true to their name, were late-night venues offering hot food and musical entertainment. Together with their imitators they were the direct predecessors of music hall. The three most famous were Evans' Late Joy's in King Street, Covent Garden, the Coal Hole in Fountain Court, The Strand, and the Cyder Cellars in Maiden Lane. All three catered for bohemian and well-heeled London society. But elsewhere, in London and beyond, variety saloons and concert halls attached to taverns offered similar fare and fun at lower cost, while pubs accommodated the working man in 'free and easies'. Evans' Late Joy's was the pioneer: it initiated an interplay between performer and audience that would become an essential component of music hall.

Evans' was situated on King Street, in the north-west corner of Covent Garden. The splendid red-bricked building, formerly the London residence of the Earl of Orford, was converted into the Grand Hotel in 1773, probably the first family hotel in London. Around the turn of the nineteenth century it became Joy's Hotel, and as a dinner and coffee room it thrived on the patronage of the noble and the notable. Nine dukes were said to have dined there on one single evening, and the social elite flocked to the huge basement dining room.

But fashions change. Towards 1820 London society began its exodus further west, and the hotel clientèle faded away. The upper rooms were converted into residential apartments, and the basement was taken over by a former singer/comedian at the Covent Garden Theatre, W.C. Evans. Evans, a bluff, ruddy-faced John Bull of a figure, was moving up in the world, and was eager to display his elevation by renaming his new acquisition to reflect his ownership; but as a shrewd businessman, he wished also to exploit the favourable reputation Joy's had earned. The uneasy compromise of the rather clumsily named Evans' Late Joy's was to launch a thousand smutty jokes.

Evans recast the great dining room into a song and supper room for gentlemen. Evans' Late Joy's opened at eight o'clock in the evening, began to fill up at ten, and was packed by midnight. It offered excellent but costly fare, which restricted its clientèle to the affluent. Night after night the hall was packed, the long tables hazy with cigar smoke and merry with good fellowship and noisy conversation. Boys from the Savoy Chapel sang unaccompanied glees. Madrigals were also popular, and choral singing and excerpts from opera enlivened many a night. In the jovial atmosphere, diners would offer their own songs or verses.

Soon professional acts were engaged – all male, naturally – to offer higher-quality entertainment. It must have been a tough assignment, for the food, drink and conviviality of the supper rooms were more important than the cabaret. Artistes had to perform over a perpetual din, and needed skill and personality to win over their audience. Some set a bawdy tone, and as the wine flowed and inhibitions fled, customers would join in to perform the rudest song or story in their repertoire. Evans himself would contribute with a song that became his signature: 'If I Had a £1,000 a Year', a sentiment that inspired many a bawdy response as the bills were settled.

Early performers at Evans' included tenor John Binge, the comedians Jack Sharpe and Tom Hudson, Charles Sloman the Jewish singer/comedian, Joe Wells, and John Caulfield, Harry Boleno and Richard Flexmore, who went on to become the principal clowns at Drury Lane and Covent Garden.

Some of these performers did not live to see music hall thrive: Hudson, the son of a civil servant but himself apprenticed to a grocer, was a popular songwriter, mimic and singer who nevertheless died in poverty in 1844. He wrote and published songs about commonplace events of life that were familiar to his audience. One historian noted that, in Hudson, the lower middle class became articulate. His forte was comedy, and a line from one of his songs, about a sailor who returns to find his wife married to another, gave further currency to the enduring phrase 'before you could say Jack Robinson'. After his death, friends arranged a benefit concert to raise funds for his widow and children, and subscriptions were offered by many notables, including the Lord Mayor, the Duke of Cambridge and Members of Parliament, as well as his fellow performers. It was a touching tribute to an engaging talent.

Charles Sloman was fiercely proud of the history of his race, which he commemorated in words and music. His career began in the pleasure gardens, but he soon graduated to the supper clubs. Sloman wrote many ballads – his most famous, 'The Maid of Judah', at the age of twenty-two – but his true gift was to 'keep the table in a roar' by conjuring a rhyme in song upon any subject shouted out to him by a well-refreshed diner. Often he mimicked the idiosyncrasies of diners or sang verses that teased or complimented them, much to the amusement of their companions. Throughout the 1830s Sloman was furiously busy as an entertainer, briefly (and unsuccessfully) as a theatre manager, and as chairman of festivities in taverns. After the 1840s his attraction declined and he was engaged in ever more downmarket venues. He died alone in the Strand workhouse in 1870.

Not everyone was a casualty of fleeting fame. Sam Collins was a firm favourite at Evans' in the late period, put his money to good use, and at the age of thirty was part-owner of the Rose of Normandy Concert Room in Church Street, Marylebone. Later he

bought the Lansdowne tavern and developed his own music hall –
Collins' Music Hall – before a premature death in his late thirties.

Others, less talented than Hudson, Sloman or Collins, were also
successful in providing for themselves. After finishing his act –
yodelling, imitations of birdsong and presenting his walking stick
as a bassoon, flute, piccolo, trombone or violin, complete with
sound effects – Herr von Joel, that refugee from Vauxhall Gardens,
mingled among the audience selling cigars and tickets for his benefit concert. The cigars were poor value and the benefit a fiction, but
no one cared. Cunning old von Joel was such an institution that –
in an age in which fraud remained a capital crime – no one
begrudged being swindled out of a few pennies.

Evans' became more raucous as a song and supper room after 1844,
when Evans retired and his successor, John Greenmore, known as
Paddy Green, built up its reputation. Green had been the musical
director during Evans' reign, and like his old employer he was a
former singer at Covent Garden Opera House. In the early 1850s he
reconstructed the hall, and spent lavish sums on enlarging the
dining room. He decorated the new ceiling, lit the room with
sunlight burners and adorned the walls with portraits of theatrical
personalities. A platform was erected to serve as a stage for the
performers, and the old supper room was downgraded to a café
lounge. The improved quality of the service, supplemented by fine
food and drink, encouraged the air of masculine bonhomie. Teams
of waiters and boys in buttoned waistcoats were on hand to take
orders. Chops, kidneys and poached eggs were typical of the fare on
offer, washed down with gin, whisky, hot brandy and water or stout.
Bills – with the exception of cigars, which were paid for on demand
– were settled on departure, with customers declaring what they'd
consumed and a waiter called Skinner, known as 'the calculating
waiter', totting up what was owed. This may have been a haphazard
system, but it was an astute piece of marketing by Green. By not
challenging what diners claimed had been consumed, he made it
unseemly for them to question the waiter's calculation. No doubt

any errors of underdeclaration and overcharging balanced themselves out.

In the swirling smoke of cigars, and amid the clink of glasses and the clatter of cutlery, Paddy Green circulated with a kindly word for the literary, sporting, commercial, political and noble diners who assembled nightly at Joy's. Posterity has been left a picture of a jovial, grey-haired elderly man moving through the room and beaming at his 'dear boys', his invariable greeting to clients, many of whose names he probably could not remember, while taking snuff and exuding an air of familiarity to all.

Green's jolly nature did not, however, always extend to the most famous of his performers, Sam Cowell. Although tolerated by his admiring audience, Cowell's habitual lateness exasperated Green. In his performances Cowell brought all his talents to bear: a gift for character, mimicry and visual expressiveness, and a strong, clear voice that enabled him to imbue narrative ballads with drama, comedy or pathos. His songs, often of thwarted love, became enormously popular. 'Villikins' and 'The Ratcatcher's Daughter', performed in character with battered hat, seedy frock-coat and huge bow cravat, were demanded by audiences at every appearance. 'The Ratcatcher's Daughter' tells the tale of two working-class sweethearts preparing to marry, although the would-be bride fears she will die before her wedding. And so she does, drowning in the Thames. Her broken-hearted lover then kills himself. We cannot be certain exactly how Sam Cowell presented this song, but its theme of love and tragedy touched the sentimental soul of Victorian London, and it's easy to see why:

> In Vestminster, not long ago,
> There liv'd a ratcatcher's daughter.
> That is not quite in Vestminster,
> 'Cos she liv'd t'other side of the vater.
> Her father killed rats and she cried Sprats
> All around about that quarter.
> The young gentlemen all touched their hats
> To the purty little ratcatcher's daughter.

Such a song could not fail. Though it (just) preceded the birth of the halls themselves, it is one of the first great music hall songs. Cowell sang it in a faux-cockney accent with, Sam Weller style, an inability to pronounce his W's. It was a model for the rich vein of cockney humour that would follow.

Despite Cowell's spectacular success, Paddy Green became so frustrated by his erratic timekeeping that he sacked his star performer for persistent lateness. Cowell never appeared at Evans' again, but found ample employment elsewhere, most famously in the first purpose-built music hall, the Canterbury in Westminster Bridge Road, Lambeth.

Even without Cowell, Evans' prospered. The principal comedian, Jackie Sharp, a specialist in unscripted, mildly risqué repartee, was at the top of his craft. Sharp's act featured topical songs that satirised the government. The most well-known, 'Who'll Buy My Images?' and 'Pity Poor Punch and Judy', were written by his friend and fellow performer John Labern, one of the foremost comic songwriters of the time. Sharp sang also of the evils of 'the bottle' at a time when overindulgence was a national pastime. Sadly, he himself did not heed the lyrics, and like so many others, he frittered away his fortune on alcohol and tobacco. At first drunkenness made him unreliable, and then unemployable. It was not long before a combination of exposure and malnutrition carried him off. He died in Dover Workhouse in 1856, at only thirty-eight years of age.

Cowell and Sharp were star attractions at Joy's, but they were not alone: on any evening, another fifteen to twenty acts – the small, sweet-voiced tenor John Binge, known as 'The Singing Mouse'; the big-voiced bass S.A. Jones; the ballad singer Joseph Plumpton – would be there to support them. Most performers were poorly paid, and would try to maximise their income by appearing at more than one venue on the same evening.

Sometime in the 1820s, William Rhodes, yet another former singer from the Covent Garden Theatre, acquired Evans' principal rivals, the Coal Hole and the Cyder Cellars – the latter of which had hosted entertainment as early as the 1690s. Maiden Lane, where the

Cyder Cellars was situated, had a famous pedigree. Voltaire and Henry Fielding had lived there, the great artist J.M.W. Turner was born there (to a wig-maker and his unstable wife), and Nell Gwynne was a resident towards the end of her life. Although the Cyder Cellars often employed the same artists as Evans', it was far less reputable. It reached the peak of its notoriety around 1840, before Paddy Green took over Evans', and remained a formidable competitor until its licence was revoked twenty-two years later.

The Cellars offered top-class food and wine, and throughout the 1840s and '50s its stars were familiar names: Charles Sloman, Tom Hudson, John Moody and Tom Penniket were among those who appeared there regularly. The entertainment was predominantly vocal, although variety was offered by conjurers and jugglers. Among the singers was one whom the more fastidious Evans' would never employ: W.G. Ross, a former compositor on a Glasgow newspaper.

Ross was a character actor-singer of enormous power. Born in Scotland, he enjoyed success in the north of England before heading south, where he found fame at the Cyder Cellars. He sang many songs – 'Going Home with the Milk in the Morning' being a representative example – but his fame rested on a dramatic ballad depicting the tragic fate of a chimney sweep: 'Sam Hall'. With this song, first sung in 1849, Ross attracted all London, and the Cyder Cellars overflowed nightly, with latecomers turned away. The most boisterous house hushed and the drinking ceased when it was announced that Ross would sing 'Sam Hall'.

Many were shocked – and even repelled – by the song, but far more were fascinated. The merciless lyrics of 'Sam Hall' explore the turmoil and emotion of a man, convicted of a capital crime, about to die an early and unnatural death while thousands look on – thousands who will then return home to their suppers, their futures, their families, while he will be dead. Hall's emotions turn from frustration to bravado to terror, and finally to hatred of those about to kill him. There is fear in the song, but no plea of innocence and no repentance. Sam Hall does not seek sympathy or express regret, he simply spits out his pent-up anger and rage.

It must have been a striking sight. A bearded Ross, in the character of Sam Hall, sitting astride a wooden chair in a cell, bearded, dressed in filthy, torn clothes and a battered hat. At first he would sit silently, his eyes darting in every direction like a terrified animal in a trap. He would then, slowly, light a grubby pipe, on which he would suck as the tension mounted. The silence was broken when he began to sing:

I goes up Holborn Hill in a cart,
In a cart,
I goes up Holborn Hill in a cart,
At St. Giles takes my gill,
And at Tyburn makes my will,
D—n my eyes.
Then the sheriff he will come,
He will come,
Then the sheriff he will come,
And he'll look so gallows glum,
And he'll talk of kingdom come,
Bl-st his eyes.
Then the hangman will come too,
Will come too,
Then the hangman will come too.
With all his bl—y crew,
And he'll tell me what to do
Bl—t his eyes.

In the repetition of the opening lines one can feel the horror that returns unbidden to the mind of the condemned man. As he curses his tormentors, he turns to spit on the cell floor. Ross's performance was a savage rendition of a bleak song, and its emotional impact made it one of the most dramatic acts ever seen on the variety stage. Its power was such that when Ross finished singing the room would empty, and for ten years it would be a cult song. Ross entered showbusiness history with his performances at the Cyder Cellars, but he did not gain – or at least keep – wealth or position. He drifted and declined until he hovered – barely recognised – on the edge of the profession. He died in obscurity in the early 1880s.

The Cyder Cellars was in close proximity to the Coal Hole, where William Rhodes had appointed his brother John, a sometime poet, as manager. John Rhodes was a big man, with a fine presence, and under his guidance the Coal Hole flourished. A raconteur with an outgoing personality, he sat at the head of the singers' table, conducted the evening's frivolities, joined in the glees and sang solos in an excellent baritone voice. Apart from being the ideal concert chairman, he had a passion for silver plate, and boasted of his collection of silver tankards, goblets, flagons and loving cups that 'the like could [not] be seen elsewhere in London'. Despite these pretensions, the Coal Hole became notorious for drunken rowdiness. Among the celebrities it attracted on a nightly basis was the actor Edmund Kean, a frequent patron and serial carouser.

In many ways, the Coal Hole was a mirror image of the Cyder Cellars. In addition to engaging the same performers, the tone was similarly low-brow. Joe Wells, a 'dreadful old creature', sang 'very coarse and vulgar' songs with great gusto; Charles Sloman improvised more spicily than elsewhere. A young singer, Joe Cave, introduced the banjo as accompaniment to 'Ethiopian' (Negro) songs in addition to his traditional fare of ballads and opera excerpts. Static near-nudes made their debut in the delphically entitled 'poses plastiques'. And from the early 1850s the self-styled 'Baron' Renton Nicholson presented his infamous 'Judge and Jury' trials. Oddly, women were admitted for the poses, which were presented, rather unconvincingly, as classical art – but not the 'trials'.

Nicholson, 'a clever, versatile, wholly unprincipled fellow', had a chequered career. He had owned a scurrilous gossip journal, the Town, before purchasing the Garrick's Head tavern, where he instituted the 'Judge and Jury Society' which later translated to the Coal Hole. The entertainment was comprised of sketches, written by Nicholson, and usually parodying contemporary events. Nicholson, in full wig and gown as the Lord Chief Justice, heard cases argued by a 'barrister' and 'witnesses'. The mock trials were witty, laced with innuendo, often vulgar and irresistible to those who recognised the victims.

At the height of the supper clubs' fame in the 1840s, the entertainment at venues like the Coal Hole may have been bawdy, even filthy, but few were offended – and certainly not the writers, journalists and intellectuals who were their habitués. If offence was taken by sensitive members of the audience, their ire could swiftly be soothed by devilled kidneys, oysters, Welsh rarebit, cigars, brandy, stout and cider, all of the highest quality.

The Coal Hole attracted a wide cross-section of society. William Makepeace Thackeray, who had a lifelong passion for the theatre, was a frequent attendee, and offers his own recollections of the Coal Hole and the Cyder Cellars. In *The Newcomes*, John Rhodes, manager of the Coal Hole, is depicted as Hoskins, landlord of the 'Cave of Harmony', with, as an added clue, Charles Sloman as 'little Nabob, the Improvisatore'. In *Pendennis*, Thackeray describes a bass singer named Hodgen who enjoyed success with a song entitled 'The Body Snatcher' – it is clearly W.G. Ross and 'Sam Hall' that is being depicted. Thackeray's description of the 'Back Kitchen' where Hodgen performs may be taken as a reflection of the clientèle of the supper clubs: 'Healthy county tradesmen and farmers … apprentices and assistants … rakish young medical students … young university bucks … handsome young guardsmen … florid bucks from the St. James Clubs … senators, English and Irish … even Members of the House of Peers'.

The song and supper clubs overlapped with the birth of purpose-built music halls which eventually forced them out of business. When William Rhodes died, his widow took over the Cyder Cellars, but it soon declined under her management. At the Coal Hole, John Rhodes was succeeded by his son, who ran it until his death in 1850, after which his widow, and later John Bruton, attempted to revive it, but its day was done. As audiences fell, the content became more lewd, and the authorities pounced: both the Cyder Cellars and the Coal Hole had their licences revoked in 1862.

Evans' Late Joy's lingered on, and Paddy Green was host to the Prince of Wales, later Edward VII, on a number of occasions – the first public nod to the supper clubs from a member of the Royal Family. One attraction for the Prince appeared to be a singer, Victor Liston, and his popular song 'Shabby Genteel', which highlighted a very British trait that still exists:

> Too proud to beg, too honest to steal,
> I know what it means to be wanting a meal,
> My tatters and rage I try to conceal,
> I'm one of the shabby genteel.

From the early 1860s, ladies were permitted to enter Evans' and listen to the entertainment from specially-constructed boxes in the gallery, provided they had a male escort, gave their name and address (as a disincentive to undesirables) and remained hidden behind a screen; notwithstanding these impertinences, many women did attend. Mrs Louisa Caulfield was the first woman to sing there, around 1860, and included 'Keemo Kino', a minstrel song, in her repertoire. At that time such songs were enormously in vogue, but were not universally popular. The poet and lawyer Arthur Munby's diary records supping at Evans' in March 1860 amid 'a hubbub of nigger howlings'. Later, Paddy Green – or his successor Mrs Barnes, it is not clear which – went even further than offering female singers, by admitting women to the floor of Evans'. As dancing was introduced, Evans' became a market for vice and a meeting place for seedy London. In 1872 the law changed and Evans' needed a licence to offer entertainment after 12.30 a.m. – which it did not obtain. This marked the end of the song and supper rooms.

3

At the Fringe

'Never was a theatre so full – never was an
audience so excited – never did the scum and
refuse of the streets so liberally patronise
the entertainment.'

J. EWING RITCHIE, WRITER AND CAMPAIGNER, ON 'PENNY
GAFFS', FROM *HERE AND THERE IN LONDON* (1859)

As well as song and supper clubs, concert halls, variety saloons and
'free and easies' in pubs and pleasure gardens were nurturing the
pre-natal life of music hall. So too, at a less salubrious level, were
the infamous 'penny gaffs'.

The Dr Johnson Concert Room in Bolt Court, Fleet Street –
named after the great lexicographer, conversationalist and writer,
who had lived in Bolt Court – had many similarities with the
supper clubs. The audience, however, comprised neither the
animated bohemians who flocked to Evans', nor the raucous lower
end of the market. The food was good, and alcohol plentiful. No
prices were advertised, and the all-male clientèle paid their bills
upon departure. A chairman kept order – the most notable being
the actor and singer John Caulfield – and the performers were
frequently the same as those in the supper clubs. Sam Cowell, Joe
Cave and Tom Penniket were regulars, often joined by the singers
John Moody and George Pervin, and variety acts like the violinists

the Brothers Holmes. The diminutive singer Jenny Hill, who learned her trade in less reputable halls, had her first upmarket booking at the Dr Johnson Concert Room, and went on to become one of the most glittering stars of the early music hall.

The variety saloons had their roots in the seventeenth century, when music flourished in the back rooms of public houses. The progression from back rooms to singing rooms to music halls took two hundred years. From the earliest days publicans have looked for legal ways to add to their takings, and – time and again – governments have unwittingly helped them with legislation that backfired. In the early eighteenth century gin was the drug of choice across all classes: 'Drunk for one penny, dead drunk for tuppence,' claimed bill-posts all over London. Hogarth's famous print *Gin Lane* was created in support of what became the Gin Act of 1751, which attempted to curtail the consumption of spirits by prohibiting distillers from selling gin to unlicensed merchants. But drunkenness remained a serious social problem, and in 1830 the Duke of Wellington's Tory government tried to alleviate it by introducing a Beer Act to promote a weaker alcoholic alternative to spirits. This well-meaning innovation had an unexpected outcome: it led to the creation of vast numbers of public houses seeking to exploit the huge demand for getting drunk. As competition became fiercer they sought to attract customers by offering increasingly opulent surroundings and more entertainment. The Rising Sun, which opened in 1830 in a Georgian red-brick house in Knightsbridge, was a typical product of the public-house revolution. Twenty years later it was licensed for music and dancing, and a concert hall was added as a 'music hall'. In 1864 it was rebuilt as the Sun music hall, reputedly one of the finest in London.

Taverns had a key role in promoting music hall. Every publican became a mini-impresario. The image of the jovial 'mine host' still persists, but a more accurate image would be of a man with a steely eye for profit. In the first half of the nineteenth century, publicans presided over small businesses catering to all comers, rich and poor. Much more was involved than selling drinks: business acumen was needed to organise fairs, Derby sweepstakes and trips to beauty spots. Pubs housed catch and glee clubs, harmonica clubs and evenings of variety. In *Sketches by Boz* (1836) Dickens describes 'Mr. Licensed Victualler', a Liverpool publican with a singing room, as 'a sharp and watchful man, with tight lips and a complete edition of Cockers Arithmetic [the accountant's bible] in each eye'. Mr Victualler's tavern has 'a plate glass window surrounded by stucco rosettes, a fantastically ornamental parapet ... a profusion of gas lights in richly gilt burners ... beyond the bar is a lofty and spacious saloon ... with a gallery equally well furnished'. Providing, as it did, a dazzling contrast to the darkness and dirt of the street and the cold and wretched home of the working man, it is no surprise that the sumptuous saloon tavern and the warm and well-lit gin and beer shop had great appeal.

Their popularity was also an unwanted, and unintended, result of government policy. To promote free trade, the duty on spirits was severely reduced in 1825. Unsurprisingly, cheaper drinking led to more drinking, and it was a boom era for publicans – by 1836 there were 36,000 licensed public houses in England and Wales – who used every inducement to promote custom. Brightly decorated windows and gas lights were installed to lure passers-by from the stinking, ordure-covered streets into warm, well-lit, ornate interiors with comfortable seating and the promise of diversion. In the land-lords' battle for customers, 'singing saloons' became an important element.

If a saloon did not have a licence to play music, the law was easily bypassed: payment was made using a token bearing the name of the pub, with a value that entitled the holder to a specified amount of food and drink, and entry to the show. When this 'wet money' expired customers were pressed either to leave or to buy more drinks as the waiters hovered and the chairman plied his trade. Soon the saloon theatres, often the more profitable part of the business, became distinct from the tavern or pub in which they were housed. Back-room theatres were upgraded to purpose-built halls with the ambience of a theatre, and public houses became a hybrid: half theatre and half public house, usually sited in their own pleasure grounds.

Among the early saloon theatres in London were the Effingham in Whitechapel Road, the Globe Gardens in Mile End, White Conduit House in Pentonville, the Bower in the Lower Marsh, Lambeth, the Albert in Islington, the Britannia in Hoxton, the Union in Shoreditch, the Yorkshire Stingo in Paddington and the Mogul Saloon in Drury Lane. Outside the capital, the Millstone inn, Deansgate, Manchester, led the way. Many of the saloons that opened in London in the late 1830s and early 1840s were either in the rough, tough, deprived East End, or at the northern and southern limits of the City. The Grecian Saloon – part of the Eagle tavern complex on City Road – became one of the most popular.

The Eagle began life as a downmarket pleasure garden, the Shepherd and Shepherdess, but its rural tranquillity was shattered in 1825 when the new City Road was driven straight through the centre of it. It was reincarnated as the Eagle tavern, and became famous when its owner Thomas Rouse, a builder by profession and a publicist by temperament, arranged balloon ascents in the garden. Charles Sloman's song acknowledged its fame:

> Up and down the City Road,
> In and out of the Eagle,
> That's the way the money goes,
> Pop goes the weasel.

Rouse was so successful that in 1831 he built the Grecian Saloon, decorating the entrance with bunting that had been used to adorn Westminster Abbey for the coronation of William IV in September that year. The interior was painted by a pupil of the famous naval artist Clarkson Stanfield, and contained an organ and the latest word in entertainment technology – an automated piano. When it opened for business in 1832 the Grecian was an instant success. It was a class above many saloons, with 'a spacious apartment containing boxes, pit, orchestra and stage, disposed as in ordinary theatres'.

The stage was small, but in the pit 'in front of each seat there is a narrow level table ... adapted [to hold] liquor and refreshments'. Rouse sat in a box, leading the applause and earning the nickname 'Bravo' for his enthusiastic endorsement of his own shows. The entertainment was varied. Concerts of music by Rossini, Handel or Mozart were accompanied by embryonic music hall fare from J.A. Cave or Robert Glindon. Musical drama and dancing were regular features, and the theatre began to attract family audiences. Up to six thousand customers passed through its doors in a single day. It was big business, fuelled by the growing purchasing power of the working population.

The entertainment at variety saloons was essentially the same as at song and supper clubs: ballads, comic songs, dance acts, jugglers and comedians performing over a hubbub of conversation and the clatter of table service to an audience intent on eating and drinking. Amid the din, a chairman kept a semblance of order and moved the show along. Once happily refreshed, the audiences joined in cheerfully with the familiar songs of favourite performers, and heckled those who disappointed. An evening in a saloon theatre had the strong participatory flavour of the early catch and glee clubs. It was, in essence, music hall proper before astute marketing labelled it as such and installed it in its own theatres.

The distinction between the entertainment offered at the various forms of theatres was minimal, but the facilities offered to them varied with the social strata the proprietors were seeking to attract. Between the upmarket song and supper clubs at one extreme, and the chaotic, ramshackle penny gaffs at the other, there was a huge gulf.

Charles Dickens, who had a lifelong fascination for the theatre, set out in 1850 to discover how the 'lower half' of London amused itself. In this quest he visited the Britannia saloon in Hoxton, and wrote of a mythical Mr Joe Whelks on an evening out. The cost of admission to the Britannia was one shilling for a box, sixpence for the pit, fourpence for the lower gallery or threepence for the upper gallery and back seats. Dickens was not impressed by the clientèle, who were, he wrote, 'very dirty people'; moreover, they smelled. A large proportion were very young, including 'girls grown into bold women before they had ceased to be children' – Dickens observed that these were more prominent in the theatres than at any other assembly 'except a public execution'.

Dickens found the audience was very attentive to the show, turning lustily on anyone interrupting it while consuming ham sandwiches, oranges, cakes or brandy-balls, and drinking porter which was passed around the galleries in a large can. He described the theatre as spacious, well-lit, and with a large stage. The organisation and management of the audience were businesslike, which was essential in order to accommodate the ten thousand customers who paid to attend the Britannia each week.

Mr Whelks also visited The Cut, Lambeth, where the Royal Victoria (now the Old Vic) could accommodate an audience of three thousand drawn from the slums crammed closely together in the nearby streets. The seat prices were similar to those at the Britannia, and so were the packed and overflowing galleries. Dickens was no kinder to the occupants of the pit at the Royal Victoria than he had been to those of the Britannia. He noted the presence of 'good-humoured young mechanics' before painting a disagreeable picture of their fellow theatre-goers. They were 'not very clean or sweet-savoured', and as they sat in their seats they ate cold fried soles and drank from flat-stoned bottles. Many of the women carried babies on their hips. The boxes, mercifully, lacked the fish-eaters and the babies, but were still not very salubrious. Among those seated in them Dickens saw pickpockets and soldiers, and observed that his neighbour 'wore pins on his coat instead of buttons', and was 'in such a damp habit of living as to be quite mouldy'. On both of his evenings out Dickens saw plays, so he did not witness the audience participating when familiar songs were performed.

*

Every karaoke evening organised today is a direct descendant of the 'free and easies' of the past. These were the poor man's song and supper clubs, situated in public houses where entrance was free of charge, with the publican relying on attracting an audience that would boost his sales of food, drink and tobacco – and thus his profits. They were similar to the singing rooms and harmonic meetings that flourished in the late eighteenth and early nineteenth centuries, and are a genuine precursor to music hall. In many free and easies customers would be invited to contribute a song, but more astute landlords recognised that popular acts were a greater draw. Often the artistes' wages were linked to alcohol sales: one singer, Thomas Weldon, earned a penny for every pint drunk by his audience while he was singing. In such an environment rousing entertainment and drunken revelry went hand in hand, but the wise landlord, conscious of the need to keep his licence to trade, tried to keep order by acting himself as chairman of the evening. Sometimes the entertainment was bawdy, but working-class audiences were often more prudish than the bohemian clientèle of the sophisticated song and supper clubs or the underclass who frequented the penny gaffs.

Apart from the landlord, the key figures in the free and easies were the chairman – familiar from the catch clubs, harmonic meetings and song and supper clubs – and the pianist who accompanied the singers. For many years the chairman would remain a central part of the music hall formula. His role was twofold: to keep order, and to pace the performance to ensure there were ample opportunities for customers to purchase refreshments.

The pianist was also pivotal. A minority could sing as well as play. Most were men, but the largest crowd-pullers were the small number of young women. They not only had novelty value, but were an obvious attraction to a largely youthful male audience. Contemporary advertisements in trade journals such as the *Era* offered a salary of up to £2 a week, with the added enticement of full bed and board. Although advertisements often specified 'steadiness' and 'gentility' as necessary qualifications for the job, prudish authority took a dim view of female pianists: as late as 1880 Bradford Council banned their employment in city taverns – perhaps the requirement to 'be agreeable to customers' aroused suspicion.

Nonetheless, whether male or female, competent accompaniment to the singers was essential. The artistes might be professional, semi-professional or amateur, but before 1850, when sheet music became cheap enough to be commonplace, many might simply hum the tune and then expect the pianist to improvise while they sang. Even with sheet music, pianists would be expected to be able to change key to match the vocal abilities of more hapless performers. It was a great relief to everyone when the pianist was familiar with the singer's repertoire.

Most of the songs were rousing choruses, sentimental ballads, patriotic anthems or celebrations of working-class people and their lives. Almost fifty years later, the theatre manager John Hollingshead recalled the free and easies of 1840, and his description reveals how closely they resembled music hall: 'The long room of the pot-house was the auditorium and, at a table larger than any other in the room was the stage, round which was seated the professional talent. The Chairman was a necessity to keep order and to draw out any volunteers who wished to distinguish themselves.'

Although the free and easies are poorly documented compared to their smarter cousins, there is one contemporary source that offers a unique insight into their world – the diaries of Charles Rice, a British Museum porter by day and ballad singer by night. They are a rich source of information written from the perspective of a performer.

Rice was born in 1817, the son of an optician, and his love of show business was evident from an early age: at eighteen he would copy out and collect performing bills from newspaper advertisements. We know nothing of his education, but his handwriting and observations reveal a certain level of sophistication. This was not reflected in his comparatively humble daytime employment, which was merely a backdrop to his evenings as an entertainer. He began at the British Museum as a twenty-year-old assistant messenger in

1837, and remained there, barely promoted for thirty-eight years, until he was sacked after lengthy periods of absence from work. His work day began at 7 a.m. – a punishingly early hour after late nights in smoky free and easies – and ended at 4 p.m. By the time he was sacked his pay had risen to £100 per annum, but in poor health and, so far as we know, without alternative employment, he died the following year at the age of fifty-eight.

Rice loved performing, and the money he earned enhanced his lifestyle. In the 1840s his salary at the museum was between £1 and thirty shillings a week. In the evenings, as a singer, he earned up to six shillings a night. There was also the fringe benefit of free drinks, at a time when alcohol was a large part of a working man's expenditure. The price of renting a room for a single man was no more than two shillings a month, and food would cost a further seven shillings or so. With total earnings of around £3 a week, Rice had significant disposable income.

He worked hard, and was in demand. In 1840 he sang at the King's Arms in Holborn on Mondays and Saturdays, at the Hope in Drury Lane on Tuesdays, at the Adam and Eve in St Pancras Road on Wednesdays, and the Horse and Dolphin, Macclesfield Road, on Thursdays and Fridays. It was a gruelling itinerary, and explains his lack of application in his job at the museum: he rarely returned home before midnight – later if he dropped in to the pie shop for a late supper, as he often did. He must have been exhausted, and probably hungover, for much of the time.

In his diaries, Rice passes judgement on his fellow performers. He writes of their songs, giving us a clear idea of the range on offer and what was popular. Amidst many anonymous names, more famous figures also appear, although not always to perform: Ross, Cowell, Sloman and other leading performers were no doubt searching for material in the free and easies, while the extraordinary Herr von Joel might have been surprised to find pub performers offering impersonations of him. Rice writes also of dancers, catch and glee singers, and 'Grecian statues' without disclosing whether or not the latter were clothed: it is likely they wore skin-tight costumes, but in view of the high necks and long skirts of the early Victorian era, figure-hugging clothing would have been quite sufficient to attract an audience.

Rice had a repertoire of around forty songs. Each evening he would sing a selection of six to nine of them, including encores. Some were adaptations of poems or narratives which he had arranged as songs for his own use. These included *Ingoldsby Legends*, 'The Jackdaw of Rheims', *Jack Sheppard* and parts of *The Pickwick Papers*, all of which suggests that he had talent far beyond what might be assumed by his intellectually undemanding work at the British Museum.

When it came to what his audience wanted, Rice had a fine judgement, and amended the lyrics of any song that might offend. The popular street song 'Billy Taylor' had many versions, some extremely rude. It tells the tale of Billy's sweetheart disguising herself as a man and joining the navy after Billy has been impressed into service. Rice chose to clean up the tale of how her gender was discovered. Similarly, he adapted W.T. Moncrieff's satirical 'Analisation' to focus on maids, young men and young wives in sentimental terms – quite different from the original.

In 1842, Rice married and moved to the emerging gentility of Somers Town, north of Euston Road, at the much higher rent of £1 a week. For eight years his diary falls silent. When it resumes, in 1850, his star seems to have waned, and he is engaged at less salubrious taverns, such as the Catherine Wheel, Whitechapel, which was better known as a haunt for prostitutes than a home for wholesome entertainment.

As purpose-built saloons, more suitable for mixed company, grew in number, the audiences at the free and easies waned. Rice did appear at larger proto-music halls such as the Yorkshire Stingo in Paddington and the Mogul Saloon in Drury Lane, but only occasionally, and well down the bill. His diary becomes increasingly bitter as he bemoans miserly landlords, incompetent pianists and inattentive audiences. Life was not going well for him: he tried to lose his dog by leaving her in unfamiliar surroundings, but the loyal animal kept returning to him. Eventually he gave her away to his greengrocer. In March 1850 Jemmy Vincent, his friend and pianist, committed suicide by shooting himself. But however tough life must have been for Rice, he could not afford to let his audience down: the evening after Vincent's suicide he was back onstage, singing at the disreputable Catherine Wheel.

In May 1850 Rice started a 'singers' republic' at his old haunt the Grapes, in Southwark, which operated on the new business model of customers paying for entrance, with 'free' drink as part of the package. He shared the gate money with his fellow performers in lieu of a flat wage, and at first the enterprise was a success, with around eighty paying customers a night. But it didn't last, and the enterprise was shelved after a mere forty-one customers turned up one late-October evening. Rice's diary ends on the last day of 1850, when he thanks the Almighty for carrying him through undisclosed 'difficulties' and adds the plaintive plea that 'things may be looking up by this time in 1851'. So far as we know, they never did.

The heyday of the free and easies ended when music hall proper began to mushroom. Even so, many continued to thrive: the King's Head, Knightsbridge; the King and Queen, Paddington Green; the Swan, Hungerford Market; the Salmon and Compass, Pentonville; the Salmon and the New Inn, both in Borough. But they were swimming against the tide. In the hierarchy of entertainment the downmarket free and easies were near the bottom, outclassing only the lowest of the low – the penny gaffs.

It is likely that the penny gaffs were given their name by the costermongers who formed a large portion of their audience. The name was not haphazard: the price of entry was a penny, and while 'gaff' has many meanings, one being a cockney term for 'place', another is a slang term for a cockfighting pit, which in its crudeness and brutality is an apt description of the barbarous behaviour that was typical of a penny gaff.

Costermongers play a significant role in the story of music hall. Colourful, definitively working-class and instantly recognisable in their short jackets, neckerchiefs, bell-bottomed trousers and peaked caps, they were a large, close-knit community of street traders who became one of music hall's most enduring stage personas. Entrepreneurial, resilient and streetwise, they earned their living selling fruit and vegetables, fish and shellfish in the formal and informal markets from which most working-class Londoners obtained their food. Their very name was a nod to the 'costard' variety of apples. Many walked the streets, selling their wares from barrows or rickety carts, earning perhaps no more than a few shillings a week.

In the 1840s it was estimated that there were about 40,000 costers in London. The social investigator Henry Mayhew gives a vivid account of a Saturday-evening market in November. The brightness was the first thing he noticed: naphtha flares, candles, gas jets, grease lamps, the fires of the chestnut-roasters. Then the noise – hundreds of traders at hundreds of stalls calling out their wares: 'Chestnuts, a penny a score,' 'Three a penny, Yarmouth bloaters,' 'Beautiful whelks a penny a lot,' 'Penny a lot, fine russets,' 'Ho! Ho! Hi-i-i. Here's your turnips.' Everything cheap and of use to the poor was there: saucepans, crockery, old shoes, trays, handkerchiefs, umbrellas, shirts. 'Go to whatever corner of the Metropolis you please,' Mayhew noted, 'and there is the same struggling to get a penny profit out of the poor man's Sunday dinner.'

It is not hard to see why costers became such powerful stereotypes. They lived their lives on the streets, and were transparently masculine in their habits. Beer shops were their natural haunts: Mayhew claimed that nearly four hundred of them catered directly for costers. Gambling was endemic, and they frequently bet their stock money against a tray of pies as they waited for the wholesale markets to open. They boxed for beer and placed side bets. Bouts were short, since the winner was the first man to draw blood. Although illegal, dog fights in beer shops were also common. Ratting was popular, as was pigeon-keeping. Many of these activities found their way into the music halls and their portrayal of the coster idiom.

Dances – tup'nny hops – were also popular, particularly with women. These too were held in the beer shops, organised

The rotunda at Ranelagh Gardens, by Canaletto, 1754. Very popular from the Restoration onward, 'pleasure gardens' provided enclosed areas with food, drink and entertainment laid on for a leisured clientèle. They would play an important role in the pre-life of music hall.

The Old Drury, Brydges Street, London, c.1830. The scene accurately captures the kind of 'singing room' familiar to contemporary commentator and performer Charles Rice.

Evans' song and supper rooms (aka Joy's Hotel, aka Evans' Late Joy's) in the 1850s, by Gustav Doré. The artist captures the intimate human scale of the very early halls, and how they would have functioned. While some watch and listen to the performance, others drink and talk.

W.G. Ross (c.1815–c.1860) achieved huge success with his 'Ballad of Sam Hall'. Even the most boisterous house hushed and the drinking ceased when it was announced that he would give his powerful performance as the condemned man.

Sheet music for 'The Ratcatcher's Daughter', composed and sung by early music hall star Sam Cowell (1819–54). Music hall seldom shrank from describing grisly realities, and we can clearly see the disappearing legs of 'the purty little ratcatcher's daughter' as she 'tumbled into the vater; and down to the bottom, all kivered with mud'.

The Eagle in City Road, Shoreditch, where Marie Lloyd (probably) made her debut in 1885. It achieved immortality with its inclusion in the song 'Pop Goes the Weasel'.

Wilton's Music Hall today. Opened in 1859 by John Wilton, it is the oldest surviving example of the style of hall built between 1850 and 1870. The void in front of the stage would have been packed with tables and chairs as the audience tucked into baked potatoes and chops, washed down with beer.

Charles Morton (1819–1904), 'the Father of the Halls'. His motto, 'Only one quality – the best', proved to be a very successful, and much copied, business model.

Morton's vision was for something more than a place to come for 'a song and a pint'. He envisaged a 'palace of entertainment', and this depiction of the interior of his Canterbury Music Hall gives a clear view of the sumptuous decoration and expensive lighting, and the ease with which patrons were able to move between the various spaces.

Ticket for the Canterbury, 1874. Most owners and managers were keen to have all comers through the doors, but apparently babes in arms were a step too far.

George Leybourne (1842–84), a great favourite at the Canterbury. His timeless hit 'Champagne Charlie' was just one of many songs that mocked the foppish and indolent 'swell'– an influential genre for early music hall artistes.

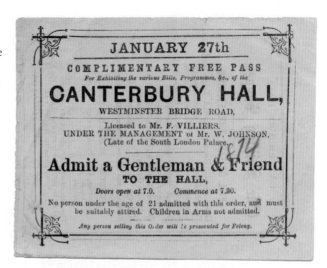

JANUARY 27th

COMPLIMENTARY FREE PASS
For Exhibiting the various Bills, Programmes, &c., of the

CANTERBURY HALL,
WESTMINSTER BRIDGE ROAD,

Licensed to Mr. F. VILLIERS.
UNDER THE MANAGEMENT of Mr. W. JOHNSON,
(Late of the South London Palace.)

Admit a Gentleman & Friend
TO THE HALL,
Doors open at 7.0.   Commence at 7.30.

No person under the age of 21 admitted with this order, and must be suitably attired. Children in Arms not admitted.

Any person selling this Order will be prosecuted for Felony.

AFTER THE OPERA.

CHORUS
"After the Opera's over,
Attending the ladies is done,
We gems of the very first water,
Commence with our frolic & fun."

WRITTEN, COMPOSED & SUNG
BY

GEORGE LEYBOURNE.

LONDON:
HOPWOOD & CREW, 42, NEW BOND STREET.

This hair-raising picture shows how close the acrobats were to the audience – and suggests that health and safety concerns were some way down the list of priorities for managers.

George Ware, one of the first music hall agents and Marie Lloyd's long-time mentor, friend and manager. He was the composer of 'The Boy i Love is Up in the Gallery', one of music hall's most cherished songs.

Jenny Hill (c.1850–96), 'the Vital Spark', was one of the earliest and greatest 'serio-comediennes'. Starting out as a child performer in the free and easies, she became a superstar to rank alongside Marie Lloyd and Vesta Tilley.

Gus Elen (1862–1940), one of the most popular 'coster' comedians. His songs told of life as most of his audience understood it – the bittersweet pleasures of courtship, mothers-in-law, wives, rent collectors and problems with work – and the police …

"E dunno where E are."

exclusively for costers. Music was provided by a fiddle, a harp and a cornopean – a kind of hooped trumpet, not unlike a French horn. They danced hornpipes, jigs, polkas and a kind of sword dance with tobacco pipes (presumably churchwardens) in place of swords. These dances acted as a kind of coster marriage bureau, where couples as young as fourteen could meet and decide to set up house together, sometimes on the same evening.

Marriage was rare; 90 per cent of costers cohabited. Men were free to do what they pleased, but women were expected to be faithful, and could be beaten up for even talking to the wrong man – or, it seems, for almost anything. Many women regretted the choices they made as girls. One eighteen-year-old woman had very strong opinions about coster men. 'They'll never go to heaven,' she told Mayhew. 'The lads is very insinivating, and after leaving them places [penny gaffs] will give a gal a drop of beer, and make her half tipsy, and then they makes their arrangements. I've often heerd the boys boasting of having ruined gals, for all the world as if they was the first noblemen in the land.' The girls' precarious existence at the hands of their male counterparts would be the inspiration for many a lovelorn 'coster girl' song.

In the process of looking at the costers and their way of life, both Henry Mayhew and his fellow social commentator J. Ewing Ritchie give us very reliable and detailed accounts of what a penny gaff would have been like. Mayhew attended one near Smithfield which he had heard was one of the least offensive. He was genuinely shocked by what he saw, even though he was more familiar than most outsiders with London's underclass. Penny gaffs were not theatres or saloons, or even rooms in pubs, but simply shops, and usually tatty ones, that had been turned into seedy temporary theatres. Despite the shortage of space, hundreds of paying customers might be crammed into every performance, of which there could be several during a single day and evening. The audience, Mayhew reported, were 'with few exceptions' young people aged between eight and twenty. The front of the shop had been removed, and replaced by paintings of the performers. A band played coster tunes as the audience paid their pennies to enter under the watchful eye of a policeman detailed to keep order.

The performance lasted barely an hour. A 'comic singer' sang a filthy song that had the boys 'stamping their feet with delight' and the girls 'screaming with enjoyment'. Another song 'coolly described the most obscene thoughts, the most disgusting scenes', causing a child nearby to 'wipe away the tears that rolled down her eyes with the enjoyment of the poison'. Each crude ditty was succeeded by another, every one being rapturously applauded and encored. The boys stamped, hollered, whistled, cat-called and sang. The dancing was no better. In a ballet featuring a man dressed as a woman, and a clown, 'the most disgusting attitudes were struck, the most immoral acts represented … here were two ruffians degrading themselves each time they stirred a limb'. The audience upset Mayhew as much as the performance. They had 'an overpowering stench'; some 'danced grotesquely to the admiration of lookers-on, who expressed their approbation in obscene terms'; the girls acknowledged such comments 'with smiles and coarse repartee'.

J. Ewing Ritchie visited two penny gaffs in Shoreditch, an area rich in theatrical history. In Elizabethan times the Curtain Theatre had stood there, and public houses had staged comedies, tragedies and histories. Close by was the Britannia saloon, which still offered daily shows and would soon be converted to a full-scale music hall. In the midst of this long commitment to quality entertainment stood the penny gaff. Since the birth of the Curtain nearly three hundred years earlier, the area had changed. It was no longer open land with a view of working windmills, but crammed with squalid dwellings, public houses, pie shops, clothes marts, shoe depots and street markets. Its crowded streets provided a ready audience, but one which was able to afford only a penny for a show.

Ritchie describes a mediocre evening of low wit and poor dancing before a grubby juvenile audience, chiefly boys, but with a sprinkling of the girls with babies in their arms who were so often present at such shows. The highlight was a pastiche of *The Taming of the Shrew* in which the henpecked husband turns on the shrew and threatens her with a cudgel as she lies cowering at his feet. This excited roars of approval from the young audience. Ritchie loathed it, believing that similar scenes would be re-enacted later in many Shoreditch homes.

The penny gaffs did not die when music hall swept into fashion. As late as 1881, dirty and dark houses were still being used as make-shift theatres. The entertainment was still tawdry, although perhaps not as brutal or degrading as forty years earlier. The penny gaffs had little to commend them, and much that was reprehensible – but they were part of the making of music hall.

By the 1840s, the ingredients for the emergence of music hall were all present. The public had a taste for community entertainment. Catch and glee clubs had popularised participatory enjoyment. Saloon theatre had offered refined singing and dancing. Song and supper clubs and taverns had familiarised audiences with risqué evenings conducted by a chairman. Food and drink had become a key component of the entertainment experience. Nevertheless, a further impetus was needed. It would soon come, and from an unexpected source.

4

The First Pioneer

'Only one quality – the best.'

CHARLES MORTON'S MOTTO

Music hall was shaped by the changing social environment, but time and the right set of circumstances were required for it to flourish.

By 1820, one quarter of the world's population was governed from London, and Britain was evolving from a rural to an urban society. Populations in towns and cities doubled and redoubled. The search for jobs drove teeming throngs of villagers to the towns, where cheap back-to-back hovels were thrown up to house them. But there were improvements: working hours fell, and wages rose.

The choice of amusements was widening. Madame Tussaud's waxworks opened in 1835. Hampton Court and Kew Gardens were welcoming visitors. The Henley Regatta and the Grand National were both held for the first time in 1839. Football was growing in popularity. Cricket was becoming a national institution as young William Gilbert Grace learned to bat and bowl in his Gloucestershire orchard. It was a new world that set the stage for music hall. One elusive element remained to be put in place, and Parliament was soon to enact it, albeit in muddled form. It would prove to be a catalyst for music hall.

The law and the theatre had been at loggerheads for centuries, and by 1840 the situation had become absurd. The Lord Chamberlain regulated legitimate theatre, but local magistrates were responsible for music and dancing licences. The scope for inconsistency was very wide. The patent monopoly, under which Charles II had granted Drury Lane and Covent Garden the sole right to perform drama, now included the Haymarket, which George III had added to the magic circle. To everyone other than the beneficiaries of the monopoly, this was absurd, and the law was regularly flouted. This led to ludicrous litigation, and the threat of actors being arrested for the heinous crime of performing Shakespeare. Parliament sought to impose order on this chaos, and in 1843 the Theatre Regulations Act abolished the monopoly of the patent theatres. Thereafter, anyone could stage drama if they first obtained the approval of the Lord Chamberlain.

So far, so good. But the Lord Chamberlain's licence gave permission only to perform drama, not to serve the audience with food and drink, or to allow smoking. The alternative of a magistrate's licence permitted eating, drinking and smoking, but did not permit the licensee to stage drama. It is clear from reading the (very limited) debates on the Bill that the legislators did not understand custom and practice in the theatres, and gave no consideration to the great diversity of performances beyond legitimate drama. The legislation succeeded only in creating confusion.

The Act was a hotchpotch. It failed to address the provision of food and drink, and left old habits and customs in place. Even the officials responsible for the law were bewildered. When the Lord Chamberlain's representative was asked to clarify it to a Parliamentary Select Committee more than twenty years later, in 1866, he told them that 'spirits and refreshments are not to be sold within the audience part of the theatre', but added, 'excepting the people who walk up and down the pit with baskets'. They were, of course, selling food and drink.

Some impresarios ignored the law. Sam Lane, who ran the Britannia on a Lord Chamberlain's licence, sold food and drink, and allowed smoking, but was never censured. It may be that the authorities were content to leave the great unwashed of the East End alone, for if the West End theatres flouted the same rules, they were closed.

The new legislation did at least present a clear choice: an impresario could produce either drama or light entertainment. The wrong choice could mean ruin – as it did for the Grecian Saloon in City Road, when it chose drama and alienated its clientèle – whereas the right choice could mean riches.

Charles Morton's Canterbury Arms, which opened in Lambeth in 1852, is generally regarded as the first purpose-built music hall. It set a trend that popularised the music hall genre, and was widely copied. Morton, born in Hackney in August 1819, grew up among the poor with an appetite for work and a sharp eye for detail. He saw his neighbours warm to street singers, cluster around peep shows, applaud itinerant performers and, when the pennies permitted, visit the cheaper inns and taverns. The theatre drew him like a magnet, and he attended shows whenever he had the means to do so. Aged thirteen, his first visit was to the Pavilion, Whitechapel – familiarly known as 'the Drury Lane of the East' – which specialised in plays catering for sailors and the large Jewish population that thronged the East End. At the nearby Old Garrick Theatre he saw the tragi-comic play *Damon and Pythias*, starring Charles Freear and William Gomershall, an actor famed for his comic impersonation of Napoleon. The young Charles Morton became a habitué of East End theatres, and grew familiar with public tastes.

Once his elementary education was over he worked as a tavern waiter, and saw at close quarters how entertainment and food and drink brought in the crowds. He earned extra cash, and a reputation for honesty, as a runner for the 'list men', the early pub-based bookmakers. At the age of twenty-one, in 1840, he became the licensee of his own pub, the St George's tavern in Belgrave Road, Pimlico. Pimlico was a brand-spanking-new development, a world away from the East End. It was close to the pleasure gardens at Ranelagh,

Cremorne and Vauxhall, where young Morton continued his education by seeing the talent available for hire.

As a licensee, Morton put all he had seen and learned into practice. His guiding principle was excellent service, food and drink,
and to these he added a 'free and easy' room with amateur talent
performing, 'For Gentlemen Only!', free of charge. These were
common features at many taverns, but Morton's astute business
brain and engaging personality made them very attractive, and as
the St George's became more profitable he hired professional acts to
lure more customers. Some of his regulars were servants at
Buckingham Palace, and they invited him to dine with them in
their quarters. He returned home with a tablecloth full of delicacies
from the royal pantry.

Morton was a natural entrepreneur who understood the power
of promotion. Bookmaking was a profitable sideline, and he
promoted his sweepstakes for big race meetings by advertising in
the *Era*.

Morton worked long hours to earn a more comfortable way of
life. He was a very visible host, but, unusually for the time, he was
abstemious, having no wish to drink away his profits. He walked
and fished for recreation, making plans as he did so. As business
prospered he traded up to the Crown in Pentonville, and then to
the far more fashionable India House tavern in Leadenhall Street in
the City. His credo was to exceed the expectations of his customers.
At the India House he abandoned entertainment to concentrate on
offering good fare in a congenial atmosphere – 'Only one quality –
the best' had become his motto, and would remain so throughout
his long life. The absence of entertainment defied convention, but
in the City, where men met to eat and drink and discuss business,
the India House was a haven – and a shrewd business move.

Despite the lack of song and dance at his City tavern, Morton
never lost sight of the profit to be gained by feeding mind and body
at the same time. He was a regular visitor to every sort of entertainment venue, and made note of money-making opportunities that
were missed. He saw that the shows catered only for men: there

were no women, no girls with their boyfriends, no families. Half the population was being ignored. Morton saw a huge untapped potential, and pondered how to exploit it without losing male patronage.

The solution was not obvious. Women had little or no money of their own, and even if they had, the social conservatism of the age would prevent them from attending taverns without a male escort. Morton realised that if men were accompanied by their wives or girlfriends, they would spend only the same sum between two customers. There was no extra profit in that. Worse, there might be a loss, since the entertainment mix would need to take account of females in the audience. The dilemma was still unresolved when Morton and his brother-in-law Frederick Stanley bought the Old Canterbury Arms in Westminster Bridge Road (then called Lambeth Marsh) in 1849. It was an ancient alehouse, once owned by the Canon of Rochester, and named as a homage to the medieval pilgrims who fed and watered there en route to the shrine of St Thomas à Becket.

The Canterbury Arms was in a squalid neighbourhood, but it had a theatrical pedigree stretching back three hundred years. It had been a favoured haunt of the Elizabethan actors of Bankside: Burbage, Henslowe, Jonson and Shakespeare were all said to have supped there. At the time of Morton's purchase it had a regular clientèle who flocked there both to hear amateur talent in the modest music room, and to enjoy the four skittle alleys at the back.

Morton took over the Canterbury Arms' licence in February 1850, but little was heard of him in the press for over two years, apart from a brief burst of publicity when a notorious skittle sharp, Joseph Jones, attracted police attention for his activities there. Morton's uncharacteristic reticence ended as soon as his new hall was complete. In the *Era* of 16 May 1852 he promoted his new venture by funding a competition to determine the 'champion swimmer of England' between George Pewters and Frederick Beckwith. 'Money ready' for the winner, it said, at 'Mr Morton's

Canterbury Arms, Lambeth'. In the news section of the same edition there is an entry: 'The Canterbury Arms. A new and elegantly fitted up hall ... and rumour speaks highly of all the arrangements.' These news snippets suggest that Morton had delayed promoting his venture until he was completely satisfied with all the preparations. Now his vision was in place, and a notice the following week informed readers that 'The Canterbury Music Hall offers superior talent ... every attention paid to comfort and amusement ... suppers, chops, steaks, etc etc. Admission by refreshment ticket, sixpence each person.'

The music room was adapted to a club room, where 'free and easy' concerts were held on Thursdays and Saturdays. With his usual attention to detail Morton set about providing excellent value in food and drink, but he was careful not to make changes that alienated the existing customers. More comfortable furniture and better lighting were introduced, and the walls were decorated with paintings and prints. There were roaring fires in the hearths, and spills to light pipes, cigars, and later the cigarettes popularised by soldiers returning from the Crimean War. Morton's Canterbury was a warm and congenial environment, far more appealing than the cold, damp, cramped back-to-back houses that were home to so many of his customers. So they came and they stayed and they spent. As his profits grew Morton commissioned a new hall, to be built over the ramshackle skittle alleys.

He also hit upon an idea to attract women to the Canterbury without losing his existing customers. Rather than facing down social convention, Morton decided to bypass it. The admission fee of sixpence, which included drinks, was his answer to the conundrum of how to profit from women patrons. Since women rarely drank their full entitlement this proved a lucrative form of entry, and he actively encouraged them to attend his hall. A 'Ladies Night' was introduced in the club room once a week, which was a triumph. Morton's brother Robert, a charmer with an excellent tenor voice, compèred evenings of entertainment that were packed to capacity. The mothers, daughters, wives, sisters, fiancées and girlfriends thoroughly enjoyed it, and their menfolk asked for the ladies to be admitted on other nights as well. Morton acquiesced, the objectors were outfoxed, and no one was offended.

Soon performances were staged every night, not just twice weekly. The Canterbury was no longer a pub, but a music hall. The package was complete: payment for entrance, refreshments available, entertainment based around comic ballads but with a wide variety of acts supporting them – and joyous, often uproarious participation from an audience of both sexes. The evening's entertainment began at 7 p.m. and ended at midnight. And the money rolled in.

The Canterbury's success was instant and overwhelming. Night after night seven hundred seats were sold and disappointed customers were turned away. Morton lined the walls with 'lists' of horses and race meetings so that customers could place bets while enjoying the show. 'Lists' were very popular, and the affinity between the turf and music hall remained strong until an Act of 1853 outlawed them.

Morton was a micro-manager who supervised everything. He booked the acts and was present at every performance. He formed his own resident choir, some members of which, including Haydn Corri, Edward Connell, St Clair Jones and Mrs John Caulfield, went on to enjoy successful solo careers in music hall. Nothing escaped his eye, and nothing was left to chance. He supervised the mobile ovens that baked potatoes, sometimes serving them to customers himself, with lashings of butter and seasoned with salt and pepper. Morton had an eye for detail, and nothing was overlooked.

The performers at the Canterbury were paid well – far more than the few shillings and free beer that were typical elsewhere – and under Morton's patronage they became stars. His most glittering performer was Sam Cowell, he of 'Villikins' and 'The Ratcatcher's Daughter' fame, who had been sacked from Evans' by Paddy Green. Much Sam cared: he knew his value, and found a better berth with Morton, who paid him lavishly – up to £80 a week at his peak – and let him draw in the crowds.

Cowell's story does not end happily. A man of weak constitution, he wasted too much of the money he earned on drink. In 1859 he returned from a gruelling twenty-month tour of America a very sick man. Long-distance travelling had left him poorly nourished, and temptation and free drinks had made him an alcoholic. His money was almost all gone. At Blandford, near Poole, he fell so ill that his wife was summoned from London, and he died in 1864, at only forty-four years of age, leaving his family nearly destitute. It was a sad ending for a man who ranks among the greatest of all music hall artistes.

Cowell was not the only refugee from the supper clubs. The old cigar con man Herr von Joel appeared, as did the mimic Charles Sloman, and song-and-supper-club regulars such as Robert Glindon and the wonderfully funny Jack Sharp. The comic singer Tom Penniket, an embryonic Dan Leno, was a frequent performer, and the tenor John Caulfield became the compère and chairman, with his son Johnny as the resident harmonium player. Many other popular artistes, such as the comedians Elija Taylor and Billy Pells, also delighted the Canterbury's audiences. The basso-profundo St Clair Jones was in and out of favour with Morton for sloppy timekeeping, much as Sam Cowell had been at Evans'. Eventually Morton dismissed him, but the wily Jones then reappeared onstage to sing 'I Cannot Leave Thee Yet'. The audience was won over – as was Morton – and Jones was reinstated.

Morton surveyed his full houses and his growing bank balance, and decided to expand. He had room to do so on his current site, but he had no wish to dismantle his theatre, lose a year's revenue, and risk his regular audience developing other loyalties. He overcame this dilemma with a radical plan to build a bigger hall literally over and around the existing premises. While building proceeded, the shows continued with no loss of income, and when the new, larger outer shell was complete, the inner walls were removed. It was a seamless transition, and the plush new Canterbury Music Hall was open for business just before Christmas 1854. It was a sumptuous sight, with a horseshoe-shaped balcony supported on pillars and accessed via a grand staircase. Chandeliers hung from the ceiling, and on either side of the imposing stage stood a harmonium and a grand piano. At a long table immediately below the stage the chairman sat with "is 'ammer in 'is 'and', his cigar and a bottle of wine.

Admission was sixpence to the body of the hall, and ninepence to the gallery. Tables seating four or more patrons were set in neat rows on the ground floor, where customers could eat and drink for a shilling and men could smoke pipes or cigars. No food or drink was served in the gallery, which made the extra threepence a worthwhile expense to the fastidious. Lavishly printed programmes announced the running order for the evening, and included the words of the songs, to encourage the audience to join in the choruses. The regulars loved it, and the increased capacity of fifteen hundred meant that they were soon joined by those who had previously been unable to get seats. Demand was enhanced by the extension of street lighting and the introduction of horse-drawn omnibuses, which allayed fears over venturing far in the dark evenings.

Morton continued to engage the best artistic talents. One of the cleverest was the Scotsman Tom Maclagan, who could sing in any style, serious or comic, dance and play the violin. Sam Collins was a regular, as was E.W. Mackney – billed by Morton as 'the Great Mackney, Negro Delineator' – one of the first artistes to 'black up' and sing what in those days were known as 'coon' songs. Among the popular female singers, billed with Victorian formality, were Miss Pearce, Miss Bramell and Miss Townley.

An additional attraction was a 'fine arts' gallery. Morton had noted the success of the National Gallery, which had opened a quarter of a century earlier and attracted 'respectable' society. Nor did he fail to notice the popularity of the picture gallery at the Grapes in Southwark Bridge Road. He had no scruples in stealing its ideas and improving on them. At first the paintings were lent to Morton by art dealers, but as profits rose he bought some of them. The gallery was not a personal indulgence, it was good business.

Morton bought fine paintings in such quantity – including Gainsboroughs and Hogarths – that by 1856 he needed an annexe to house them all. This was celebrated in *Punch* as 'the Royal Academy over the Water', and the publicity was a further boost to Morton's reputation.

It was in fact much more than a picture gallery, containing a reading room with books, periodicals and newspapers. Oysters, chops, baked potatoes, and bread and butter were among the refreshments that were eagerly consumed for the price of a sixpenny refreshment ticket. The gallery was open seven days a week, including Sunday night – a privilege granted to Morton, presumably because of his reputation, that caused resentment among other theatre managers denied the same indulgence.

Morton continually sought to widen the entertainment he offered. To the usual fare of ballads, comic songs, madrigals and glees, Morton – who had a great admiration for the celebrated Swedish soprano Jenny Lind – added selections from opera. Popular arias from *Il Trovatore, La Traviata, Lucia de Lammermoor* and *Un Ballo in Maschera* became a regular part of the evening's entertainment, sung by Augustus Braham, Signor Tivoli and Miss Russell, an excellent dramatic soprano and a favourite of the audiences. Gounod's *Faust*, premiered in Paris in 1859, had never been heard in England, and proved to be a popular sensation when Miss Russell sang excerpts from it. Contemporary rumour suggested that Colonel Mapleson, manager of Her Majesty's Theatre in the Haymarket, brought the celebrated German prima donna Thérèse Tietjens to the Canterbury to see if *Faust* was worthy of his stage. An opera making its British debut in a music hall added to Morton's reputation, and helped lure fashionable and wealthy patrons across the river to the dank location of the Canterbury.

Morton was an influential figure in music hall for the rest of his long life. He was probably the first to offer the complete music hall experience, although others were not far behind. His reputation was built on his early work, and enhanced by charitable hindsight. He was a kindly man, bow-tied, long-jawed and with muttonchop whiskers framing his friendly face. On his eightieth birthday in 1899, many prominent members of the profession paid warm tributes to him. An ode recited by Mrs Beerbohm Tree gives the flavour:

> His Harbour Light was a vista view of things as they
>   ought to be,
> The pleasures of England should be pure and Art, it
>   must be free
> He took with pluck this parable up, at Duty's bugle call
> And swore he would lead to paths of peace the
>   dangerous Music Hall!

This depicts Morton as a cross between Sir Galahad and Mr Valiant-for-Truth. He was a good and honourable man, but above all he was an astute businessman with an eye on the main chance and the bottom line. His virtues were real, but were puffed up in a rose-tinted biography by his friend and admirer H. Chance Newton, which was published in 1905, just after his death. In it, Morton is celebrated as the 'Father of the Halls'. The appellation stuck. Morton's record was remarkable, and he has an honoured role among the founders of music hall.

5

Explosion

'I have seen the future, and it works.'

LINCOLN STEFFENS, JOURNALIST (1866–1936)

The opening of the new Canterbury was the moment when music hall put down firm commercial roots, even though its golden age lay over a quarter of a century ahead. In the early 1850s the greatest names of music hall were either children or not yet born. The road from the Canterbury to the popular memories they would engender, and to the great empires of Moss, Stoll and Thornton, was long and thorny, but at the end of it lay stars still fondly remembered, and songs that have endured.

Music hall was a new industry that needed a support structure. New theatres were built in every part of the country, requiring architects, builders and designers. Singers, musicians and songwriters were needed for these theatres. Lawyers were employed to advise on the awkward legal division between legitimate theatre and music hall. Disputes over matinées and Sunday performances had to be settled. Health and safety regulations had to be met.

Taverns, concert halls and song and supper clubs were converted into music halls, and Charles Morton soon had rivals. The most formidable was Edward Weston, owner of the quaintly named Six Cans and Punch Bowl tavern in Holborn, who purchased two adjacent properties and in November 1857 opened the purpose-built Weston's Music Hall on the site. It was launched amid huge publicity, with an elegant dinner for three hundred guests and a little theatrical larceny: Weston engaged the former chairman of the Canterbury, John Caulfield, as his musical director, and Sam Collins as his star attraction. Contemporary advertisements suggest the setting was sumptuous, with high-quality fixtures, fittings, food and drink, all for an entrance fee of sixpence. It was a none-too-subtle declaration of war, and Morton was swift to respond.

Being at Holborn, Weston's was on the threshold of the West End, where music hall had not yet penetrated. The challenge was irresistible for Morton. In partnership with his brother-in-law Frederick Stanley he bought a seventeenth-century inn, the Boar and Castle, on the corner of Oxford Street and Tottenham Court Road. Despite a legal challenge from Weston, whose music hall was only a few hundred yards away, Morton built the Oxford Music Hall on the site, and opened it in March 1861. Constructed in the Italian style and reputedly costing £35,000, it was the most glamor-ous music hall yet, described by the early music hall historians Charles Stuart and A.J. Park as 'a point of architectural beauty'. One of the chief features was the lighting, with twenty-eight brilliant 'crystal' stars. Its huge capital cost notwithstanding, the Oxford was a highly commercial proposition, with a restaurant area in the audi-torium offering sufficient space for 1,800 customers to eat and drink in relays until 1 a.m., served by attractive barmaids. This was typical Morton: the best artistes packaged in an environment with fringe attractions.

At the Canterbury, the additional lure had been an art gallery and library; at the Oxford it was attractive barmaids and bars deco-rated with flowers. The Oxford also offered Morton an important revenue saving: from the outset he employed the same stars to sing opera selections for both the working-class audience at the Canterbury and the more cosmopolitan customers at the Oxford, transporting them between the two venues in broughams. As at any one time they might include a tenor (Mr St Aubyn), a bass (Mr

Green), a soprano (Miss Russell), a contralto (Miss Walmisley) and a mezzo (Miss Fitzhenry), it is evident that a great deal of serious music was juxtaposed with more familiar music hall fare. John Caulfield was recaptured from Weston's as resident chairman, and his son Johnny was one of the pianists. Miss Fitzhenry enjoyed early success singing 'Up the Alma Heights', which delighted every soldier in London, and 'Launch the Lifeboat', which enchanted the naval men. With other performers including George Leybourne, Tom Maclagan, Nelly Power and 'Jolly' John Nash, all tastes were met.

One of Morton's innovations at the Oxford was foiled by the magistrates. When he tried to stage matinée performances on Saturdays, he was warned that his licence permitted him to open only after 6 p.m. He had to drop the idea, only to see it become common practice a few years later.

Although the Canterbury, Weston's and above all the Oxford remained pre-eminent, competition was growing as music halls of every size were opening all around them. In 1860 the South London Palace, designed internally to resemble a Roman villa, opened at the Elephant and Castle, with the black-faced E.W. ('the Great') Mackney topping the bill. Harry Hart's Lord Raglan at Bloomsbury also made its debut, followed swiftly by John Deacon's Music Hall at Islington, with Fred Williams as chairman.

The former chimney sweep Sam Collins, one of the early stars at the Canterbury and the top of the bill at Weston's, opened establishments of his own: the Rose of Normandy public house in Edgware Road, alongside which he built the Marylebone Music Hall. At the beginning of his musical career Sam had earned a few shillings a night as a pub singer; in 1863, at the age of thirty-five, he became the respected and much-loved owner of the newly built Collins' Music Hall in Islington, known colloquially as 'the Chapel on the Green'. Sadly, Sam was able to revel in his new status only briefly, for he died two years after it opened. He was one of the many music hall pioneers who did not live long enough to enjoy the rewards of the trail they had blazed.

In 1859 the London Pavilion was opened in Tichborne Street, Haymarket, by Emil Loibl and Charles Sonnhammer. Originally a stable yard, it had been converted to the Black Horse tavern two years earlier, run as a song and supper room, and then rebuilt as the much more substantial London Pavilion, with an audience capacity of two thousand. It became the home of variety under Sir Charles (C.B.) Cochran, and would end its life as a cinema three quarters of a century later. But the intervening years wove it into the fabric of music hall history.

The boom continued throughout the 1860s with the debut of the Alhambra Palace, Leicester Square, together with the Bedford Theatre in Camden, immortalised in oils by Walter Sickert. The Royal New Music Hall, Kensington, the Royal Standard at Pimlico, the Oxford & Cambridge in Chalk Farm, the Regent in Regent Street, the Royal Cambridge in Commercial Street, Whitechapel (where Charlie Chaplin is thought to have made his debut as a solo-ist) and Hoxton Music Hall all opened in 1864. Gatti's-in-the-Road, in Westminster Bridge Road, and Gatti's-under-the-Arches, in Villiers Street, opened in 1865 and 1867 respectively. The latter year brought the Panorama in Shoreditch, Davey's at Stratford, the Royal Oriental at Poplar and the opening of the Virgo, otherwise the Varieties Theatre, Hoxton. Later known as the Sod's Opera, this was a seedy, rowdy hall with an insalubrious audience. The pace slowed thereafter, but new building continued. By 1875 London hosted thirty full-time music halls, and double that number by the turn of the century.

Outside London, public demand for music hall was similarly fierce. Old taverns and 'free and easies' had been swiftly adapted: the Adelphi in Sheffield had formerly been a circus, and Thornton's Varieties in Leeds a harmonica room. In Sheffield, the curiously named Surrey Music Hall – formerly a casino – opened in 1850, and proud locals pronounced it to be the most handsome in the coun-try; sadly, it burned down in 1865. Undaunted, its owner, a former Irish labourer, Thomas Youdan, took over the Adelphi and opened it as the Alexandra Music Hall. Manchester boasted the Star at

Ancoats, 'the People's Concert Hall', which had opened in the early 1850s, and the London Music Hall in Bridge Street.

The old 'free and easies' in Nottingham had built up a huge appetite for music hall, and the venerable and grubby Theatre Royal in St Mary's Gate was renovated as the Alhambra Theatre of Varieties. A little later St George's Hall attracted local audiences. Its resident chairman was Harry Ball, father of music hall's greatest male impersonator, Vesta Tilley, who made her debut there in 1868, aged four. Music hall made its Scottish debut with the Alhambra in Dundee, although Scottish old-time music hall continued to centre on Glasgow.

All of the theatres that followed the opening of the Canterbury faced many of the same problems. One was the law. By sharpening the distinction between drama and music hall the 1843 Theatre Regulations Act had opened up opportunities, but it presented problems too. Charles Morton's experience was higher-profile than most, but was not unique. The Canterbury, as a music hall, was unlicensed for drama, but at Christmas 1855 Morton staged a dramatic sketch which, under the absurdities of the Act, was illegal. Rival managers, keen to undermine him, pounced, and Morton was hauled before the local magistrates. He lost the case on the flimsy grounds that the sketch had two speaking parts; if one actor had played both roles it would have been legal.

Such trivial prosecutions were to continue spasmodically until 1912. Morton suffered again when he staged an abbreviated version of *The Tempest* and was fined a nominal £5 by a reluctant magistrate who had seen and enjoyed the show. But, as he pointed out to a disgruntled Morton, the law was the law. Law or not, it was often flouted without action being taken, especially in the less fashionable halls that posed no threat to legitimate theatre. But the banning of drama did have the beneficial side-effect of preserving undiluted music hall fare in the halls.

Morton's mini-drama over *The Tempest* had one lasting consequence. *The Times* reported the court case, and in doing so described the performance. This was the first time the foremost newspaper in the land had acknowledged the existence of music hall. Once it had done so, Morton, seeing an opportunity, offered it an advertisement for his theatre. *The Times*, perhaps acknowledging the force that music hall was to become, accepted it. Other theatres followed suit, and a new advertising outlet was born, assisted by the abolition in 1853 of tax on press advertisements.

Despite Morton's foray into the fashionable West End, and *The Times*'s preparedness to accept his money, music hall was not yet respectable, nor would it be for many years. Some strands of opinion regarded it as a malign influence on the working man. In 1831, the Lord's Day Observance Society had been established to combat 'the multitudes intent on pursuing pleasure on the Lord's Day'. The society's members, led by the vicar of Islington, whose parish was not far from the heartland of enthusiasm for music hall, had in mind such wickedness as coach and steamboat trips and visits to tea rooms and taverns. The vicar's concern was that such indulgences would 'absorb much of the money which should contribute to the more decent support of wives and children'. It is not clear when the society thought the working man – whose only day for leisure was Sunday – should enjoy himself, or whether he should at all. In any event, the society was to be a powerful and hostile lobby throughout the life of music hall.

But the killjoys had powerful opposition. In 1836 Charles Dickens wrote a biting pseudonymous essay, 'Sunday Under Three Heads', mockingly dedicated to the Bishop of London: 'The day which his Maker intended as a blessing, Man has converted into a curse. Instead of being hailed by him as his period of relaxation, he finds it remarkable only as depriving him of every comfort and enjoyment.' Others agreed. A current song commented:

> No duck must lay, no cat must kitten,
> No hen must leave her nest, though sittin'.
> Though painful is the situation
> She must not think of incubation
> For as no business must be done on a Sunday
> Of course, they'll have to put it off till Monday.

Such ridicule had no more effect on the morally upright than
Dickens' disdain. Many Victorians took the Fourth Commandment
seriously: Sunday was a day of rest from enjoyment as well as from
work, and if it was the only full day of leisure for the working man,
that was just bad luck. It was bad luck for the music hall proprietors
as well, robbing them of full houses and a day's revenue. Sunday
opening was a battle that would outlast music hall, but the proprietors did not always lose to pious opinion. After a long campaign
the ban on opening during Lent was relaxed in 1875, and ten years
later the Lord Chamberlain permitted performances on Ash
Wednesday – but not Good Friday.

As competition grew, the design of music halls evolved. Up to the
1850s embryonic music hall mostly found a home in converted and
extended taverns. These were usually very basic, although there
were exceptions, such as Evans' Late Joy's. Early music halls were
generally a commercially driven exercise in maximising profit from
limited space. Typically, two or more rooms would be knocked into
one large space with a rudimentary stage, and a long table (or
tables) at right angles to it where the customers sat and were served
with food and drink. The chairman compèred the evening from a
seat at a table parallel to the stage.

This primitive set-up was succeeded by adapted, and later
purpose-built, halls, often constrained by an existing site – which is
why so many music halls were no more than roofed-over yards –
but on a grander scale. The second Canterbury Music Hall, built in
1854, was the exemplar: a hall with balconies, a stage and a void in
front of it packed with tables and chairs. The design had more in
common with a Methodist chapel or a concert hall than a public
house or a modern theatre. The Canterbury had other assets, in its
gallery, lounge and library, but the actual presentation of the entertainment was still simple.

This style of hall can still be seen today in Wilton's, built in 1859
by John Wilton across the back gardens of five terrace houses situated behind the Prince of Denmark public house in Whitechapel. It

was very similar in structure to the Canterbury, and although it is now in disrepair it is the only surviving music hall built between 1850 and 1870. It remained a music hall only until 1879, when it was transformed into the East End Mission of the Methodist Church. As the result of a campaign mounted in the 1960s by the poet John Betjeman, together with performers and conservationists, Wilton's has survived demolition* and is currently undergoing restoration.

We can see from contemporary pictures and descriptions that the Canterbury, Weston's, Wilton's and the Oxford all conformed to the same structural elements: main auditorium, balcony, easy access to the bar, and a raised platform for the performers. The only variants were the differing levels of interior splendour. There were a handful of other more sophisticated halls: the South London Palace at the Elephant and Castle and the Alhambra Palace in Leicester Square were circular halls with the deep proscenium we are familiar with today.

The Canterbury, having passed from Morton to the impresario and self-styled 'People's Caterer' William 'Bill' Holland in 1867, saw many changes. It was rebuilt and expensively furnished, with a thousand-guinea carpet, fit – so the advertisements said – 'for people to spit on'. This odd comment followed suggestions that the luxury of the carpet might make some of the humbler patrons feel awkward.

The upgraded Canterbury focused on comedy acts, George Leybourne being a particular favourite, before it was sold on nine years later to George Villiers, who introduced ballet as a key attraction. It passed to a further four owners in the next fifteen years, outliving its contemporaries only to be destroyed by Hitler's bombs in the Second World War.

The Alhambra, a building of Moorish design, had begun life in 1854 as the Royal Panopticon, a showcase for contemporary achievements in science and the fine arts. It closed after only two years, and

* It was subsequently cared for by the London Music Hall Society, and later by Broomhill Opera and the Wilton's Music Hall Trust. It was reopened as a performance space in 1997, but not for music hall, although in 2009 Dame Norma Major staged a charity performance for Mencap featuring Elizabeth Mansfield as Marie Lloyd.

in 1858 E.T. Smith, the lessee of the Drury Lane Theatre, added a circus ring and reopened it as the Alhambra Palace. The son of an admiral, Edward Tyrell Smith was a restless eccentric with an original mind and an appetite for risk. He had previously been a policeman, auctioneer, land agent, publican, wine merchant, picture dealer and – briefly – owner of the *Sunday Times*. He had directed Cremorne Pleasure Gardens, and as a publican in 1850 had enticed customers by dressing his barmaids in bloomers, which shocked some but attracted far more.

Taking on the Alhambra was a brave venture, for it was situated in the French quarter of Leicester Square, which had an unsavoury reputation. In 1859 the journal *Peeping Tom* reported: 'London cannot boast of another spot where an equal amount of aspiring fallen humanity vegetates' – plainly the author had not visited parts of the East End. 'What a chronicle of misery and woe … of innocence betrayed and vice made more vicious would not Leicester Square yield if it could be made to speak … Its internal filth and outward show are all French and even the dirty urchins who wallow in its gutters are tainted with French notions. "Ici on parle francais" is written on every front, upon every window, on every shopwoman's and shopman's countenance.' Francophobia, it seems, was alive and well in mid-Victorian London.

Smith had been refused a licence to run the Alhambra Palace as a theatre for legitimate drama, but was granted a music licence by local magistrates. At a cost of £120,000 he converted the circus ring to an open area for tables and chairs, and added a proscenium and a stage. The Alhambra became one of the largest music halls, with a capacity of 3,500, and Smith employed the pugilists Tom Sayers and John Heenan to give exhibitions of boxing there. Sometimes popular taste outran official approval: in 1870 the theatre fell foul of the London County Council when the Colonna Group, featuring 'Wiry Sal', danced the can-can with an enthusiasm that was far too racy for officialdom. For a brief time the theatre was closed.

The shape of the Alhambra reflected its past. In contrast, the South London Palace not only had a circular structure with the proscenium, but at the rear of the hall, beyond the tables and chairs set out for dining, were benches ranked 'theatre style', with shelves on the back of each to hold glasses. It also offered arm-height shelves around the perimeter of the hall, where customers who chose to stand could place their drinks. This was a glimpse of the future, but further refinements had to await sites in the prosperous suburbs, where land was cheaper and space was less of a constraint.

The building programme in the quarter of a century following the opening of the Canterbury was frenetic, but many of the new music halls had short lives. Some were lost to new development, or poor management, or changing fashions. But the greatest hazard was fire. Like its namesake in Sheffield, the Surrey Music Hall in Blackfriars was destroyed by fire in 1865. The Royal Standard, Pimlico, burned down in 1866. The South London Palace, where the interior resembled a Roman villa, was destroyed by fire in March 1869, but reopened a mere nine months later with its audience capacity tripled to around four thousand.

Charles Morton's Oxford was burned down in February 1868. The audience had left, and Morton was making a final check of the auditorium when he noticed a flickering light in the gallery. By the time he reached it a couple of seats were on fire. He tried to extinguish the flames, but they soon defeated him. Horse-drawn fire engines arrived in short order after the alarm had been raised, but the fire spread to the paint on the Corinthian columns supporting the extravagantly ornamental roof, which was soon ablaze. Furniture and fittings, hangings and carpets, the wardrobe full of costumes, the contents of the bar, which helped to fuel the flames, were all consumed. Only the wine and spirits in the cellar survived. Just a month earlier, Morton had sold or sub-let the Canterbury to William Holland, so he now had no theatre to manage, and the jobs and prospects of the entertainers and support staff at the Oxford were lost. Morton being Morton, he arranged a benefit concert at the Crystal Palace to help those in need. This provoked its own controversy, and a famous impersonation. Morton sold the ruin of the Oxford and moved on.

It is reasonable to speculate that the fire at the Oxford was caused by an unextinguished cigar. Smoking was commonplace during performances, and with fumes from gas lighting,* wooden construction and a large number of people in a confined and poorly ventilated space, it made a combustible mix.

A new Oxford, rebuilt by M.R. Syers and W. Taylor, and designed by the architects Edward Paraire and William Finch Hill, opened in August 1869, only to be burned down once more three years later. Syers, who by then had parted company with Taylor, opened a third Oxford in March 1873. Once again designed by Paraire, it differed from its predecessor in one very important detail: the tables and chairs for eating and drinking had been replaced by rows of comfortable seating. This was part of a trend. The simplicities of the earlier designs – an empty floor space bordered by grandeur – no longer met the demands of management or audience, and music halls began to move recognisably towards the variety theatres of later days. The third Oxford was renovated again in 1892, reopening a year later. It survived as a theatre until 1927, when it became a Lyon's Corner House.

The worst disaster in the history of British theatre occurred when a fire broke out at the Theatre Royal, Exeter, on 5 September 1887. During a performance of the romantic comedy *Romany Rye* a naked gas flame did its worst and flames billowed from the stage. There was panic in the auditorium. One hundred and eighty-six people, mostly in the upper galleries, died from asphyxiation or being caught in the crush to get to the upper tier's only exit. Just two years earlier the first Theatre Royal in the town had burned to the ground, without loss of life, but lessons had not been learned. On the morning of 6 September all that remained of the theatre was a smouldering shell. Blame for the tragedy was placed upon the lack of a safety curtain and insufficient exits.

Partly as a consequence of the fires that destroyed so many theatres, health and safety requirements were a perennial irritant for

---

* Astley's Equestrian Amphitheatre was reputedly illuminated by 200,000 gas jets.

owners. In 1878 the Metropolitan Board of Works (later the London County Council) introduced a Certificate of Suitability which had a profound effect on the economic viability of music halls. Most of the new regulations were sensible and simple, but expensive enough to destroy profitability, and music hall was always a business: no profits, no performance. Up to two hundred halls closed down because their owners could not afford to reinforce shaky floors or install safety curtains as a barrier to fire. But the old halls were unsafe, and many of the new breed of owners saw the legislation as a catalyst for new development and the plusher facilities we now associate with the golden age of music hall. Vast emporiums of gilt, with upholstered seats and decorations of nymphs and cherubs, became fashionable. They were made so by Frank Matcham.

In the vast explosion of theatre-building after 1850, Matcham was the leading figure. He was not the first Victorian architect to specialise in designing theatres: that distinction goes to C. J. Phipps, who built the Garrick and Her Majesty's in London, as well as regional theatres including the ill-fated Theatre Royal, Exeter. But Matcham become the pre-eminent architect of music halls, and was responsible for the design of more than two hundred theatres. His first success was the Elephant and Castle Theatre in south London, which introduced elephant motifs and the Moorish and Indian styles that went on to characterise so many Victorian and Edwardian buildings. His designs were in huge demand. In 1888 alone he was working on the Alhambra, Brighton; the Mile End Empire and the Grand Theatre, Islington, in London; a major remodelling of the Grand Theatre, Douglas, Isle of Man; and preparatory work on theatres in Blackpool, Bury, Halifax and St Helens. It was exhausting, but Matcham was changing the face of theatre. The Matcham style spread even more swiftly once he began to build for the syndicate-owners Oswald Stoll and Edward Moss in around 1890.

Matcham introduced many innovations: more and better exits to reduce fire risk, push-bar bolt exit locks, and the use of steel to support balconies, which brought to an end the need for pillars that obstructed sightlines. His style had important aesthetic benefits, with curved tiers that seemed to float on air and were visually very attractive. He increased the number of seats, much to the delight of the owners. Matcham's greatest attribute was his ability to create a different ambience for each theatre. He used a dazzling array of styles, both interior and exterior, drawn from all manner of historical and cultural sources. He was able to create theatres of such elegance and style that even the largest auditorium felt intimate. Sadly, many of his palaces have fallen victim to German bombs and soulless planners. Unenlightened eyes saw his theatres as gaudy, kitsch and deserving of demolition; others, sometimes too late, regarded his designs as temples of pleasure as worthy of preservation as a Roman bath complex. Matcham worked consistently until 1920, leaving a legacy of theatres including the Coliseum, the London Palladium, the Victoria Palace and the Grand Theatre, Blackpool.

Just as architecture and design were changing, so too were music hall performances. Between 1870 and 1890 the chairman disappeared. He had become an anachronism who slowed down the show. Scenery was introduced. Glees were dropped from the programmes and the number of opera selections fell away. Novelty acts, comedians and comic-ballad singers became ever more popular. To increase capacity, rows of theatre seats replaced tables for eating and drinking. As refreshment moved from the auditorium to the bars, the audience became static and quieter. Waiters and cigar-sellers disappeared. Seats were raked to improve sightlines. The house lights were lowered to increase the focus on the performers.

These organic changes, which were commercially motivated, focused attention upon the stage and the performers. The audience might not have been aware of it, but music hall was entering a 'golden age', when a new breed of artistes with extraordinary talents would explode into people's hearts and minds.

6

The Swells and the Costers

'The main thing is catchiness. I will sacrifice
everything – rhyme, reason, sense, sentiment, to
catchiness. There is ... a great art in making
rubbish acceptable.'

FELIX MCGLENNON, LYRICIST AND SONGWRITER,
THE *ERA*, 10 MARCH 1894

Music hall was, first and last, an intimate medium, in which
performers and audience were locked in an enduring embrace.
Today we can only glimpse this symbiotic relationship through
grainy black-and-white photographs and tinny gramophone
records in which the singers, mostly past their prime at the time of
recording, struggle to perform in the absence of the factor that
made them great – the audience.

That bond between artiste and audience – the secret heart of
music hall – was so profound that many artistes were not allowed to
leave the stage until they had sung their 'signature' songs. Their
public would join in, and would then whistle them all the way
home. Refrains such as:

A sweet tuxedo girl you see
A queen of swell society

or

> Oh! I'm in such a mess – I don't know the new address –
> Don't even know the blessed neighbourhood

or

> Observed by each observer with the keenness of a hawk,
> I'm a mass of money, linen, silk and starch

are largely forgotten now, but a Victorian music hall audience would await each with the greatest anticipation. Popular songs entered the national canon, and even today we know their choruses: 'Ta-ra-ra Boom-de-ay', 'My Old Man Said Follow the Van', 'The Man Who Broke the Bank at Monte Carlo'.

From the early days of music hall the songs, and the artistes who performed them, were the backbone of every bill. When appearing at Evans' or the Cyder Cellars, artistes such as Sam Cowell and W.G. Ross invariably sang 'The Ratcatcher's Daughter' or 'Sam Hall', and the audience expected to be indulged over and over again with encores. In an era before recorded music, the live experience was all there was.

It was the combination of singer and song that created stars, and a colossal business sprang up around them. Artistes bought their songs from songwriters, often for a pittance, and those that struck a chord with the audience became closely identified with the artiste throughout their lifetimes, and are today our only remembrance of them. Hall-owners paid handsomely for artistes to sing the songs that had caught the public imagination, and the sheet music was sold with the artiste featured prominently on the cover.

One such singer was Charles Coborn, born Charles Whitton McCallum into a relatively prosperous family in Stepney, east London, in 1852. His father was a shipbroker and a Freeman of the City of London. Coborn's early life was a model of middle-class convention. He was privately educated, and employed in clerical jobs in the City between 1866 and 1871, subsequently becoming a commercial traveller in women's accessories. If it were not for his yearning to perform, he might have been just another name in the births, marriages and deaths columns.

After a brief flirtation with the legitimate stage, his early music hall act was based on an impersonation of a drunken man. Its success brought him a debut at the Alhambra, Greenwich, in 1872, under the name Charles Laurie, but this was swiftly changed to Charles Coborn – apparently after Coborn Road, Poplar – because McCallum believed it sounded more sophisticated. He struggled at first to find work, and had to wait three years for his first week-long engagement at the Gilbert Music Hall, Whitechapel. Thereafter, word-of-mouth spread quickly, and he was given the soubriquet 'the Comic of the Day' by the Oxford Music Hall manager J.H. Jennings.

Coborn's first big hit was 'Two Lovely Black Eyes', which he co-wrote with Edmund Forman in 1886. It is a cautionary tale explaining why it is wise not to get too closely involved in party politics. After receiving 'two lovely black eyes' from political enthusiasts for arguing about policy, he warns:

> The moral you've caught I can hardly doubt,
> Never on politics rave and shout.
> Leave it to others to fight it out
> If you would be wise.
> Better, far better it is to let
> Liberals and Tories alone you bet,
> Unless you're willing and anxious to get
> Two lovely black eyes.

On the strength of this song Coborn became a much-sought-after act, and was soon booked into long engagements at the Trocadero and the Pavilion. His stage persona was a fortuitous fit with his only other great hit, 'The Man Who Broke the Bank at Monte Carlo'. Written by Fred Gilbert in April 1892, it was based on the exploits of a serial fraudster, Charles Wells, who managed to *'faire sauter la banque'* – literally 'blow up the bank' – at a marathon session at the gaming tables of Café de Paris Casino, Monte Carlo, in July 1891.* To add spice to the tale, the £4,000 Wells used to bet with was fraudulently obtained through a scam. He is said to have won twenty-three times from thirty spins of the wheel, making a million francs. The casino was convinced he had used a system, but Wells merely shrugged his shoulders and said it was a lucky streak. He later returned to the Café de Paris, but his luck had run out. He was accused of defrauding investors in a marine engineering swindle, convicted of fraud at the Old Bailey and sentenced to eight years in jail in 1892. Subsequent frauds committed in France led to a further five years' imprisonment, and he died penniless in Paris in 1926. But Gilbert's song achieved immortality for both Wells and Coborn.

As a performer whose act was based on a drunken man, Coborn was the perfect exponent of a song based on the louche milieu of Monte Carlo. Onstage he wore a rakishly-set top hat, tailcoat, watch chain, buttonhole, immaculate dickie, monocle and well-groomed handlebar moustache, set off perfectly by his nearly off-balance stance, faraway look and expansive gesticulations. An airily held cheroot and splayed-out fingers completed the look of a man not quite in charge of all his faculties. We are left in no doubt about the affluence of the singer:

> I've just got here, through Paris, from the sunny
>   southern shore;
> I to Monte Carlo went, just to raise my winter's rent
> Dame Fortune smiled upon me as she'd never done
>   before,
> And I've now such lots of money, I'm a gent
> Yes, I've now such lots of money, I'm a gent.

---

* It has also been suggested that the song was based on one Joseph Jagger, apparently a distant relation of Mick Jagger, who after careful scrutiny of the Café de Paris' roulette wheels noticed a bias in one. He exploited the weakness, and in 1875 won £75,000 (around £4 million today) at the tables.

The chorus echoes still:

> As I walk along the Bois Boolong
> With an independent air
> You can hear the girls declare
> 'He must be a millionaire.'
> You can hear them sigh and wish to die,
> You can see them wink the other eye
> At the man who broke the bank at Monte Carlo.

Coborn sang of affluence onstage, and exercised influence offstage. He was joint founder of the Music Hall Benevolent Fund, set up in 1888 to help performers in distress, and in the early twentieth century he was a firm supporter of the Variety Artists' Federation. He remained a devoted adherent of the Scottish Kirk throughout his long life.

Coborn sang his two most famous songs thousands of times, in many languages, for over half a century, but he was never able to repeat their success. He slipped from the top of the bill – and often, off the bill – but he sang on, enjoying a career of sufficient length for him to entertain troops in three wars – the Boer War and both World Wars – before dying at home in Paddington in 1945, aged ninety-three.

'The Man Who Broke the Bank at Monte Carlo' was an example of one of the first definable genres of British music hall: the 'swell' song. In many ways these were a powerful illustration of the gentrification sought by early entrepreneurs like Charles Morton. Artistes like the Great Vance, George Leybourne, G.H. MacDermott, Arthur Lloyd and Harry Rickards dominated bills in the early days of the halls, and became known as 'lions comiques', a term attributed to J.J. Poole, manager of the South London Music Hall.

Gloriously aping their social betters, 'swells' were the theatrical peacocks of their day, swaggering around the stage in spats, sporting monocles and outrageous suits of garish cloth. Nearly all the lions comiques – in essence, comic singers – adopted variants of this dress, and wore 'Dundreary' whiskers (also known as 'Piccadilly Weepers'), absurdly long 'lambchop' sideburns, often a foot in length.

The inspiration for these adornments came from the stage actor Edward Askew Sothern, who deployed them in his performance of the dim, ineffectual 'toff' Lord Dundreary in Tom Taylor's 1858 play *Our American Cousin*.* This simple physical shorthand was also used to identify dudes, swells and mashers, and many in the audience came to believe that this was how the socially elevated looked and behaved.

Some of the young men in the audience took inspiration from the stage swells. Their songs told of undreamed-of sophistication and idleness. They sang of free-flowing champagne, fine food, beautiful girls and late nights in fashionable districts of London and Paris. It was a heady ideal for the clerks and drapers' assistants who were among the habitués of music hall.

Alfred 'the Great' Vance was one of the first swells to come to prominence, and with George Leybourne he can be credited with pioneering the swell style. Vance was born Alfred Peek Stevens in 1839, and, like Charles Coborn and 'coster laureate' Albert Chevalier, he came from a middle- rather than a working-class background. Unable to settle in his job as a solicitor's clerk, he began a career on the stage in the early 1850s. At first he played clowns in pantomime, before turning to music hall, touring all over the country in second-rate halls while creating and refining a multi-character one-man show. Like many others, he adopted a black-face act in 1860, appearing with his brother billed as 'Alfred G. and C. Vance – Negro Comedians'. He went solo four years later at the South London Palace, singing mainly 'coster'-style songs, years before the term was widely used.

---

* Sothern's performance was a sensation, and gave rise not only to the eponymous whiskers but to a vogue for 'Dundrearyisms', a sort of nonsensical mixed metaphor, like 'Birds of a feather are worth two in a bush.' Today *Our American Cousin* is chiefly remembered because it was during a performance of the play at Ford's Theatre, Washington DC, on 14 April 1865 that Abraham Lincoln was assassinated.

Vance was an accomplished dancer – although a school of dancing he had opened in Liverpool had failed – and his experience on the legitimate stage made him a formidable character actor. Unlike many contemporaries, he changed costume for every characterisation. This led him to advertise the merits of his tailor, no doubt for a discount on purchases, in his first hit, 'Chickaleary Cove'. His move upmarket to the 'swell' persona, at the other extreme of the performance demographic, occurred shortly after – and possibly as a response to – the rise in popularity of George Leybourne. Vance soon enjoyed a huge success with 'Slap Bang', a nonsensical song that became a lifelong signature tune for him.

George Leybourne, born Joe Saunders in Gateshead in 1842, came from humbler stock than Vance. Having trained as a mechanic, he gave up the security of that job to go onstage. He built a local reputation as a performer, and after being spotted performing in Manchester he was brought to London in 1864 by the agent Charles Adolphus Roberts.

Unlike Alfred Vance, George Leybourne was a superstar. The historian Harold Scott argued that, together with Marie Lloyd and Dan Leno, he held 'a supreme place in music hall history'. That is a contentious claim, but it is evident that contemporary opinion idolised him. He was variously billed as 'Lion of the Day' then 'Lion of a Comic', and finally, in the name that stuck, the original 'Lion Comique'.

It was during an engagement at Collins' Music Hall in Islington in 1865 that Leybourne met Alfred Lee, who wrote his first hit, 'Chang, the Chinese Giant', for him. When he performed the song on stilts at the Canterbury, the astute William Holland, who had taken over managing the theatre from Charles Morton, saw an opportunity to create a megastar. He booked Leybourne for an entire year from June 1868, and relentlessly promoted him as the quintessential swell. The long-legged Leybourne was slender, handsome and charming, with a fine baritone voice, and Holland dressed him in smartly tailored suits, along with hats, gloves, cane and winder (an eyeglass), and arranged for him to be taken everywhere in a brougham.

Vance and Leybourne enjoyed a friendly rivalry, often working with the same teams of writers and composers, especially Frank Green and Alfred Lee, and appearing on the same bills. They also shared the same song publisher, the British and American Music Publishing Company. A song would be written for one of them and responded to by the other, often using the same team of writers. Following Leybourne's 1866 smash hit 'Champagne Charlie' – he favoured Moët – (music by Alfred Lee and lyrics by Leybourne), Vance came back in 1867 with 'Clicquot' (written by Green and Jules Rivière), to which Leybourne replied in 1868 with 'Cool Burgundy Ben' (written by Green and Lee).

While 'Champagne Charlie' was a hit, William Holland of the Canterbury persuaded the makers of Moët to supply endless quantities of their product, which Leybourne was seen to drink at all times: 'Moët's vintage only satisfied the champagne swell', as it says in the song. It was superb advertising for Moët, and for Leybourne:

> Whenever I'm going upon the spree,
> Moët & Chandon's the wine for me.

Vance's 'Walking in the Zoo' tells of a 'swell' taking his alluring 'cousin' to the zoo, only to have his amorous intentions foiled by a bite from a cockatoo. Leybourne responded with 'Lounging at the Aq[uarium]' (by Lee). Their rivalry served them both well – much like the insults traded between Bing Crosby and Bob Hope over half a century later. 'Walking in the Zoo' was soon forgotten, but its abbreviation of 'zoological' added a new word to the English language, just one indication of the influence of music hall on popular culture. The expression 'OK' also made an early appearance in the same song.

Leybourne and Vance continued to trade song for song, with Leybourne's 'The Dark Girl Dressed in Blue' responded to by Vance's 'The Fair Girl Dressed in Check'. Vance wrote several of his own songs, but also collaborated with both Green and Lee to produce songs like 'The Naughty Young Man', 'Idol of the Day' and 'May the Present Moment be the Worst of Your Lives'. Similarly, Leybourne collaborated with Lee to produce 'Sweet Isabella' and the enduring hit, which offered a new phrase to the English language, 'The [Daring Young Man on the] Flying Trapeze', written as a tribute to Jules Léotard.

Leybourne was so popular that he sometimes played six halls a night, and had to plead with audiences to allow him to leave the stage to keep to schedule. Jenny Hill, his friend and contemporary, said he had 'a curious faculty for filling a stage'. He had a faculty for filling his pockets, too. At the height of his fame he was earning the unheard-of sum of £120 a week at the Canterbury. Unfortunately, having filled his pockets, he emptied them, spending as much as he earned on hangers-on and high living, and helping to pay the bills of acquaintances who were poor or sick.

Like all the lions comiques, Leybourne sang topical songs. Apart from 'The Flying Trapeze' there was 'Zazel' (about the Great Farini's human cannonball act) and 'Up in a Balloon' (ballooning was a hugely popular attraction at the time), both written by G.W. Hunt. Sometimes he cast aside his lion comique manner and sang sentimental and dramatic songs and ballads in a rich baritone – often to the surprise of an audience unaware of the depth of his talent.

Inevitably, the hard-living swell persona he was forced to adopt rubbed off on Leybourne. He drank too much, too often, with too many 'friends'. By the 1880s his star had begun to wane, although his money continued to be spent recklessly. After a spell as a double act with his daughter Florrie – who married Albert Chevalier – he died aged forty-two in 1884, penniless and understandably bitter about false friends. One of his last hits was 'Ting Ting, That's How the Bell Goes'. This song, set in a tea shop, led early music hall historian McQueen-Pope to suggest ironically that 'Maybe the tea killed him.' But it didn't. It was the fame.

Vance never quite hit the heights of Leybourne, but he was a regular bill-topper who remained popular throughout his

all-too-short life. He died onstage from a heart attack at the Sun
Music Hall, Knightsbridge, on Boxing Day 1888. He was only
forty-nine.

Another performer gifted at satirising the upper-class toff was
'the Great' MacDermott, a specialist in topical comment. Born John
Farrell in London in 1845, he worked as a labourer before joining
the navy, where he learned to entertain his shipmates. He could
dance and sing, wrote plays (including a version of Dickens' unfin-
ished *The Mystery of Edwin Drood*), and appeared on the legitimate
stage before turning to music hall. He developed a 'swell' persona,
and styled himself 'the Statesman of the Halls'.

MacDermott was often unpopular with managers because of his
tendency towards vulgarity, but he is mostly remembered for singing the G.W. Hunt song 'By Jingo', which was intended to move
public opinion in favour of intervention in the Turkish–Russian
conflict of 1877–78. The song proved so influential it merited a
leader in *The Times* and was quoted in the House of Commons.
When MacDermott harangued the Liberal leadership in songs like
'W.E.G.'s in a State of Lunacy' (W.E.G. being William Gladstone),
there were rumours he was funded by the Conservative Party. There
is no evidence for this, and it is unlikely. Music hall audiences were
often Conservative – the Conservatives under Disraeli had cut the
hours of work, while Gladstone's Liberals had cut the hours of
drink. 'By Jingo' famously popularised the word 'jingoism', although
it was not a new word – as has been suggested – but had been in use
for many years.

> We don't want to fight but by jingo if we do.
> We've got the ships, we've got the men, and got the
>   money too!
> We've fought the Bear before, and while we're Britons
>   true,
> The Russians shall not have Constantinople.

Whatever MacDermott's politics may have been, the song shows the power of a good tune and catchy lyrics. In his book *The Psychology of Jingoism* (1901), J.A. Hobson commented on this phenomenon: 'A gradual debasement of popular art … has raised … the music hall to [a] most powerful instrument … Its words and melodies pass by quick magic from the Empire or the Alhambra over the length and breadth of the land, re-echoed in a thousand provincial halls, clubs, drinking saloons, until the remotest village is familiar with air and sentiment.'

MacDermott was a natural to sing the topical songs written by Fred Gilbert – already famous for 'The Man Who Broke the Bank at Monte Carlo' – and neither man shied from political controversy. In 1885, when the Liberal MP for Chelsea Sir Charles Dilke was accused of having an affair with his sister-in-law *and* her nineteen-year-old sister, it was too good an opportunity for Gilbert and MacDermott to pass over. 'Charlie Dilke Upset the Milk' was their far-from-subtle commentary on the scandalous divorce case. The judgement partly absolved Dilke, but after a press campaign continued to stress his impropriety he went to court to clear his name. After a merciless cross-examination he lost the case, and was ruined, ensuring that the song became a phenomenon:

> Master Dilke upset the milk
> When taking it home to Chelsea;
> The papers say that Charlie's gay*
> Rather a wilful wag!
> This noble representative
> Of ev'rything good in Chelsea
> Has let the cat – the naughty cat
> Slip out of the Gladstone bag.

* A euphemism at the time for sexually active.

The song caused a serious stir, but, undeterred, Gilbert and MacDermott continued to add new verses as more information came out in court.

Onstage, MacDermott was a great exponent of the 'call and response' idiom, where he would involve the audience in dialogue. In 'Not Much (It's Better Than Nothing at All)' he would sing, 'Not what?' and the audience would sing back, 'Not much!' His 'Dear Old Pals' was a lasting hit, and far more mellow than his more controversial songs. When MacDermott retired from the halls he became a theatrical agent and hall manager, and unlike many contemporaries died comfortably well-off, in 1901.

MacDermott's collaborator G.W. Hunt wrote for many artistes. One of his biggest hits, 'The German Band', was written for the last of the 'big four' lions comiques, Arthur Lloyd, and transformed Lloyd's fortunes. Lloyd was one of the most popular artistes of his day, and his songs, many of which he wrote himself, sold in their thousands – yet outside music hall circles he is barely remembered.

Arthur Lloyd was born in Edinburgh in 1839 into a theatrical family, and toured the country as a straight actor, a comic and a singer before arriving in London in 1862. He made his debut at the Sun Music Hall, Knightsbridge, playing the Marylebone Music Hall and the Philharmonic Music Hall in Islington later the same evening. His impact was immediate, and in a matter of months he was appearing at the Pavilion, the Oxford and the Canterbury. In 1868 he became one of the first music hall artistes to perform before royalty – in his case the Prince of Wales at a private party in Whitehall, together with Jolly John Nash and Alfred Vance. An interview he gave the *Era* offers a flavour of the occasion:

> We were not required until two o'clock in the morning, and when we were, a screen formed by curtains made a sort of sanctum between us and the audience. The Prince was seated with a blue sash round him in a lounge chair, whilst the rest were all ranged round him with their chairs turned behind-before, and

the occupants leaning over the back. Nash was very nervous and persuaded me to go first. I went and sang a song, of which the chorus ran 'It's the sort of thing you read about but very seldom see.' After two or three verses I sang the following: 'I must now award a word of praise to a gent who's sitting there/I mean that worthy party who so ably fills the chair,/See how sweetly now he smiles, as pleasant as can be,/It's a sort of smile I read about but very seldom see.'

As I sang it the Prince leant forward to listen, and all those round him turned and clapped their hands towards him. He seemed immensely amused, and when I had finished the last verse he applauded very good humouredly.

It is a vivid vignette of Victorian deference to the future King.

Arthur Lloyd wrote most of his own material, and was deeply frustrated when it was 'stolen' by other performers. In July 1863 he published a warning in the trade press: 'Comic singers who steal the ideas and songs of others, look out for your time is short.' The warning was justified, but ineffective.

Lloyd was a highly accomplished man, but not all his offstage enterprises were successful. He ran a successful touring company, and took a three-year lease on the Queen's Theatre in Dublin in 1874, but when he bought the Star Music Hall in Glasgow in 1881 the remodelling costs and artistic failure reduced him to bankruptcy in only fourteen weeks. Notwithstanding such setbacks, he remained a successful performer and songwriter. His self-composed hits 'Not for Joseph', 'The Song of (Many) Songs', 'Pretty Lips' and 'Immensikoff, the Shoreditch Toff', not to mention his break-through hit 'The German Band', were hugely popular. While 'The Dark Girl Dressed in Blue' was successful for Alfred Vance, Lloyd's 'Not for Joseph', which tells of a swell who is careful with his money, was the first comic song to sell 100,000 copies:

I used to throw my cash about,
In a reckless sort of way;
I'm careful now what I'm about,
And cautious how I pay:
Now the other night I asked a pal,
With me to have a drain,
'Thanks Joe,' said he, 'let's see, old pal
'I think I'll have Champagne'
[*Spoken*: 'Will ye,' said I, 'oh, no –']

CHORUS:
Not for Joe, not for Joe,
If he knows it, not for Joseph,
No, no, no, not for Joe,
Not for Joseph, oh, dear no.

It was a philosophy many of his fellow performers would have been wise to follow.

Sadly, none of Lloyd's songs live on in the same way as others from the 'swell' canon, which is why, despite his enormous success during music hall's heyday, he is less well-known today than he deserves to be. He died in July 1904, widely respected for his talent and his lifestyle, having made his last appearance only a few months previously at the Palace Theatre, Hull. His *Era* obituary noted that his 'Song of Songs' 'had a most extraordinary career of popularity, but did not bring its author and composer the large fortune that one sometimes hears of as the guerdon [reward] of a comic song, for he sold the rights of publication for a mere trifle'.

Other lions comiques enjoyed their day in the sun, not least Harry Rickards (born Henry Leete in Croydon, 1841). Although a minor figure compared to the 'Big Four', surviving pictures show he affected to be the swellest of the swells, and he had a number of hits in lion comique style: 'Strolling in the Burlington', 'Oxford Joe', 'Lardy Dardy Do', 'Captain Jinks of the Horse Marine', 'Cerulea the Beautiful', 'That's the Sort of Man We Want in England Here Today' and 'In England Now'. Unfortunately for Rickards, he began to believe his own 'swellegant' publicity, telling the press he was the son of Norfolk nobility, had been educated at Eton and destined for the Church – none of which was true. After some unwise investments in the 1870s he went bankrupt and fled to Australia, where he reinvented himself as a successful agent and hall manager and was responsible for enticing major stars, including Marie Lloyd and Little Tich, to tour the country. He also made a notable contribution to music hall by promoting the early career of Florrie Forde, a little-known singer from his adopted city of Melbourne, but destined to become one of the most beloved of performers. In many ways, the bad boy made good.

While audiences enjoyed the 'swell' songs that lampooned their social betters, great performers like Gus Elen, Albert Chevalier, Harry Champion and Alec Hurley sang of hard and humorous life as the audience knew it. Costermongers were a fixture of every street corner in London, and the 'coster' singers were their minstrels. They perfected the 'cheeky cockney chappie' persona that made tough lives bearable.

Whereas 'swell' singers – apart from the male impersonators – were exclusively male, women did sing 'coster' songs. Marie Lloyd sang of 'A Coster Girl in Paris'. Being Lloyd, the coster girl was on her honeymoon and her mother was demanding details, but the only information she received in reply was:

> I'd like to go again
> To Paris on the Seine
> For Paris is a proper pantomime,
> And if they'd only move the Hackney Road and plant it
>   over there
> I'd like to live in Paris all the time.

Kate Carney, big-boned and stocky, was born in Southwark in 1869. Her career began in 1889 singing Irish ballads, but success came when she started to specialise in songs about working-class girls and their lives, about which, being one herself, she knew a great deal. 'Three Pots a Shilling' (1895) was her biggest success, but 'Sarah', 'Oysters a Shilling a Dozen' and 'Are We to Part Like This, Bill?' were all hits. With her sonorous voice and big hats, Kate Carney was one of the great characters of music hall, and ideal as a 'Coster Queen'. She and her husband, the comedian turned theatrical agent George Barclay, lived in comfort on Brixton Hill, and threw lavish parties for the music hall aristocracy. She was still performing during the Blitz in the Second World War, ignoring the bombs that fell on London. Late in life she went into management and ran the Clapham Grand, but continued to perform irregularly until her death in 1950.

Also much loved was Gus Elen, born in Pimlico in 1862 and one of the greatest 'coster' stars. He was born to the part, having worked as a coster before becoming a street performer in The Strand, complete with barrel organ. He worked in pubs, in minor halls and in the provinces. In 1891 he got his big break when he was taken on by Hugh Didcott, one of the most powerful agents in music hall history. With Didcott in charge, Elen's publicity in the trade press went into overdrive, and after his first hit, 'Never Introduce Yer Donah to a Pal', he was booked solid for the next eighteen months. Elen's songs were direct and unpretentious. Most of them celebrated ironic and resigned self-knowledge – one of his most famous being 'If it Wasn't for the 'Ouses in Between', written by Edgar Bateman and George Le Brunn in 1894. Here Elen makes much of his house's position and accommodation:

> Oh it really is a wery pretty garden
> And Chingford to the eastward could be seen;
> Wiv a ladder and some glasses,
> You could see to 'Ackney Marshes,
> If it wasn't for the 'ouses in between.

A similar sentiment can be found in Elen's 1905 hit "'Arf a Pint of Ale', written by Charles Tempest, in which he pretends to be abstemious but accompanies every meal, however small, with 'arf a pint of ale. In 'It's a Great Big Shame', he milks the stereotype of the nagging wife and the henpecked husband, together with – to the modern ear – some very politically incorrect views on how to restore male supremacy in the home. Elen sings of a pal he's lost to marriage; the meat of the song is in the chorus:

> It's a great big shame, an' if she belonged to me,
> I'd let 'er know who's who.
> *[Here Elen mimes slapping her]*
> Naggin' at a feller wot is six foot three
> And 'er only four foot two!
> Oh! they 'adn't been married not a month nor more
> When underneath her fumb goes Jim.
> Oh isn't it a pity that the likes of 'er
> Should put upon the likes of 'im!

Albert Chevalier was much more sentimental than the down-to-earth, proud-to-be-working-class Elen. Chevalier fell into the coster persona by accident. Born in Notting Hill in 1862 to Welsh and French parents, he was given the extraordinary name of Albert Onesime Britannicus Gwathveoyd Louis Chevalier. He toured with several legitimate theatre companies before finding fame in 1887 with a song he wrote himself, 'Our 'Armonic Club', which he first performed at the Strand Theatre in London in a production of *Aladdin*. Unlike many of his contemporaries, he had no burning ambition to be a professional entertainer until circumstances, in the form of a lengthy period out of work and the success of his song, intervened. He was soon singing songs like 'Tink a Tin' and 'Funny Without Being Vulgar', co-written with his brother-in-law Charles Ingle.

In February 1891 Chevalier appeared at the London Pavilion in full coster regalia – peaked cap, neckerchief, tight-fitting jacket and bell-bottomed trousers trimmed with pearl buttons – singing 'The Coster Serenade'. He was an instant sensation, hailed as 'the Kipling of the Halls' and 'the Coster Laureate'. 'My Old Dutch', written with Charles Ingle, was another early big hit. Chevalier's style benefited from his background in straight theatre, and was more polished and mannered than Elen's. Chevalier became something of a 'cross-over' artiste, giving lucrative private recitals and exclusive matinée concerts at non-music hall theatres like the Queen's Hall in London and the Free Trade Hall in Manchester. He attracted audiences who would never normally have gone to a music hall, and became a great favourite of the royal family. Improbably, the stately Queen Mary was said to be a fan of his song 'Knocked 'em in the Old Kent Road'. She was evidently a good judge, because the song has lasted through the generations and been widely covered. Shirley Temple sang it in *The Little Princess* (1938), Marlene Dietrich recorded it, and Fozzie Bear sang it – in coster costume – on *The Muppet Show*. Always a class act, Chevalier teamed up with the French singer Yvette Guilbert in 1906, and they toured America with great success, even playing Carnegie Hall. He married George Leybourne's daughter Florrie – the inspiration for 'My Old Dutch' – and died in 1923.

Alec Hurley, 'the Coster King' – Marie Lloyd's only faithful husband – made another London street, not far from the Old Kent Road, equally famous in 1899. Written by E.W. Rogers, 'The Lambeth Walk' became a quintessential music hall crowd-pleaser. Hurley milked the coster idiom almost to death with songs like 'My London Country Lane', 'No More up at Covent Garden', 'Cockney's in Japan', 'The Cockney Sportsman', 'The Coster's Banquee-et', 'The Coster's Beanfeast', 'The Coster's Family Tree' and 'The Coster's Sister'. Both 'The Lambeth Walk' and 'Knocked 'em in the Old Kent Road' remain irresistibly catchy, and a tribute to the craft of the songwriters. The power of the melodies, and the unforgettable choruses, transcend the performers to take on a life of their own.

Harry Champion was in many ways a 'professional cockney', rather than a coster singer *per se*, who inserted his idiosyncratic songs into a classic patter/song format. He was one of music hall's great survivors. Like Elen, Chevalier and Hurley he had a store of amazingly catchy songs that he famously trotted out at alarming speed. Born William Henry Crump in Bethnal Green in 1865, he, like Elen, started off as a black-face performer, but quickly honed an act that put him at the top of the bill for nearly fifty years. He became Harry Champion, 'Quick and Quaint', in 1887, and his songs have become a part of English cultural life. 'Any Old Iron', 'Boiled Beef and Carrots', 'Ginger, You're Barmy', all written by Charles Collins and/or Fred Murray, can all be brought to mind with little or no prompting. 'Any Old Iron' has been covered by Peter Sellers and the Monkees, and, again, by Kermit the Frog and Fozzie Bear on *The Muppets*. Another of Champion's popular songs, 'I'm Henery the Eighth, I Am', was covered by the pop group Manfred Mann in 1965, when they were the best-selling act in the US. It became one of their biggest hits, with its sexually liberated comic payoff:

> I got married to the widow next door,
> She's been married seven times before
> And every one was an Henery,
> She wouldn't have a Willie or a Sam
> I'm her eighth old man named Henery,
> Henery the eighth, I am!

Champion had a liking for songs involving obscure foods, some of which, popular at the time, are now forgotten and have little evident appeal: 'Baked Sheep's Hearts Stuffed with Sage and Onion', 'Hot Tripe and Onions' and 'Hot Meat Pies, Saveloys and Trotters'.

The 'swells' and 'costers' included many artistes now long forgotten, or remembered only for a single song or chorus or phrase – but they too helped sustain the growing phenomenon that was music hall.

7

The Serio-Comediennes

'Every art contributes to the greatest art of all,
the art of living.'

BERTOLT BRECHT, *A SHORT ORGANUM FOR
THE THEATRE* (1948)

No one in the history of British entertainment embraced 'the art of living' as well as the female stars of music hall. Coming from humble backgrounds, they sang about life as it was for the vast majority of their audience, bringing to life the ups and downs, ironies, agonies and gritty realities of a woman's lot in Victorian Britain. Marie Lloyd was by every measure the leading lady, but her path to stardom was eased by the success of predecessors like Jenny Hill, Bessie Bellwood, Kate Carney and Ada Lundberg. These four can be categorised broadly as 'coster' singers and early serio-comediennes.

The expression 'serio-comic' (often shortened to 'serio') means, literally, part serious, part comic, and became attached to those female music hall artistes who drew material from their personal experiences. Julia Harcourt was one of the first to advertise herself as a 'serio-comic vocalist', in the *Era* in October 1856. Initially the term was applied to both men and women, but by the end of 1860 it was exclusively used for female performers, in reviews, advertisements and 'wanted' notices.

Some of the earliest serios are shadowy figures. Ada Lundberg ran away from home in Bristol to join a circus, where she appeared in static near-nude *poses plastiques* at the tender age of eleven. In songs like 'I'm Alright Up Til Now' she specialised in portrayals of women at the very bottom of the social ladder – chars, slaveys and the most downtrodden of kitchen maids. She was in fact an attractive girl, and audiences reacted favourably to the contradiction between her natural beauty and the rags she wore. Ada was popular in the London halls from the early 1870s, and appeared in America as late as 1893. Her last appearance was at the Tivoli, Manchester, in June 1899. She died later that year, in her mid-fifties.

Kate Harley was billed in 1863 as 'the Best Serio-Comic Singer of the Day'. Unlike Ada Lundberg she was short, stocky and unprepossessing, and sang some numbers in male dress. Two of these, 'Granny Snow' and 'Away Down Holborn Hill', were big hits for her. In June 1866 a reviewer was smitten: 'Few can compete with her refinement in style but it is to her undoubted histrionic abilities that her success is principally due.' Her 'clever impersonations' were well received at the Tyne Concert Hall, Newcastle, and she later toured with Vance's Varieties for three years. It may be that her relative anonymity today results from her performing outside London, but there can be no doubt of her popularity and talent.

More is known of Annie Adams, a big girl with a voice to match. She specialised in ballads and arias from opera, and was neither suited for nor attracted to the mild vulgarity and suggestiveness that were then so popular among the 'coster' serios. Born in 1843, at the age of eighteen she was singing arias from *Il Trovatore* at the Theatre Royal, Southampton. She was famed for her expensive dresses, and to protect them and keep them clean her husband, the comedian Harry Wall, whom she married at nineteen, habitually lifted their hems when she left the stage. Songs like 'The Merriest Girl' and 'Are You Gazing on this Little Beauty' earned Annie great popularity. An appearance at Turnham's Hall, Edgware Road, in January 1863 had the *Era* purring: 'Her vocalization is as bewitching as her pretty face.' The ballad 'If They Only Saw Me Going' was taken up by the whole audience and sung with gusto. Such spontaneous participation creates a charming picture that conjures up the best of early music hall. In 1871–72 she toured the United States, becoming a popular sensation from New York to San Francisco, and earning a great deal of money. Back in England she appeared regularly across the country until the late 1870s, when she disappears from sight.

One of the greatest of the serios, the petite and sharp-featured Jenny Hill, was the daughter of a Marylebone 'cab minder', whose lowly and poorly paid job was to hold the horses of carriages waiting in a cab rank. There are few reliable details of her early years, but it is clear they were not easy. Music hall journalist and writer Chance Newton recalls her as a 'child serio', a very young 'keen eyed little Cockney' singing in free and easies; other reports suggest she appeared in pantomime as young as six. Another legend is that at or about the age of nine Jenny left London to be apprenticed to a publican at the Turk's Head Inn in Bradford. It is said that her job was to sing to the customers in between scrubbing floors and washing up, and that she was sometimes expected to sing until two in the morning, beginning work again three hours later. Even if this account is exaggerated, it suggests a deprived and exploited childhood. Her biographer, Henry Hibbert, claims she was discovered as a child by Bob Botting, manager of the Marylebone Theatre, while making artificial flowers in his factory, and that she made her London debut at the age of twelve, at Dr Johnson's Hall in Fleet Street.

In her mid-teens Jenny Hill married an acrobat, Jean Pasta (real name John Woodley), but when she became pregnant he deserted her. Alone and with a baby to care for,* and not yet twenty, she was desperate for work and prepared to try anything. There are differing versions of what happened next. The more colourful story is that, penniless and half-starving, she pestered the early music hall agent Ambrose Maynard, who sent her with a note to Emil Loibl, the manager of the London Pavilion. Loibl let her perform that night, to rapturous applause, following which he showed her Maynard's note,

* The baby was Peggy Pryde, later to be a music hall star in her own right.

which described her as troublesome and advised him not to see her. She fainted. This story may be true, but in his unreliable memoirs the grand old man of music hall, Chance Newton – who claimed to have known Jenny since she was a child – makes no mention of it. Instead, Newton credits theatrical agent Maurice de Frece with booking her into the Oxford and a succession of other theatres. The truth will probably never be known.

Despite the mystery of her early years, the teenage Jenny was soon touring relentlessly and receiving excellent notices for her 'comic characterisation'. A word of caution came in March 1865 from a reviewer at the Prince's Concert Hall, Leeds, who advised that she 'would do well to eschew all tendency to vulgarity'. It was advice she ignored. Managers were so wary of her unscripted patter that clauses were written into her contracts forbidding her from speaking direct to the audience. Even so, the social comment in the lyrics of her songs had the force of a piledriver.

Jenny Hill specialised in characters drawn from the working-class audience she knew so well: shop girls, servant girls and factory workers. She brought them vividly to life, giving them strength and stature despite their lowly position in life. 'I've Been a Good Woman to You' must have appealed to many of her audience:

> I've been a good woman to you,
> And the neighbours all know that it's true,
> You go to the pub,
> And you 'blue' the kids' grub,
> But I've been a good woman to you.

But Jenny was never a doormat, even in character:

> He's out on the fuddle, with a lot of his pals,
> Out on the fuddle, along with other gals,
> He's always on the fuddle,
> While I'm in such a muddle,
> But I mean to have a legal separ-a-tion.

Jenny did not sing the 'chorus' songs so beloved of music hall audiences, which may explain why her songs did not sell in sheet music form. Most of her material was strongly narrative, and reflected the lifestyle of her working-class world: 'Every Pub We Saw We Went Inside', 'Four Ale Sal', 'The Coffee Shop Gal', 'Boy about Town'. In 'Bai Jove' (1880) she takes a broadside at the swells, mocking their lazy, unproductive lifestyle:

> No intellect troubles the 'chappie',
> For to work or to think would be 'low',
> He prefers to be more or less 'sappy'
> And delights but in tinsel and show.
> Some say he's no use in creation,
> And his graces and airs they deride,
> But a fig for such sermonisation,
> There's nothing like putting on 'side'.
>
> Bai Jove! Bai Jove! notice our side
> As along through existence we glide,
> We drink S and B –
> And it's easy to see,
> That we glory in putting on side.

'Side', of course, is 'show', puffing oneself up, pretending to be what one is not, or boasting about what one is. To the hard-pressed, hard-up working classes, this was a provocation, and a legitimate target for the 'coster' boys and girls.

In ''Arry' (1882) the lyrics mock the social aspirations of the clerks and shop boys who idolise such swells, but while satirising their pretentions it reminds the audience (which would be full of such boys) of their real worth:

> 'Arry likes a jolly good joke
> Quite right 'Arry,
> 'Arry won't mind the fun that I spoke,

What say 'Arry?
The 'Upper Ten' may jeer and say
What 'cads' the 'Arries are,
But the 'Arries work and *pay their way*
While doing the La-di-da ...

'La-di-da' – putting on airs – stuck in the English language, and even now I can hear my mother using it to mock the socially pretentious.

Jenny Hill scoffed at social mores with great effect. In a throwback to W.G. Ross and his ballad about the convicted murderer Sam Hall, the lengthy narrative song 'The City Waif' (1889) tells a dark tale of urban misery, prosperous exploitative 'toffs' in their 'caffys', dispossessed agricultural workers and put-upon costers scratching a living. It is Victorian melodrama, but also an indictment of social conditions. It appeared in the year following the famous match-girls' strike at Bryant & May, which received huge public support. The song tells of a 'waif and stray' observing city life:

Alone, in the streets of London, my papers! I sell each
    day,
And notice each sight around me, though only a 'waif
    and stray'.
I ain't 'ad much eddication. It's wasted on such as me,
Except what the Ragged School gave me, or else the
    reformat'ry ...
I'd never no mother nor father
To love me, like some I see,
And what does this big, cold world care
For a poor little chap like me.
Out of my bed in a doorway,
Bobbies all hunt me down,
And no home have I beneath the sky
But the streets of London town ...

The song then moves into the waif's first moral tale:

> Well, Johnson he was a bumkin, he opened cab-doors
> and sich.
> And his 'ands was as a lady's, or fellers what's grand and
> rich.
> Well, the chaps, they all sneered and chaffed him, says
> they, 'He's a toff, he is.'
> Till he cried, 'If you're men, you'll hear me, and learn
> how I came to this!'
> Then he told how he'd tramped to London, along with
> his poor, sick wife,
> In search of some work to keep 'em, but it cost him his
> darling's life.
> He told how she sank by the wayside, one sigh! and her
> soul was gone,
> But up in his arms he took her, and carried her on and
> on,
> Then, as he sobbed while he told us how he came down,
> down, down,
> All our eyes were dim with tears for him, in the streets
> of London town …

The next verse tells how one of the many thousands of 'working girls' on the streets of London saved the waif's crippled sister:

> One night, in the depth of winter, my sister she lay jest
> here,
> Poor kid! she's a cripple, she is, and she was so faint and
> queer,
> She lay in the snow quite 'elpless, and, oh! how my poor
> heart bled.
> For I knew that my little sister was a-dying for want of
> bread.

Then up comes Sal Brown at that moment,
And rough as she is, says she,
'Take this money, here! run for food, boy,'
Then she took Kitty on her knee;
She saved the life of my sister,
And though people run her down.
She played an angel's part that night
In the streets of London town.

The song finally turns to the subject of the good working-class
girl 'ruined' by a 'gentleman':

One night, it was on midnight, I was minding a cabby's
     'orse.
Outside of a big swell 'caffy', in a street off of Charing
     Cross,
When a shaboyish sort of a feller, he comes up and says
     to me,
Describing a man and woman, 'Have yer seen sich a
     pair,' says he.
Jest then a gent comes from the 'caffy' with a lady all
     jools and lace.
And the shabby cove turns in a moment, and meets the
     pair face to face,
My father! My child! You villain! the shabby chap
     'oarsely cries,
'I've found you, my child's betrayer,' then straight at his
     throat he flies.

He snatched up the old cabby's 'orsewhip,
And the swell he turned white and blue,
As the shabby chap laid the lash on,
He 'owled as a kid might do;
He ruined a poor man's daughter,
Trampled her good name down.

And we said he deserved all he got that night
In the streets of London town.

It is easy to see why Victorian audiences took Jenny Hill to their
heart. In her, the downtrodden had a champion. She was a herald
who trumpeted their grievances. She was also more than a great
performer – she was a feminist trailblazer, a professional success at
a time when women could neither vote nor borrow money without
a male guarantor; when the professions were closed to them and
their only employment choices were low-paid factory or shop work,
or domestic service. Jenny Hill not only earned success on her own
merits, she remained in control of her career: there were no
Svengalis for her. She did it her way, and took the knocks.

In 1891, at the height of her fame, Jenny became one of the first
female music hall stars to play New York, but five years later she was
a fallen star, overwhelmed by arduous years playing her heart out
every night of the week, combined with a little too much liquid
anaesthetic. The strain crippled her defences, and tuberculosis
swarmed over them. She died, in her mid-forties, in 1896.

To those who saw her in the golden days of music hall, Jenny
Hill was a superstar to be ranked alongside Marie Lloyd and Vesta
Tilley. John Hollingshead described her as 'the one woman of real
genius who ever enlivened the music hall stage', while Percy
Fitzgerald tells of a performance that was watched with 'breathless
attention from beginning to end'. Harry Hibbert acknowledged her
as 'the supreme genius' of her generation, and Chance Newton –
admittedly never far away from a superlative – described her as 'the
most artistically "realistic" comic and pathetic singer on the music
hall boards'. Even Vesta Tilley revered her: 'If I were asked who ...
was the greatest artist we ever had on the Variety stage, I would
unhesitatingly plump for Jenny Hill.'

Bessie Bellwood, 'Queen of the Halls', was cut from similar cloth,
but of a coarser weave. Born Katherine Mahoney, probably in 1857
to Irish parents living in London, she had a sharp tongue and a
unique ability to deal with hecklers. As a child she earned her living

as a rabbit-skinner in Bermondsey, and supplemented her income by singing in taverns. Her onstage life began, rather incongruously, at the Star, Bermondsey, as Signora Ballantino, 'world-famous zither player', but she quickly gained a reputation for spicing up her act with lewd allusions. Theatre managers feared her 'blue' stories would deter patrons, but many in the halls loved them, and – like all great artistes – Bessie responded to her live audiences. Vulgar, loud-mouthed and proudly working-class, Bessie had numerous affairs with aristocrats. A sincere Roman Catholic, she was generous with her time and money to those in need, but was never far from a public brawl. Her biggest hit, 'What Cheer 'Ria' (1885), co-written with Will Herbert, was sung in the multi-coloured skirts of a typical factory girl. Its first verse gives us a very clear idea of the confident urbanised 'coster girl on a spree' that became Bellwood's signature:

> I am a girl what's doing wery well in the wegetable line,
> And as I'd saved a bob or two, I thought I'd cut a shine.
> So I goes and buys some toggery, these 'ere wery clothes
>   you see,
> And with the money I had left I thought I'd have a spree.
> So I goes into a music hall where I'd often been afore,
> I don't go in the gallery but on the bottom floor;
> I sits down by the Chairman and calls for a pot of Stout,
> My pals in the gallery spotted me and they all
>   commenced to shout
>
> CHORUS:
> What cheer, 'Ria? 'Ria's on the job.
> What cheer, 'Ria? Did you speculate a bob?*
> Oh, 'Ria she's a toff
> And she looks immensikoff,
> And they all shouted, What cheer, 'Ria?

* A shilling was the price of a seat in the stalls.

The lyrics of the song tell us a lot. We see the confident, hard-working young woman, her aspirational choice of the more expensive seats at the music hall, her firm bond with her 'pals', the healthy disrespect of the audience for 'toffs', and ultimately her self-deprecating acceptance that her 'place' is with her own kind – all of which would have resonated with her audience. The spoken 'patter' in between the verses shows Bessie reaching across the footlights. It is one of the few examples of 'patter' to have survived, as it was never included in song sheets:

> You don't catch me going chucking my money away, trying to be a toff any more – the way they served me wasn't so very polite. They brought the chucker-out and he said, 'Come on. 'Ria, you've been kicking up a pretty row,' he says. 'Come on, outside.' I says, 'Shan't, shan't! There you are! Shan't!!' He took hold of me and handed me out, just as though I'd been a sack of taters. When I got outside, my young man was waiting. So he says, 'Serves you jolly well right, 'Ria! You shouldn't try to be a lady, 'cause it don't suit yer.' Just then my pals were coming out of the gallery and they all commenced shouting:

> What cheer, 'Ria? 'Ria's on the job.
> What cheer, 'Ria? Did you speculate a bob?
> Oh, 'Ria she's a toff
> And she looks immensikoff,
> And they all shouted, What cheer, 'Ria?

The aspirational working-class ethic is seen in another of Bessie's popular songs, 'He's Going to Marry Mary Ann', written for her by Joseph Tabrar in 1885. Here she proudly lists everything her husband-to-be, Fred, is going to buy for her:

> He went right off to Maples where the furniture is grand,
> He said he meant to have new things, not common
>   second hand.

We've got one chair, one table and one chest of drawers,
two mugs,
Two plates, two cups, two saucers and a pair of water jugs.

The chorus lists other items on the wedding list, and finishes touchingly with:

And he's going to marry Mary Ann, that's ME!

As with Jenny Hill, critics warned Bessie against vulgarity. In April 1882 one reviewer from the *South London* wrote: 'she sails as close to the wind as possible in the way of suggestiveness'. Another, seeing her at Lusby's in Mile End Road in February 1883, enthused: 'For low comedy she is not surpassed on the Music Hall Stage.'

Bessie's life was no less racy offstage, and her solicitor was a busy man. In spite of her high earnings, she was summonsed frequently for non-payment of debts, on one occasion narrowly avoiding going to Holloway Jail. In 1891 – for once a plaintiff, not a defendant – she unsuccessfully took the Duke of Manchester's estate to court for money she had lent him (there were rumours that she was paid off to avoid a public scandal). In 1895 she was in court again, for non-payment of doctor's fees for treatment of her live-in lover, the Marquis of Ailesbury. Bessie claimed the charges were excessive. Expert witnesses said they were not. Again, she lost. In 1889 she claimed damages of £1,000 – a significant sum – from a Middlesex magistrate named A.G. Crowder, who had written to the Canterbury demanding she be dismissed on grounds of indecency. Crowder's letter claimed that she had been dismissed from the Royal, the Cambridge and the Pavilion for the same reason. This was not true, and she sued for libel. In court, Crowder apologised and accepted that he had been misinformed. He was ordered to pay Bessie's costs, and her action went no further. In the same year she was back in court once again, for punching a cab driver in the face after an altercation. This fracas involved Lord Mandeville, another lover, and one of *his* debts.

The cab driver may have got off lightly. The music hall historian Theodore Felstead tells of how, after Bessie's nose had been put out of joint by famous racing manager George Masterman, she accosted him while he was lunching at Romano's: 'I hear you have been going around calling me a "so and so".' Masterman, not having heard the question properly, bent his head towards Bellwood, who allegedly bit off a part of his ear. 'That'll teach you a lesson,' she is reported to have said. 'Next time you talk about me, remember I'm still Bessie Bellwood.' If the story is true, she was lucky not to find herself in court again. When she died in 1896 of 'cardiac disease exhaustion' at only thirty-nine, thousands followed her funeral cortège.

Later serios were less pugnacious, even though, in a tough profession, they had to be prepared to fight for their interests. They tended to fall into one of two categories: the streetwise 'woman of the world', a buxom graduate of the school of hard knocks; or the innocent 'little girl lost', often wearing a child's smock dress and frilled bonnet.

Artistes like Vesta Victoria were adept at both these roles. 'Our Lodger's Such a Nice Young Man', written in 1897 by Fred Leigh and Victoria's brother Lawrence Barclay, is a perfect example of the 'ingenue' genre:

> At our house not long ago a lodger came to stay,
> At first I felt as if I'd like to drive him right away;
> But soon he proved himself to be so very good and kind,
> That, like my dear mamma, I quite made up my little
>   mind …

The young singer clearly has no suspicions of the lodger; the more worldly-wise audience is left to make up its own mind, while heartily joining in the infectious chorus:

Our lodger's such a nice young man, such a good young
    man is he;
So good, so kind, to all our family!
He's never going to leave us
Oh dear, oh dear no!
He's such a good, goody, goody man,
Mamma told me so.

Born Victoria Lawrence in Leeds in 1873, Vesta Victoria was the
daughter of black-face comedian Joe Lawrence – whose speciality
was to sing while standing on his head – and singer Marie Nelson.
Like Vesta Tilley and Marie Lloyd she was onstage as a child,
appearing at the age of six weeks with her father, as 'Baby Victoria'.
For her solo debut, aged around ten, as 'Little Victoria', she was
billed as 'Champion Clog Dancer of the World and Queen of Lady
Serio Comics'. She was later billed as 'the Minnie Palmer of the
Halls', and a glance at the sheet music for Minnie, the American
child star who came to the UK in 1883, shows a similar portrayal of
an innocent young girl in smock and bonnet.

'Little Victoria' grew up, and her last performance in that guise
was at the Washington Music Hall, Battersea, in June 1888. Only one
month later, advertisements appear for 'Vesta Victoria', remarkably
described as 'the Greatest Lady Artiste in the World', which confirms
that Joe Lawrence had a fine line in hyperbole. At the time Vesta
was fourteen, and had been onstage regularly for eight years. Two
years later she was topping bills across London, and so in demand
that she turned down an offer from Tony Pastor to appear in New
York in 1891. The big boost to her career came that same year with a
song, 'Good for Nothing', based upon a hopeless, wayward child
called Nan, a character in a play of the same name by John Baldwin
Buckstone. The song tells of a grubby tearaway who yearns to be a
boy. Vesta claimed immodestly: 'The idea for the song and the
dance was, I might say, quite my own … It trebled my earnings in a
week.' When she performed it at the Canterbury, the *Era*'s critic
wrote: 'Miss Vesta Victoria's impersonation of a "good for nothing"

girl ranks among the best things this clever serio-comic has done, and is likely to considerably enhance her reputation ... She is dressed as a little girl, and does quite a merry romp around the stage. She makes odd little grimaces: and, to show what a genuine don't-care sort she is, she makes the back of her hand the table cloth, and all that sort of thing. It's a very fresh and pleasing turn.'

In 1892 Vesta made the first of many tours to America. She took with her Joseph Tabrar's 'Daddy Wouldn't Buy Me a Bow-Wow', which was a huge hit:

> I love my little cat, I do
> With soft black silky hair
> It comes with me each day to school
> And sits upon the chair
> When teacher says, 'Why do you bring
> That little pet of yours?'
> I tell her that I bring my cat
> Along with me because
> Daddy wouldn't buy me a bow-wow! Bow-wow!
> Daddy wouldn't buy me a bow-wow! Bow-wow!
> I've got a little cat
> And I'm very fond of that
> But I'd rather have a bow-wow
> Wow, wow, wow, wow.

My father, who heard Vesta sing the song, said that, as performed, it was not the innocent number it seemed, being full of innuendo that audiences would readily have understood.

America made Vesta a rich woman. By the early twentieth century she was among the most highly paid stars on both sides of the Atlantic, and a significant property-owner in America.

The success of 'Bow-Wow' had an unexpected side-effect. The sheet music made clear that the song could be sung 'without fee or licence, except at music halls'. The prohibition did not exclude theatres, and this was seized upon by the producers of the successful musical comedy *In Town*, who included the song every night, without fear of prosecution for copyright infringement. This infuriated Vesta, who hated her songs being printed, because familiarity could shorten their shelf life. She told an interviewer: 'In this particular instance, I consented. Of course, it was too late to rectify the mistake [omitting theatres], but nonetheless I was excessively annoyed.' It was not a mistake she would make again.

Vesta's career prospered with a string of memorable songs, most of which tapped in to her 'ditsy girl' persona. It was so successful she remained in a smock and bonnet well into her thirties. She also began to specialise in 'victim' songs of women 'done down' by events.

In 'Poor John' (1906), where her character had managed to snare a man, the girl's meeting with her prospective mother-in-law did not have the positive outcome for which she might have hoped:

> John took me round to see his mother!
> His Mother! His Mother!
> And while he introduced us to each other,
> She weighed up everything I had on,
> She put me through a cross-examination,
> I fairly boiled with aggravation,
> Then she shook her head, looked at me and said,
> 'Poor John! Poor John!'

Even worse was to come. In 'Waiting at the Church' (1906) the bride suffers every girl's worst nightmare:

> There was I, waiting at the church,
> Waiting at the church, waiting at the church;
> When I found he'd left me in the lurch.
> Lor, how it did upset me!
> All at once, he sent me round a note
> Here's the very note, this is what he wrote:
> 'Can't get away to marry you today,
> My wife won't let me!'

In 'Now I 'Ave to Call Him Father' (1908), a young girl has to suffer the ultimate ignominy of being passed over in favour of her mother:

> He used to come and court his little Mary Anne
> I used to think that he was my young man
> But Mother caught his eye and they got married on the
>   sly
> Now I 'ave to call him Father

Offstage, Vesta Victoria's life was as far from innocent as were the lyrics of 'Bow-Wow'. Her marriage to music hall manager Fred McAvoy in 1897 was unhappy from the outset, and they separated after only three years. Divorce followed in 1903 after a hearing that painted McAvoy as a violent adulterer, a poor father to their daughter, and possibly a liar, since the judge dismissed his cross-petition that Vesta had an affair with the black-face performer Eugene Stratton. Vesta was no luckier with her second marriage, to Herbert Terry – a member of the famous theatrical family – in America in 1912, which proved to be bigamous. When his lawful wife died she remarried him, but the marriage failed, and he left her in 1926. Unsurprisingly with these setbacks, drink became a consolation to Vesta, and remained so for the rest of her life. Much of her fortune was frittered away, though she was never left in need, and she died, aged seventy-seven, in 1951.

A single hit song could keep a performer at the top of music hall bills for years. A famous instance of this is Lottie Collins' 'Ta-ra-ra Boom-de-ay', first performed in October 1891, when Lottie was twenty-five. Until then she had been down the bill for fourteen years, firstly as a member of a singing trio with her sisters, and then as a black-faced soloist. Within a few months of the song's first performance in October 1891, her song and dance routine became a craze. Her agent, Hugh Didcott, advertised widely to ensure that managers all around the country were aware of the excitement only Lottie could generate. Above her name he splashed: 'It's not exactly what she does, but the way in which she does it!'

The song chronicles the private, unspoken thoughts of an outwardly demure 'tuxedo girl ... a queen of swell society'. She is:

> Fond of fun as fond can be
> When it's on the strict Q.T.
> I'm not too young, I'm not too old
> Not too timid, not too bold
> Just the kind you'd like to hold
> Just the kind for sport I'm told ...

The chorus, 'Ta-ra-ra Boom-de-ay', was repeated eight times to the accompaniment of a frenetic dance, with the audience roaring out the familiar words. Lottie's dance, performed at breakneck speed, with much high kicking and displays of petticoats, stockings and garters, was never captured on film, but was very similar to the can-can. For the audience it was exhilarating, but for Lottie it was exhausting to perform such a routine three times a night, with numerous encores, and for months at a stretch. The sheer physical effort would have been tiring for a fully fit, healthy woman, but Lottie had a suspect heart and was known to faint, or collapse in distress, at the end of her performance. But 'Ta-ra-ra Boom-de-ay' had made her a star, and night after night for eighteen years she danced on, ignoring the cost to her health. Her daughter Jose (later the star of the musical *Maid of the Mountains*) believed the routine hastened Lottie's death, in 1910, aged only forty-four.

The song still causes dispute. Richard Morton wrote the lyrics, but the identity of the composer is less clear. It was thought the music had been composed by Henry Sayers, manager of the George Thatcher Minstrels, but he denied authorship, claiming that he had heard it sung in the 1880s in a well-known St Louis brothel by a black singer, 'Mama Lou'. Others believed it to be a variant of a Tyrolean folk song. However, when the English composer Alfred

Gilbert heard this 'new' melody being played by a friend, he claimed it to be his own composition, from his cantata *Abdullah, the Last Moorish King*. The publishers agreed with Gilbert – or, at least, were unable to contest the claim – and he was bought off with a cheque for £250 in lieu of royalties.

When Lottie Collins was a teenager singing with the Collins Sisters she was supported by a very young Ada Reeve. Ada was not solely, or even predominantly, a music hall star, but that is where she began, aged only four, in melodramatic plays in her native East End. 'The breathless silence during [her] recital and the hearty applause at the conclusion was a triumph,' said the *Eastern Post and Weekly Chronicle* in February 1884, following a performance by the ten-year-old Ada in Bristol. In September 1886 the *Era* wrote: 'We were particularly pleased with this little girl's elocution: it is particularly free from cockney taint.' By fourteen she had become 'Little Ada Reeve' the ingénue 'child serio' in the inevitable smock and frilled bonnet, with songs like 'What Do I Care?', 'She Glories in a Thing Like That', 'She Was a Clergyman's Daughter' and 'I'm a Little Too Young to Know'. But these outwardly innocent songs were accompanied by winks and gestures indicating more knowledge than might be assumed from her appearance.

Reeve was wide-eyed and toothy (rather like Marie Lloyd) and had a pronounced squint, but she moved smoothly up the bill. At nineteen she was on Broadway, returning to London to share top billing with Albert Chevalier, Dan Leno, Herbert Campbell, Eugene Stratton, Bessie Bellwood, G.H. Chirgwin, Little Tich and George Robey. In 1894 she moved from music hall to musical comedy when she was invited by George Edwardes to play the lead in his Gaiety show *The Shop Girl*. Ada's reviews were excellent. Once again her diction, 'free from the music hall twang', impressed reviewers, and the *Sporting Mirror* congratulated Edwardes for 'again travelling "to the halls" for his principal lady'. Nearly all of them commented on the success of bringing a 'saucy' artiste 'from the 'alls' to play an archetypal rags-to-riches story.

Ada went on to star in a string of Edwardes' musicals (*All Aboard*, *The Gay Parisienne*, *Milord*, *Sir Smith* and *San Toy*), all sharing the theme of poor girl made good. Thereafter, her long career moved effortlessly between musical comedy, music hall, legitimate theatre and radio. She toured extensively and was very popular in America, South Africa and Australia (where she lived for fifteen years and was managed by the expatriate debtor Harry Rickards). In 1935 she returned to England, and later appeared in several films, none of them very distinguished.

Ada's long and varied career was underpinned by her strong and robust personality. As she aged she became cantankerous, but she remained an irrepressible performer. Her final appearance onstage was on her ninetieth birthday at the Players' Theatre (formerly Gatti's-under-the-Arches, where she had made her West End debut in 1888). She died two years later, in 1966, one of the last of the serios who had been at the heart of music hall.

8

Marie Lloyd

'No other comedian succeeded so well in giving
expression to the life of [the] audience, in raising
it to a kind of art. It was, I think, this capacity for
expressing the soul of the people that made Marie
Lloyd unique, and that made her audiences …
not so much hilarious as happy.'

T.S. ELIOT, 1922

Marie Lloyd was born in Plumber Street,* Hoxton, on 12 February
1870, the eldest of what would eventually be the nine children of the
then twenty-two-year-old John Wood, a maker of artificial flowers,
and his eighteen-year-old wife Matilda. The new baby was named
after her mother, but was known from birth as Tilly. Beyond a tiny
circle of family and friends, it is unlikely that anyone noticed her
birth, or cared much about it. Yet when she died fifty-two years
later, tens of thousands lined the route of her funeral cortège, and
she was mourned as far away as Australia and South Africa. A light
had gone out, leaving a legend that will endure as long as show
business has a memory. 'She was,' wrote the *Stage*, 'as much part and
parcel of her time as Dickens and Thackeray.'

* Some have said mistakenly that she was born in nearby Peerless Street, which would have
been appropriate.

There may have been few luxuries in Tilly Wood's young life, but she was never short of affection. Hoxton, a mere mile from St Paul's Cathedral, was a district without pretensions, but amid the pawn shops and street markets it was a centre for the blossoming music hall. The famous Eagle Music Hall was one of many halls and pubs offering entertainment to the nearby East End of London.

Neither John nor Matilda Wood was gifted with artistic talent, but Tilly's aunt, a dancer who performed as 'Madame Louise Patti', put the possibility of a career in entertainment in front of the children's eyes as an escape route from the tedious labour that barely earned their parents a living. After leaving school Tilly worked in a series of dead-end jobs: she made boots for babies, curled feathers for hats and made bead trimming for dresses. None lasted beyond a few days. Tilly had other ambitions.

John Wood supplemented his meagre earnings working as a barman in the Eagle Music Hall, and it was there* that the fifteen-year-old Tilly Wood made her professional debut, probably on Saturday, 9 May 1885. The timing was perfect. Music hall was poised to begin its high summer of popularity, and Tilly was soon earning fifteen shillings a week singing at local halls under the name Bella Delmere. She was swiftly taken up by the theatrical agent George Belmont, but after a contract dispute he was replaced by George Ware, who became her long-term mentor, friend, manager and occasional songwriter. Controversy accompanied her from the very beginning. In 1885 she 'borrowed' a song – 'The Boy I Love is Up in the Gallery' – from Nelly Power, a heinous offence at the time, as singers 'owned' their songs, and depended on them to get work. Marie apologised, pleading naïveté, and was forgiven, but would subsequently make the song her own.** Ironically, the song was written by George Ware, who suggested she change her stage name.

---

* Or at the nearby Grecian Theatre – it is unclear. Marie claimed it was the Grecian, but the manager she named was in fact the manager of the Eagle.

** Poor Nelly Power died two years later, in poverty, aged only thirty-two.

The exotic-sounding Bella Delmere, once plain Tilly Wood, adopted the name that history remembers – Marie Lloyd.

Marie Lloyd began life at the bottom of the bill, but she did not remain there for very long. She was soon appearing with established stars like Charles Coborn, Bessie Bellwood, G.H. MacDermott and the large and jovial Herbert Campbell. Critics praised both her singing and her dancing, and her gift of instant rapport with her audience was already apparent. Encores – many of them, night after night – were routine. By mid-1886 she had graduated to the West End, with the critic of the *Encore* writing approvingly that she 'got all there was' out of her material. It was the first recognition that Marie Lloyd could lift a song out of its natural orbit – a skill that would propel her to the very top of her profession.

Life was tough in the poorer districts of London. The work-houses were crowded. The population was soaring, and much of it crammed into the streets of the East End. Chinese, Irish, Lascars, Malays all jostled with Jewish refugees from Tsarist Russia. Ships docked at the Port of London to unload the wealth of the East for the consumers of the West, and their crews filled the pubs and theatres. Crime and drunkenness were rife. So was fear, as Jack the Ripper marauded in the streets of Whitechapel. Amid it all, music hall boomed as the motley populace thronged to the theatre. In this atmosphere the young Marie Lloyd flourished.

There is no one alive today who saw the young Marie Lloyd perform, but contemporary reports and later memoirs confirm her talent. She began her career with the poise and self-confidence of youth. In appearance she was pretty but not beautiful, with a smile made more charming by slightly protruding teeth and a pronounced nose. Her hair was long and fair, set off by large blue eyes. She was short, comely, well-scrubbed and fresh, and exuded an air of cheerful good humour. The whole package was real, not a concoction, and to her working-class audiences she was always one of 'them'.

From the outset, Marie was blessed with a precociously strong voice that could soar over the noise and clatter that were the invariable accompaniment to music hall. She danced energetically – on one occasion at Collins' Music Hall she forgot the words of her song, but a looming disaster was turned into uproarious triumph with an impromptu hornpipe. Some critics compared her to Lottie Collins, and George Bernard Shaw wrote that she had 'an exceptionally quick ear for pitch and rhythm. Her step-dancing is pretty.' Years later, the caricaturist and writer Max Beerbohm added a comment that captured the essence of her appeal: 'Rhythm was one of her strong points. She had an acutely sensitive ear, impeccable phrasing and timing. But sheer joy of living was always her strongest point of all.' That *joie de vivre* was conveyed to her audiences. Marie loved being onstage, and her public enjoyed the vitality of her performances.

As her reputation grew, her act became more saucy, her ad-libs riper – 'I haven't had it up for ages,' she declared as she unfolded her umbrella, and the most innocent of lyrics could be transformed with intonation, a facial expression or a gesture. The prolific songwriter Joseph Tabrar wrote the apparently innocent 'A Bird in the Hand' for Marie in 1894, and it is easy to imagine how she interpreted the apparently innocent lyrics to set the house in a roar:

> He bought me a diamond ring
> Well, you can understand
> He had the bird in the bush
> And I had the ring on my hand.

Another song, 'Johnnie Jones', was performed dressed as a schoolgirl:

> What's that for, eh? Oh, tell me Ma!
> If you won't tell me, I'll ask Pa!
> But Ma said, 'Oh, it's nothing, shut your row.'
> Well, – I've asked Johnnie Jones see
> So I know now.

So did the audience. The lyrics of Marie's songs were never crude, but they were sufficiently suggestive to encourage the mind to wander. She could, said one impresario, have recited the Twenty-Third Psalm and made it indecent. The writer Harry Greenwall described Marie's performance of the song 'The Tale of the Skirt': 'It was a marvellous piece of acting ... it was often possible to have revealed to one a woman's social status by the way in which she handled her skirts ... Marie, without a word, but with a wink and a flash of the ankle, would leave no doubt in your mind that ... she was one of those ladies who trod the pavements of Piccadilly late in the evening.' Such suggestiveness delighted Marie's admirers but infuriated many a prim Victorian mind. As a result she had frequent brushes with authority, although some of the most famous stories about her are apocryphal – she inspired legend, as great talent often does.

Marie Lloyd swiftly became a music hall favourite. Equally important for box office receipts, her private life was public property. When, aged only seventeen, she ditched one boyfriend for another, it inspired a song, 'Never Introduce Yer Donah [i.e. girlfriend] to a Pal'. Poor George Foster, her hapless boyfriend, made that mistake, with the result that his close friend Percy Courtenay became Marie's first husband. Courtenay was twenty-five, slim, well-dressed and present-able, but beyond that he is a shadowy figure, known to history only through the hostile recollections of Marie's family and friends, who regarded him as a wastrel and an idler. Marie married him at seven-teen – she gave her age as eighteen on the marriage certificate – probably because she was pregnant, for their daughter Myria was born seven months later. There was no honeymoon. Two days after the wedding, Marie was appearing in Dublin.

By the age of eighteen, the ingénue of three years earlier was a wife, a mother, and in demand as a rising star. Her big breakthrough would come when a single song propelled her to the top of the bill and established her style for the rest of her career. 'Wink the Other Eye' had lyrics by W.T. Lytton and music by the prolific George Le Brunn, who was to become a continuous source of melody for

Marie. It was a classic Marie Lloyd song – innocent if sung without inflexion, but in her hands alive with innuendo:

> Say, boys, whatever do you mean
> When you wink the other eye?
> Why, when you tell where you've been,
> Do you wink the other eye?
> You preach your wives such stories
> You can tell them just a few:
> 'Just met an old acquaintance'
> Or 'The train was overdue'
> Then you wink the other eye …

If 'Wink the Other Eye' exposed the misbehaviour of men, Marie was prepared to balance it by describing the misadventures of women. 'The Wrong Man', another Le Brunn melody with John Harrington as lyricist, became a highlight of her early act:

> One night, my beau was rather late in calling round for
>   me
> And, when I heard a loud rat-tat, thinks I 'That must be
>   he.'
> So, I rushed to the passage and no chance of courtship
>   missing
> All in the dark I kissed him twice – then found that I'd
>   been kissing
>
> CHORUS:
> The wrong man! the wrong man! Wasn't it awful rum?
> The wrong man! the wrong man! Oh, Jerusalum!
> I never was in such a plight before
> Pity me if you can
> I thought I should fall
> I'd given them all
> To the wrong, wrong man.

Both these songs were written for the twenty-year-old Marie in 1890, a pivotal year that sealed her reputation and led to an invitation to appear in New York. She set off on an eight-week visit, the first of five she made to America. Within a mere five years of her debut, Marie had moved from fifteen shillings a week to £50, an enormous sum for the time. And she was worth it. She was, said an admiring *New York Sun*, the best representative of music hall that the city had ever seen.

Marie did not hoard her new-found wealth. It ran through her fingers like quicksilver. Her husband, Percy, was on hand to help spend it, and her large family shared in the financial rewards brought by her success. Each time Marie and Percy moved home – eventually to a big house in Brixton, via Dalston and New Cross – the family came too, which must have damaged her ailing relationship with her husband. All her life Marie was open-handed to people in need, especially those who shared her profession or the backstreets of her youth. Her legendary generosity added to the public's affection for her, and no doubt contributed to tolerance of her excesses.

Marie may have spent her money easily, but she worked hard to earn it. From the onset of her career she would sing at three or four halls a night, speeding between them by horse-drawn carriage. It was a gruelling routine, but was not unusual. Like other artistes, Marie needed a regular supply of new and pertinent songs, as well as humorous patter between them. Audiences were raucous, and only artistes at the top of their game stayed at the top of the bill.

Upon her return from New York, Marie was the hottest ticket in town. George Le Brunn wrote a string of new songs for her, and the auditoriums were packed to hear her sing 'Never Let a Chance Go By', 'How Dare You Come to London?', 'I Was Slapped' and 'Actions Speak Louder than Words'.

Marie was ready for further challenges. From the mid-1880s the impresario Gus (later Sir Augustus) Harris had been casting music hall stars in leading roles in pantomime, and in 1891 Marie appeared at Drury Lane in *Humpty Dumpty** alongside Little Tich as Humpty, with Herbert Campbell and Dan Leno as the King and Queen of Hearts. Success was assured with such casting, and Marie was paid £100 a week. The pantomime was a triumph, but not every critic was enthralled by Marie. The *Daily Telegraph* commented that she was 'prettily coquettish ... but some of her attitudes need a little toning down and are unsuitable ... to Drury Lane'. She brushed aside such criticism, and Gus Harris was sufficiently impressed by her performance to rebook her for the next two years. In 1892 she appeared as Little Red Riding Hood in *Little Bo Peep*, and in 1893 as Polly in *Robinson Crusoe*.

By 1892, only seven years after her debut, Marie Lloyd was the biggest female star in music hall. New songs like 'Twiggy Voo'** and 'Oh, Mr Porter' were huge hits in sell-out tours in the north of England. 'Twiggy Voo' yet again showcased her gift for innuendo:

> When a girl goes to be wed
> She is nearly off her head
> And, upon my word, she don't know what to do
> She is frightened for Oh lor'
> She's never done such things before
> Twiggy Voo, my boys, Twiggy Voo ...

The cheery good nature of Marie's songs was belied by her private life. Her marriage was failing. Percy Courtenay's ill nature had worsened, and his behaviour had become openly abusive and privately violent. He had no career of his own or involvement in Marie's, and was fobbed off with a weekly allowance of £3 which he invariably overspent. To be 'a kept man' was embarrassing for him, and humiliation followed when he discovered that Marie was

---

* The full title was *Humpty Dumpty, or The Yellow Dwarf and the Fair One With Golden Locks*. Marie played Princess Allfair, 'the Fair One'.

** The expression 'twiggy voo' may be bastardised French – 'Do you twig [understand]?' – but this is only a guess.

having an affair with the coster singer Alec Hurley. According to one source Percy burst into her dressing room during an interval of a performance of *Humpty Dumpty* in 1891, assaulting her and threatening to murder her. Another source has the assault occurring outside the theatre in 1893, after a performance of *Robinson Crusoe*, and the threat to kill her being made in a public house later the same evening. Whichever is true – perhaps both are – the marriage had become unsustainable. Courtenay was charged with assault, and they parted for good.

Marie was learning that fame had its drawbacks. Her marital troubles, her relationship with Hurley and her risqué act were all newsworthy, and she attracted the attention of the vehemently anti-music hall National Vigilance Association. Although well aware of their hostility, she did nothing to tone down her act, probably assuming that her popularity placed her beyond censure. Nonetheless, it was an irritant that would dog her as she became ever more identified with vulgar behaviour.

Throughout the 1890s Marie performed all over the country, as well as touring Europe, America and South Africa. Her gift of layering tiers of meaning onto apparently innocuous lyrics was not always well received. The Moss Empire banned her 'coarse and vulgar' act from its flagship London theatre, the Coliseum. Bournemouth too rejected her, the Town Corporation deeming her appearance 'not consistent with the dignity of the Corporation'. It is likely that these pinpricks cemented her hold on her public. As later cynics observed, there's no such thing as bad publicity. Nor did Marie take these criticisms placidly. When the manager of the Norwich Hippodrome said to her, 'This is a cathedral city … we don't want anything to cause offence,' she asked for a train timetable so she could return to London. The manager backed down, and a full house cheered Marie to the echo.

In 1901 Marie toured Australia with her lover Alec Hurley in tow. The tour, arranged by the former bankrupt-turned-impresario Harry Rickards, was extended from three to six months. Adelaide and Sydney accepted her warmly, but the more refined Melbourne was less enthusiastic. Marie and Alec sailed home in November, satisfied with their successes but scarcely richer: their large salaries had passed rapidly through their hands, much of it on Australia's racecourses.

Two years later, in 1903, Marie made her first recordings, some of which survive today. They are of poor quality, but reveal a strong voice that is a little worn after nearly two decades of singing in rowdy music halls without a microphone. But the records do reveal one of her secrets: her diction is impeccable, and every word can be heard. Other secrets remain hidden, since only a live performance could ever fully display the whole package that was Marie Lloyd. The recordings lack that spark, and without it, it is impossible to experience her true appeal. She lived, as much as any artiste ever did, in her rapport with her audience, and without that only a portion of her magic is on show. Her empathy, her ad libs, her asides, her gestures, her facial expressions, her meticulous attention to detail in her costumes – all are missing.

In 1904, ten years after they had separated, Marie and Percy Courtenay were divorced. Two years later Marie married Alec Hurley. At the peak of her fame she lived contentedly with Hurley in north London where they both enjoyed the fruits of success, entertaining friends on a pair of houseboats moored on the Thames near Hampton Court. But twenty years of touring, performing and living in the public gaze were beginning to take their toll. Marie was exhausted. Dates were cancelled due to illness. Then there were emotional stresses. Close friends died: jovial Herbert Campbell of a heart attack; Dan Leno, exhausted and insane; and her long-time favourite songwriter George Le Brunn, penniless despite his prolific output. For Marie, increasingly alone on her pedestal, drink became a familiar companion.

Marie's role in the music hall strike of 1907 was quixotic. The dispute arose over payments for matinees. Although big stars like Marie were unaffected, she was a strong supporter of more poorly paid performers, and because of her prominence became identified as a leader of the strike. Her involvement angered the big impresarios and theatre-owners, a grievance that laid the ground for a retaliation that would come years later.

After the strike was settled, Marie toured abroad: first in Paris and later in America, where her younger sister Alice had enjoyed great success the previous year. Marie was seen merely as Alice's sister, which must have both surprised and irritated her following her own past successes in the USA. Her reception was good, but not ecstatic, with some critics observing – truthfully but unkindly – that she was getting fat. The six-month tour was not the triumphal progress to which she was accustomed.

Upon her return home, the frustrations of her tour of America were dwarfed by the fall-out from Marie's relationship with Bernard Dillon, a young Irish jockey eighteen years her junior. Her marriage to Alec Hurley was crumbling. Work often kept them apart, and when they were together Marie's love of company meant they were rarely alone. There were rows, reconciliations and more rows. Court cases and contract disputes added to the strains between them. It is possible, too, that Marie's matronly appearance and the growing theatrical success of her younger sisters Alice and Rosie may have unsettled her. The attraction for Marie of the young, handsome Bernard Dillon was evident, and when Alec returned from a tour to South Africa he found an empty house. Marie had left him. The cruel homecoming began a downward spiral for Hurley that would have a tragic end.

As a leading jockey, Bernard Dillon, known as Ben, was a celebrity in his own right. The alliance of racing and music hall, and of two public figures of whom the puritanical middle class disapproved, was very newsworthy, and became a scandal when it was highlighted by Dillon's Derby win on Lemberg in 1910. At this point Alec Hurley was declared bankrupt – betting and generosity to friends had eaten away his money. He sued for divorce, citing Dillon as co-respondent.

It was a wretched time for all three of them. Hurley was ruined, sick and drinking far too much. Marie was once again being charged with vulgarity, and the tolerance so often granted to her formerly was reduced. 'I couldn't see,' wrote the novelist Arnold Bennett, 'the legendary cleverness of the vulgarity of Marie Lloyd.' A year later Dillon was effectively banned from racing by the Jockey Club after being sued by a trainer over a gambling scam. His career was over, and Marie's reputation was severely compromised.

The big impresarios, notably Edward Moss and Oswald Stoll, were striving to make music hall more respectable, which they believed would widen its audience. One guarantee of social acceptability was royal recognition, and the two men convinced Buckingham Palace to advise the King to attend a 'Royal Command' performance to be held in Edinburgh in 1911. After fire destroyed the intended venue, the Empire, the event was rearranged at the Palace Theatre, London, the following year. The cast comprised the glittering aristocracy of music hall, but with one omission: Marie Lloyd, the vulgar, the bawdy, the adulteress, and above all the strikers' friend, was not invited to appear. The impresarios had taken their revenge.

It was a staggering insult, and Marie responded with vigour. She threatened to write to the King, but there is no evidence that she did so. On the evening of the 'Command' performance, legend suggests that she appeared onstage at the nearby Pavilion in Piccadilly with placards proclaiming 'Every performance by Marie Lloyd is a performance by command of the British Public'. If this is true, I can find no proof of it. A hundred years later, her omission seems both sad and vengeful.

Nevertheless, the snub did Marie no harm with her public, or with overseas impresarios. In 1913 she set off on her fifth tour of America for the handsome fee of $1,750 a week. She and Dillon travelled to New York as a married couple, but, tipped off by a journalist, the US immigration officials challenged that status under legislation relating to 'moral turpitude'. After an acrimonious row on the quayside, and not before she had spent an uncomfortable few hours of internment on Ellis Island, Marie was granted leave to enter New York, but Dillon was not. Humiliated and angry, she appealed against the decision, but with only partial success, as they were both granted leave to enter New York, but only if they lived apart and returned to Britain as soon as the tour ended. Marie had no choice but to agree, even if through gritted teeth, because if she failed to fulfil her obligations she ran the risk of being sued for breach of contract. The bad publicity did, at least, ensure a full house when the tour opened at the Palace Theatre in New York.

This embarrassment was followed by sad news from England. At only forty-two, Alec Hurley had died, still professing his love for Marie. He was living at Jack Straw's Castle, a large public house near Hampstead Heath, with only his dog for company. After Marie had left him in such a cruel fashion and he had been declared bankrupt, he began drinking heavily and his health declined. Marie's public response to the news, if accurately reported, was graceless: 'It means,' she supposedly told the press, 'that Bernard Dillon and I can marry.' It is hard to believe that could really have been the response of such a warm-hearted woman after the death of someone who had shared her life for so long.

The tour stumbled from crisis to crisis. Reviews were mixed. Marie's gestures were too suggestive, said critics, and she was asked to withdraw certain songs from her show. When she refused, she was banned from performing in Vancouver: she never sang there again. In explaining herself she became foul-mouthed and intemperate, causing a storm of protest. To make matters worse, she had unwittingly broken her immigration agreement by leaving the US for Canada, and was barred from returning to fulfil her contract. She appealed again and was re-admitted, but Dillon was refused re-entry. To stave off further problems she defiantly – and foolishly – married Dillon. Once the Dillon story lost its traction, pure fiction created more headlines. After a dreadful review in the *Vancouver Sun*, Marie was reported to have horsewhipped the editor. This was wholly untrue, but caused a sensation on both sides of the Atlantic. Marie learned the perennial truth that once you are a target, any dart will do.

Following the outbreak of war in 1914, Marie was tireless in entertaining the troops. She took part in Sunday concerts for them in London theatres, arranged special performances elsewhere, paid for outings for troops and plied them with drink and cigarettes as if she knew their lives would be brutal and short. Her support for the young volunteers was wholehearted and genuine. For Dillon, an Irishman – many of whose countrymen were in rebellion against the Crown – the war years were a disaster. He joined the British Army, but applied for exemption from service in 1916. He was frequently in court accused of assault and drunkenness, and his previously slender frame turned to fat. Marie suffered a breakdown brought on by overwork, stress and domestic unhappiness.

The war was the catalyst that hastened the death of music hall. Cinema and revue-based entertainment had been undermining it for years, and theatres were closing. Marie still drew crowds, but her health was worsening. Ageing, sick and lonely, she had only her public to sustain her. But her career was to have a late flourish. She was once again overlooked for a Royal Command performance in 1919, but Charles Collins and Fred Leigh wrote one of her most enduring songs, 'My Old Man (Said Follow the Van)', the lament of a woman who becomes separated from her husband after they flee their home, having been unable to pay the rent. Once again, Marie tapped into the experience of many Londoners.

> We had to move away
> 'Cos the rent we couldn't pay.
> *The moving van came round just after dark.*
> *There was me and my old man*
> Shoving things inside the van
> Which we'd often done before, let me remark …
>
> My old man said: 'Foller the van,
> And don't dilly-dally on the way.'
> Off went the van wiv me 'ome packed in it
> I walked be'ind wiv me old cock-linnet.
> But I dillied and dallied,
> Dallied and dillied,
> Lost me way and don't know where to roam …

It was one of her most memorable songs, but her mainspring was running down. Marie and Dillon separated in 1920, and Virginia Woolf, who saw her in 1921, noted in her diary that she was 'scarcely able to walk, waddling, aged, unblushing'. But one great song remained: 'One of the Ruins that Cromwell Knocked About a Bit'. It would be the last song she sang. On Wednesday, 4 October 1922, Marie collapsed onstage at the Edmonton Empire, complaining of stomach pain. Unconscious, she was taken to her home in Golders Green, where she died three days later of suspected stomach cancer. She was fifty-two. Vast crowds lined the route of the cortège from her home to St Luke's Church, Hampstead, and thence to Hampstead Cemetery.

Unlike her successors George Robey, Harry Lauder and Gracie Fields, Marie Lloyd received no honours. She did not marry into society and respectability. But what she did, as T.S. Eliot declared, was to 'express the soul of the people'. And the people knew it. Her songs were their experiences. Her virtues and hardships were theirs. She tapped into their world. And when she leaned across the footlights, confiding in them and drawing them in, they became part of hers. Fame and wealth did not drive her from them. To the end, she preferred eels, winkles and kippers from a street stall to champagne and caviar at the Café Royal. She made mistakes in her life – as they did. She drank – as many of them did. She loved unwisely – as many of them did. Her language could be basic – as theirs was. She lived their lives vividly and in public, and they loved her for it.

Was Marie Lloyd vulgar? Yes, she was, in a 'Carry On' sort of way, and her jokes would have fitted into any of those films' scripts. The impresario C.B. Cochran spoke of 'the delicacy of her indelicacies'. Her act had the sauciness of the seaside postcard, but never the crudeness of a Chaucer. And, in a London of three thousand brothels and eighty thousand ladies of the night, it was scarcely offensive – except to those who wished to be offended. Her first biographer, Naomi Jacob, wrote: 'I watched and listened and realised that here I was seeing artistry that could be classified with the dignified grandeur of Henry Irving, the delicious comedy of Ellen Terry [and] the tragedy of Sarah Bernhardt.'

T.S. Eliot wrote: 'Although I have always admired the genius of Marie Lloyd, I do not think I always appreciated its uniqueness: I certainly did not realise her death would strike me as the important event it was.' Lloyd's pre-eminence, he felt, was due to 'the people's recognition of the fact that she embodied the virtues which they genuinely respected most in private life'.

The woman who was laid to rest in Hampstead Cemetery was a sad relic of the Marie Lloyd who had enchanted audiences for over thirty years. In her later years she became stout, balding and arthritic, all physical attraction gone, but memories of her past glories were too bright to be extinguished. The fire was out, but in its prime the blaze it created warms the memory still. Marie Lloyd was the Queen of the Halls, and we who did not see how truly great she was can only lament our loss. On her gravestone, the following words are carved:

> Tired she was, although she didn't show it,
> Suffering she was, and hoped we didn't know it,
> But, He above – and understanding all,
> Prescribed 'long rest', and gave the final call.*

* Written by Catherine Greene, Marie's daughter's old headmistress.

9

Dan Leno and Little Tich

'The greater the genius, the greater the
unsoundness.'

J.F. NISBET, *THE INSANITY OF GENIUS* (1893)

The man who would be billed as 'the Funniest Man in the World'
was born to Dan and Louisa Galvin on what is now Platform One
of London's St Pancras Station. In 1860 it was a short terrace of
houses, and the tiny rented back-to-back at 4 Eve Court was his
birthplace. The baby was christened George, but history reveres
him as Dan Leno. His story is one of the most touching in the
history of show business.

Eve Court was one of many transitory dwellings for the Galvins.
They were itinerant players travelling the country in search of brief
engagements in low-rent penny gaffs and tavern back rooms. More
often than not the baby's cot was a drawer in the pokey room of a
dingy lodging house. George Galvin may have been born into show
business, but it was on the very bottom rung of the theatrical
ladder. His parents were billed as Mr and Mrs Johnny Wilde,
'Singing and Acting Duettists', and earned no more than a few shillings a week. In music hall, cruel disappointments were a way of
life, and George's father turned to drink with every one of them. He
died when George was four years old, leaving Louisa and her two

boys in a parlous situation. She soon remarried. Her new husband, a Lancashire man, William Grant, was also a music hall artiste, who performed under the name Will Leno – sadly, with the same lack of success as Johnny Wilde. He shared the same love of alcohol as well: it was an occupational hazard.

Life was no less hard for the Lenos than it had been for the Galvins, and to generate income the children became part of the act. Three-year-old George made his debut at the Cosmotheca Music Hall, Paddington, as 'Little George, the Infant Wonder Contortionist and Posturer'. Two years later, dressed in costumes made from old petticoats and umbrella linings, he and his older brother Jack were a double act, 'the Great Little Lenos'. Occasionally they appeared well down the bill in popular halls such as the Britannia in Hoxton, although for every such booking there were many more evenings spent earning a few pennies as street performers.

Jack Leno loathed the life of an itinerant, and as soon as he was old enough he left to learn a trade. He was replaced by George's uncle Johnny Danvers, who was only a month older than George. The two boys had no toys, and knowing nothing but the theatre, invented routines as their childish play. Years later, Dan Leno recalled some of their lines:

> Dan: I once had an IOU.
> Johnny: So had I. But now I have only got a U left.

The zany turn of mind that was to fuel Dan's theatre of the absurd was already at work. It was a gift that, many decades after his death, would inspire the Goons, Monty Python and *Blackadder*.

Dan and Johnny were a natural double act, and enjoyed a deep and lasting friendship. Years later they would be reunited in pantomime, but they were not only a double act – they performed both together and separately on the same bill to earn two fees. Dan appeared in many guises: as 'Young Leno', 'Master George Leno' or 'Dan Patrick – Descriptive and Irish Character Vocalist', and as a member of 'the Brothers Leno' and 'the Leno Family'. His fees usually went to satisfy the thirst of his stepfather Will Leno, and swell the profits of the wine trade.

The main family act was slapstick. In the 'Torpedo Bill' routine, a father (Mr Leno) wants his son (Dan) to follow his trade as a cobbler, but his mother (Mrs Leno) wants him to better himself by becoming an inventor. Chaos follows. The son invents a series of unfeasible items, all of which go wrong, and ends by blowing up the entire family. Dan also played the role of Pongo the Monkey, a rebellious simian who thwarts the best efforts of his master in an act that was typical of many in the bottom half of the bill.

Success eluded the Lenos, and their prospects worsened as Will became ever more dependent on drink. Ireland proved no more lucrative than England, although Dan was noticed there by Charles Dickens, who remarked to him that he would one day 'make headway'. It may have been the only understatement Dickens ever made. The family act toured for years in the north and the Midlands, playing well down the bill anywhere that paid. Like many working-class families in mid-Victorian England they were poor, but not destitute.

From the age of six, Dan danced in clogs, which were all around him in the northern mill towns, and he became a skilled dancer. He had no set routine; his dancing was the extempore performance of a man with rhythm in his soul. He entered clog-dancing competitions, a regular feature of music halls in the north, and in 1880 in Leeds Dan won a cash prize and a leg of mutton. Encouraged by this success, he entered another competition which was intended to be a dance-off between clog-dancing champions Tom Robson and Tom Ward. The prize was a boxing-style belt worth £50 and the right to the title 'Champion Clog Dancer of the World' – albeit, in truth, rather a small world. To everyone's surprise except perhaps his own, Dan won. He defended his title three times, but then lost it to a disputed decision. When the victor failed to defend his title (and lost the belt) a replacement was made, and a new contest was held at the People's Concert Hall, Oldham, in May 1883. After a week of competition Dan regained the title and took the new belt. He kept it for the rest of his life.

Clog dancing gave impetus to Dan's rise to fame. He shot up the bill, and was soon outstripping the other Lenos. In 1883 he married Lydia Reynolds, a comedy vocalist, at St George's church, Hulme, Manchester. It was a modest affair. They walked to the church, were married in front of two witnesses, and returned home for the wedding breakfast; but it was a marriage that lasted.

Dan's act was now in demand in London, and he and Lydia moved south. His parents settled down in the suburbs of Manchester, confident that regular contributions of cash from Dan would ensure they would never be in need again. Will Leno never tired of boasting of his stepson's fame as he helped to spend his fortune in the pubs of Manchester.

Dan Leno's adult debut in London was at the Foresters' Music Hall, Mile End, on 5 October 1885; the same year that Marie Lloyd made her first appearances a couple of miles away. He was engaged to perform his award-winning clog dance and two comic songs for a fee of £5 a week, but found that the southern audience was unmoved by clog dancing. The comic songs, however, were a success. Dressed as a woman, Dan sang 'Going to Buy Milk for the Twins': onstage cross-dressing would underpin his career. His second song, 'When Rafferty Raffled his Watch', was typical of many hilarious numbers that would follow. The same evening he also performed at the Mogul tavern, Drury Lane, where he was so well received that he was booked for the following two weeks. Theatre bills began to advertise him in glowing terms: there was, however, no mention of the clogs.

Dan's skill in female impersonation encouraged George Conquest to book him to play Jack's mother in the pantomime *Jack and the Beanstalk* at the Surrey Music Hall, Blackfriars, with Lydia engaged to play Mercuria. They received a joint salary of £20 a week, and were delighted to find Dan's childhood friend Johnny Danvers in the cast. Dan received rave reviews, and was re-engaged by Conquest for *Sinbad and the Little Old Man of the Sea* in 1887.

Augustus Harris was as impressed by Leno as Conquest had been, and booked him for the 1888 Drury Lane pantomime *Babes in the Wood*, playing the role for which he was ideally suited, the pantomime dame. Another *Jack and the Beanstalk* followed in 1889, and *Beauty and the Beast* in 1890. All were huge box-office hits, running from Christmas until well into April each year.

In pantomime, Dan was now sharing top billing with Marie Lloyd, Little Tich and the former 'nigger minstrel' Herbert Campbell. The partnership between the vast nineteen-stone Campbell, a baritone and a well-loved raconteur of earthy comic tales and songs, and the nimble Leno, a mere five foot three inches, was inspired, and provided the template for later duos such as Laurel and Hardy, Morecambe and Wise and the Two Ronnies.

The Drury Lane pantomimes were lavish spectacles in which Leno and Campbell interchanged the male/female roles. In *Humpty Dumpty* in 1891 – in a star-studded cast that also included Marie Lloyd and Little Tich – Leno was Queen Sprightly and Campbell the King. Three years later in *Dick Whittington*, Leno was Idle Jack and Campbell was Eliza the Cook. The following year saw Leno cast as the Baroness and Campbell as the Baron in *Cinderella*. In the 1896 *Aladdin* Leno played Widow Twankey, setting an enduring standard for that character. The Leno/Campbell double act often played on Leno's gift for farce. This exchange from *Bluebeard*, written by Hickory Wood in 1901, is typical of the repartee that so appealed to audiences:

SISTER ANNE [LENO]: *Where are you going?*

BLUEBEARD [CAMPBELL]: *I'm going to a place called Puzzleton.*

ANNE: *How do you get there?*

BLUEBEARD: *That's what I'm trying to find out. Here you are. There's a train at 9.40 marked 'B'. What does that mean?*

ANNE: *'B'? Cattle only.*

BLUEBEARD: *That's no good.*

ANNE: *There's one at 10.30 marked 'J'. See what 'J' means.*

BLUEBEARD: *'J – see page 406.'*

ANNE: *There it is. 'J – see page 108.'*

BLUEBEARD: *Why, that's where we started from.*

ANNE: *So it is. What silly things guides are.*

BLUEBEARD: *Here you are, 'J' – I've got it, 10.30 train to Puzzleton. 'This train runs on Sundays, Wednesdays and Fridays only during September and July, except on the 15th of each month, then it runs on Tuesday and Thursday and Saturday from the 9th of June to the 8th of August, except on Bank holidays and Sundays, when it starts at 6.50. On all other occasions it runs as usual.'*

ANNE: *That's a very good train.*

BLUEBEARD: *Yes, but I don't think I'll go by it.*

ANNE: *Let me see. I understand these things. Look here! You start by the 11.30 express; that takes you to the edge of the desert in time to catch the 2.30 camel; the camel brings you across the desert to Tra-ra-ra Junction, where you meet the 5.16 elephant that brings you to the 9.20 steamer.*

BLUEBEARD: *That isn't a steamer; it's a balloon.*

ANNE: *So it is. Well! The 9.20 balloon brings you as far as Muddle Circus, where you take the blue bus with the umbrella over the driver. See? Look for yourself.*

BLUEBEARD: *11.30 express. Here we are. 'Z' – what's that? 'Z – Shrove Tuesday and Christmas Day only'.*

Outside pantomime, Dan Leno lifted the tradition of music hall to a higher level of performance and creativity than any predecessor. In performance he was the direct descendant of Sam Cowell and W.G. Ross, who perfected 'in character' songs as chimney sweeps, ratcatchers, etc. Leno went further. He honed the comic-song format to a perfect balance of singing and 'patter', becoming so effective at the technique that many of his performances resembled a comic story, bookended by a verse and a chorus. In the process he would create wholly fictitious offstage characters who became personalities in their own right – most famously, Mrs Kelly.

You know Mrs. Kelly? ... You know Mrs. Kelly? ... Good life.
Don't look so stupid. Don't – you must know Mrs. Kelly! ...
Don't you know Mrs. Kelly? ... Well, of course, if you don't you
don't, but I thought you did, because I thought everybody knew
Mrs. Kelly – and what a woman. Perhaps it's just as well you
don't know her. Oh, she's a mean woman. Greedy. I know that
for a fact. Her little boy, who's got the sore eyes, he came over
and told me – she had half a dozen oysters and she ate them in
front of the looking glass to make them look a dozen. Now that
will give you an idea what she is.

It is a form of patter that would be familiar to later audiences of
Max Miller, Al Read, Les Dawson, Larry Grayson or Frankie Howerd,
all of whom owe a great deal to Dan Leno. Its essence is that it draws
everyone into the artiste's confidence. He creates a world that
includes the audience, even though that world is entirely fictitious.

Dan Leno's physique was an important part of his appeal. While
his big mouth and large ears were comical, they were counter-
pointed by his bright, sad eyes – 'the saddest eyes in the whole
world', observed Marie Lloyd; 'If we had not laughed we would have
cried.' He was unthreatening, loveable. To see him was to smile. He
was born and shaped to bring pleasure into the lives of others.

It is impossible, without seeing him live, to fully appreciate
Leno's genius, but it is clear that he had the gift of being able to
submerge himself entirely in both male and female characters,
making them real people and not simply caricatures. He created
individuals familiar to his audience: railway guard, driver, detective,
fireman, huntsman, cobbler, seaside holidaymaker, abused parent,
shrill wife and henpecked husband. He shared his audiences' lives
through these surreal characters, and they loved him for it. His
women were never grotesque, but were instantly recognisable as
family members or neighbours, and his male characters were
equally familiar as work colleagues or husbands.

Dan Leno dealt in absurdity. His songs and digressions left audiences mesmerised, fearing to laugh in case they missed the next

line. Part of his appeal was the degree of hopelessness in all his characters. They were fragile and needed protection. Something would always go wrong. They would get lost when going to an important meeting, burn their hand on the teaspoon, faint in front of the landlady, all in a continuous stream of absurd consciousness.

Leno made his American debut in 1887 at Hammerstein's Olympia Music Hall in New York, billed as 'the Funniest Man in the World'. He would recall the month-long engagement as a highlight of his career, but the hyperbole of American advertising made him uncomfortable – probably because it raised expectations too high – and the lucrative tour was never repeated. For the rest of his life he stayed in England. The week after his return to London he played the Canterbury, the Pavilion and the Tivoli – every night.

He starred in his own touring shows, in which a token plot was merely a vehicle for his talents. *Orlando Dando* ran for six weeks in 1898, and was a runaway success, followed by *In Gay Piccadilly* and *Mr. Wix of Wycombe*. His fame and popularity were showcased in *Dan Leno's Comic Journal*, featuring cartoons of his acts and advertising for his shows, which sold 350,000 copies when it was published in 1898. Dan Leno mugs, jugs and other memorabilia were widely sold. These were big money-spinners, and by 1900 Lydia was able to retire from the stage and supervise their new house in Clapham, which had extensive gardens, conservatories and stables, together with a cook and housemaids.

But there were setbacks. Leno, Herbert Campbell and the comedian Harry Randall purchased or leased several halls across London. At first the enterprise thrived, but ruthless rival managers began to put 'barring clauses' into the contracts of performers to prevent them from playing in Leno's halls, which were forced to close, with the loss of a great deal of money. Thereafter he stuck to what he did best: performing.

In November 1901 Dan faced the grandest audience of all when he was commanded to entertain King Edward VII at Sandringham

House, Norfolk, a recognition of his pre-eminent talent as well as his unimpeachable reputation and material – he was never too risqué. This earned him the gift of a diamond pin, and public acknowledgement as 'the King's Jester'. It was a proud moment, the pinnacle of his fame, but from that high point the fates deserted him.

His lifestyle was physically draining. Over two decades he had undertaken an unrelenting routine of travel, full days of rehearsals and the tension of one or more performances a day, followed by the inevitable encores. Genius demands enormous mental energy, and Dan Leno never stinted in his search for perfection. The more he gave to his art, the more his mind and body suffered. His working habits, already crippling, were accompanied by too much entertainment of friends, much of it liquid, followed by late suppers and even more drinks with others who were only too happy to entertain a celebrity. Drink had killed his father, and it was now overwhelming Dan. Ill health, alcohol and frustration with his increasing deafness made for violent scenes, followed by tearful remorse. His behaviour became erratic: he gave money and valuables away to complete strangers, including the precious diamond pin presented to him by the King.

It is not clear whether it was overwork – and a reckless lifestyle – that began to destroy Dan's mental equilibrium, or the onset of the brain tumour that would eventually kill him. In any event, as his mental health worsened he was admitted to a nursing home in Camberwell. An illusory recovery saw him return to play Queen Sprightly in *Humpty Dumpty*, the 1903 Christmas pantomime at Drury Lane, which was now under the management of Arthur Collins. He wasn't the old Dan: he was erratic, and missed his lines and entrances. But the audience still loved him and forgave him. Dan was back, and the theatre rocked with laughter. He – and Herbert Campbell as the King – closed the final night on an optimistic note:

In the Panto of old Drury Lane
We have both come together again,
And we hope to appear
For many a year
In the Panto of Old Drury Lane.

It was not to be. Campbell died in July 1904, and Dan Leno swiftly followed his old friend. His mind and body were burned out, and he died in the arms of his wife Lydia on 31 October 1904, at the age of forty-three. His death was national news: the *Daily Mirror* devoted its full front page to seven pictures of him, under the heading 'Death of Mr. Dan Leno, the Famous Comedian'. To those who were unaware of the state of his mind and body it was a shock, and thousands gathered outside his home in Atkins Road, Balham. At his funeral, his coffin was accompanied by a huge procession of carriages and mourners that passed slowly by shops that were closed in respect. Tearful crowds lined the roads. The tiny man with the melancholy air and the squeaky voice had been a bright and welcome part of their lives. For many, a light had gone out, and they tearfully bade him farewell.

Tributes came from every side. The actor-manager Herbert Beerbohm Tree, no mean judge of character acting, wrote, 'No actor of our time deserved immortality so well as he.' W.J. Macqueen-Pope observed, 'He never had a rival, he will never have a successor.' But the final word came from another great clown: 'He was,' said Chaplin, 'the greatest comedian since the legendary Grimaldi.'

Another man, even smaller than Dan Leno, also enchanted music hall audiences. Harry Relph was born in 1867, the fifteenth and last child of an aged and prolific father, the seventy-seven-year-old landlord of the Blacksmith's Arms in Cudham, south of London, and his thirty-two-year-old wife. He was a curiosity from birth, having an extra finger on each hand. He was also double-jointed, pigeon-toed and overweight, and by the age of ten had stopped growing, condemned to be a mere four foot six inches for the rest of his life. Physically, nature had not treated Harry well, but he had an excellent brain, and learned to make the most of his minor oddities. His early days at the Blacksmith's Arms had one beneficial effect, rare in the world of music hall: all his life, Harry loathed alcohol.

In 1874 the Relph family moved to Gravesend in Kent, where the seven-year-old Harry had his first experience of singing parlours, penny gaffs and free and easies. He excelled at school, but was forced to leave at the age of ten because his father, now eighty-seven, needed him to contribute to the family budget. One can only imagine what went through the young Harry's mind. What was a diminutive, pigeon-toed, ten-fingered, two-thumbed boy to do with his life?

In later life Harry was apt to say that he had drifted into show business, but he had a compulsive need to perform. As a young boy he quickly learned what made people laugh or cry, and his gift soon brought rewards – firstly with a few coins thrown to him in penny gaffs for an expressive dance to his own accompaniment on a tin whistle. He learned clog dancing and black-face or 'burnt-cork' routines, and as his repertoire expanded he moved on to better venues. Although still only twelve, he soon graduated from the penny gaffs to play at the Royal Exchange, Gravesend, and the pleasure gardens at nearby Rosherville, performing for audiences which included many day-trippers familiar with London music hall, who had travelled out of town by paddle steamer and train.

By now Harry was being advertised as 'the Infant Mackney' or 'the Great Little Mackney', a pocket version of the original black-faced comedian, and was booked to play in Chatham for thirty-five shillings a week. It was at this time that he changed his name to 'Little Tich'. Legend has it he did so at the suggestion of Mackney – and who was he to argue with such a big star? Being plump and small, Harry had been teased since his Cudham days with the name 'Little Tichborne', after the famous portly claimant to the Tichborne baronetcy, who had been the subject of a notorious and much publicised trial in 1871–72. The abbreviation to 'Little Tich' was inevitable, and a new term for 'diminutive' entered the English language.

Following his engagement in Chatham, times were hard for the newly-named Little Tich. Life was a constant struggle for work, often in seedy houses and sometimes only for board and lodging. But he was persistent, and continued to add to his skills, learning to play the piano and the cello, to read and write music, and to dance *en pointe*. He could tumble and perform magic tricks, but most importantly he could tell jokes and get the measure of his audience. His talent was developing, and by the time he was seventeen he was earning £2 a week or more, several times the average working-class wage. Harry was becoming a prosperous young man.

In his personal life, he was less at ease. He was self-conscious about his lack of height and his extra fingers, and deeply offended by any suggestion that he was a freak. But his commercial instinct told him these deficiencies were exploitable, and during his wilderness years he promoted himself as 'a six fingered ... novelty' and 'grotesque dancer'.

In November 1884 'Little Tich, Negro Comedian' made his London debut at the Foresters' in Mile End and the Marylebone. A lengthy review in the *Era* of his performance at the Marylebone, where he was billed as 'the most curious comic in creation', concluded: 'We shall probably hear a lot more of Little Tich.' Before Christmas he was playing four theatres a night.

Harry began to fill up his calendar with visits to the provinces, and it was on one of these that Tony Pastor, one of vaudeville's greatest impresarios, spotted him in 1886 during his annual scouting trip for talent to take to America. Pastor booked him for a three-month tour of the States the following year as part of his Gaiety Company, at a guaranteed £10 a week.

In America Little Tich played to houses all over the midwest and the eastern seaboard. His agility, comic timing and sure hand with the audience made him a smash hit with the public and critics alike. He abandoned burnt-cork make-up, which was no novelty in America, and perfected a boot dance to which the audiences responded enthusiastically. It was to become famous. Tich's 'big boots' were unique. They were long and ski-shaped, and he experimented with various lengths to enable him to stand on tiptoe, bend forward to touch the ground or contort his body into extraordinary positions. Nothing like it had been seen before: the routine became central to his act and was demanded everywhere. In later life he joked that he had asked for size two and a half boots, but the cobbler had misheard and made them two and a half feet in length.

Harry met his first wife, Laurie Brooks, while touring America with the Chicago Opera House Company, and for a time he seriously considered settling in the States, where he was more celebrated and better-paid than in Britain. But in 1889 he returned with his pregnant wife so their son Paul could be born in England. News of his celebrity in the USA had boosted his reputation at home. He appeared at the Pavilion, and so impressed Tom Charles, the manager of the Prince's Theatre, Manchester, that he was offered the part of Bantam in *Babes in the Wood* in the 1889–90 pantomime season. Harry stole the show. For the first time in his career, Little Tich was getting the recognition he felt he deserved in England. The *Manchester Guardian* wrote glowingly: 'His dance in long flat wooden shoes is a triumph of eccentric step dancing – with many elaborate gymnastic contortions … It is certainly the most striking thing in pantomime, and was loudly encored.'

Little Tich would later say, 'I am sure my engagement with Mr Charles was the making of me.' He had become *the* act everyone demanded, and halls he had only dreamed of playing were now clamouring for him. From 1891 to 1893 he was engaged by Augustus Harris for three consecutive pantomime seasons at Drury Lane, where together with Marie Lloyd, Herbert Campbell and Dan Leno he was part of a remarkable cast. For 'vulgar' music hall artistes, such a booking was so desirable that some were prepared to work for nothing simply so they could style themselves as 'from Drury Lane'. But for Tich it was too much hard work for too little reward. He wanted £100 a week for the 1894 show, which was more than

Harris would pay. He never appeared at Drury Lane again, and the following year was back in Manchester.

Between 1896 and 1902 Tich rarely performed in London. He was never a fan of the capital, partly for practical reasons. His act was physically very demanding, and he did not think it was worth his while 'going back to London to do three or four turns [a night] when I can get as much in the provinces for one'. His reasons were not purely mercenary. He cared passionately about his art, and wished to demonstrate his versatility: 'You are only allowed, say ten minutes in each hall [in London]; when you are in the provinces you can have half an hour in which to do your turn.' This also explains why he was paid more in provincial theatres.

By now Tich was the most successful British star in Europe. He toured extensively in France, Germany, the Netherlands, Spain and Hungary, and from 1894 he kept a flat in Paris (when he was in London he stayed in a hotel). The Parisians took him to their hearts. They were drawn to the artistry and sophistication of his act, and responded enthusiastically to its visual nature. The French critic Lorrain described him as 'the miraculous dwarf', and as resembling something out of a painting by Goya. Tich became friends with Toulouse-Lautrec, who painted a picture of him which unfortunately does not survive. He also captured the imagination of other artists, and was painted by Jan van Beers in 1898. He would later inspire the second movement of Stravinsky's *Three Pieces for String Quartet* (1914) after the composer saw him in London. Stravinsky said: 'The jerky spastic movements, the ups and downs, the rhythm – even the mood or the joke of the music – was suggested by the art of the great clown.'

Tich flirted with film, making a brief appearance in *Le Raid Paris: Monte Carlo in Two Hours* by cinema pioneer Georges Méliès in 1905. In 1900 another Frenchman, Clément-Maurice, had taken rare footage, which survives today, of the 'big boots' dance. But music hall remained Tich's natural home, and when he made his entrance on a first night at the Alhambra in the 1920s, the French classical actor Lucien Guitry stood up, turned to the audience and demanded: 'Get up, all of you, in homage to the world's greatest genius.' This genius was recognised by the French government in 1909, when he was awarded the prestigious Ordre de l'Académie, the Napoleonic decoration for men of letters and science and those who 'advance education'.

In 1901 Tich returned to America for two weeks in New York, but it was to be his last visit. The audiences there, so supportive of his early career, had moved on. In Britain he was still top of the bill, and evolved two new dances. 'The Serpentine Dance', a spoof of the 'skirt and scarf' style of the Americans Loie Fuller and Isadora Duncan, was a huge hit at home and abroad. The second new routine was a parody of the Spanish *otero* style. These two dances joined the big boots among the most popular parts of his act.

In 1909 Charlie Chaplin, at that time a young artist touring with Fred Karno's troupe, saw Tich in Paris. Chaplin was captivated by the physicality of Tich's act, and several French critics have suggested that his famous 'little tramp' owed much to Harry Relph: the cane, the expressive walk, the bowler hat and the use of mime were all incorporated into the young comic's developing act. Harold Nicolson wrote that 'Chaplin could never be an imitator' – perhaps not, but he could observe, and he did borrow.

If so, it is not surprising. At his peak Little Tich was one of the highest-paid performers in music hall, regularly commanding three or four hundred pounds a week; many performers consciously or not, may have been influenced by his style. In private, Little Tich was not an extrovert, possibly because of his sensitivity about his height, but he was active in support of charities. He was a leading member of the Grand Order of Water Rats and the Music Hall Artistes' Railway Association, and a founder member of the Variety Artists' Federation. He appeared as a star of the first Royal Command Performance in 1912.

What made Tich's act so special? We can see the grainy footage taken by Méliès and Clément-Maurice, and listen to sound recordings made by him, but it is impossible to capture the full flavour of what he did. Like George Robey's and Dan Leno's his was a 'total'

performance. He did not rely on catchy and memorable songs –
indeed, his songs were generally quite weak. Nor was he a character
comic, like Robey or Leno or Sam Cowell. His patter was in character, but when you read it without the timing and the visual impact,
it is not very funny.

Typically, his later act included either the Serpentine Dance or
the *otero*, and always the 'big boots' routine. He would add a character song, in the role of a park-keeper, a doctor or a gamekeeper,
interrupted with patter and sung briskly in a highish pitch. The
lyrics were written mostly by Alf Ellerton with music by Will
Mayne, but Harry himself wrote a few. Part of the appeal of his act
seems to have been his infectious laughter. Tittering, giggling, then
guffawing, sometimes starting by laughing silently and building up
to a great belly laugh in a crescendo of hilarity. His communication
with the audience was absolute.

Those who saw him praised his extraordinarily nimble feet, his
agility, flexibility, poise, animated expressions, comic diversions and
adroitness. The great dancer Nijinsky often saw Tich perform in
London, and referred to him simply as 'Little'. Everywhere the big
boots were the highlight. He would use them to contort his body
into gravity-defying extremes of posture, leaning forward to put a
hat straight onto his head from the ground, bowing horizontally
with his feet flat on the ground. Sitting down, he would use them to
obscure his face, splaying them apart or peering around them to
play peep-bo with the audience. Having learned to dance *en pointe*,
he would stand on tiptoe, almost doubling his height, although
doing this every night of the week (sometimes three or four times a
night), the strain on his leg and stomach muscles must have been
intense. Unsurprisingly, as he grew older he performed this feat
only rarely.

Harry Relph's personal life, like that of so many in his profession, was rarely tranquil. His physical abnormalities made him shy,
sensitive and even peevish. His unhappy first marriage to Laurie
Brooks ended in 1897 when she left him and their young son Paul
for an actor named Francois Marty. She died four years later

without Harry or Paul ever having seen her again. In the year she left, Harry started a new relationship with Spanish ballet dancer Julia Recio. It is probable that they married quietly in March 1904, and he always referred to her as his wife, but the marriage was a failure. For more than twenty years Julia and Harry lived together but apart, in adjoining flats just off Tottenham Court Road. Each had other homes and other lovers. Theirs was a loveless relationship, and throughout it Julia was so extravagant that it put serious pressure on Harry's finances.

One of Harry's mistresses, Ivey Latimer, or 'Win', would be the love of his life. They met while performing in *Sinbad the Sailor* at the Royal Court, Liverpool in 1915. In Win, Harry had found his soulmate, and she was devoted to him. When he had difficulty finding gloves, she made some herself; when he ran low on silk socks she had Rowe's, the children's outfitter in Bond Street, make them specially for him. Harry and Win lived a very discreet life. She had her own flat, and when they travelled they always made separate bookings. Eighteen months into their affair Win discovered she was seven months pregnant. Their daughter, Mary, was born on 23 February 1918 while Harry was playing in Brighton. Attitudes towards unmarried mothers at the time were harsh. Win's family ostracised her, and refused to take her into their home in Hove. She and her daughter lived in a flat paid for by 'Uncle Harry', who visited regularly.

Despite his enormous success, Tich never received the recognition in England that he did in France. He saw classical actors and managers decorated for their work onstage, but believed there was an institutionalised animus against music hall performers – variety artistes like George Robey and Harry Lauder, and managers like Oswald Stoll, were decorated not for their talent as icons of music hall, but for their war work. After congratulating Robey on his CBE in 1918 he went on to say, 'It is time this unwritten law, this survival of snobbishness, was abolished. Because a man wears grotesque make-up on the stage it doesn't follow that he will do or does anything derogatory to good taste or incompatible with a title.' The comment gives us a glimpse into the mind of this highly intelligent man. He was proud of his act, which he believed was undervalued. He hated being patronised, and sided instinctively with the underdog. One can assume that his size and his deformities caused him much agony of mind.

At the end of the war Tich continued to top bills, even as the decline of music hall accelerated. His personal life with Win was stable. He bought her a house in Hendon in 1925, and when Julia died a year later, they married. Harry, still able to command £300 a week, carried on working, but in November 1927 a new routine with a mop went wrong, and he received a bump on the head. Although his head ached, it didn't overly bother him, and he finished the week's engagement. The following Sunday he was in his bathroom at home chatting to Win when, out of her sight, he failed to answer a question. She found him bent over the sink. He had had a stroke, and was paralysed down his right side. He would never speak again. Doctors told Win the mild bump had triggered a long-standing condition. He was expected to make a gradual recovery, but this was not to be. Harry Relph – the immortal Little Tich – died at 6.26 a.m. on 10 February 1928. J.B. Priestley, a lifelong admirer, said that Little Tich's loss affected him more than the recent deaths of Thomas Hardy, Prime Minister Herbert Asquith or Field Marshal Douglas Haig.

Little Tich left an indelible mark on music hall. '"Little Tich" was enormous,' wrote Sir Ralph Richardson fifty years later, 'a wonderful artist, with a rich deep voice and with great command. [His] was a bizarre art ... but he was accepted ... as being no more than a little odd.' Perhaps the definitive tribute comes from the French actor and director Jacques Tati: 'Little Tich was professor to ... comics ... his big boots act remains a foundation for ... comedy or the screen. [He was] the giant of creation.'

In the history of theatre, Little Tich can stand tall.

10

The Comic and the Minstrel

'We, at home, will never understand what the
name George Robey means to them … in the
silence of no-man's land.'

SIR MAX PEMBERTON, JOURNALIST
AND NOVELIST (1863–1950)

'So long as the world loves singing,
so long will Harry Lauder live.'

NEW YORK TIMES, FEBRUARY 1950

Even as music hall declined, it produced stars who endured. George
Robey and Harry Lauder rose to great fame and fortune in the halls,
but also prospered in variety, revue, radio and cinema.

Robey was born George Wade in the pleasant, lower-middle-
class surroundings of south London's Herne Hill in 1869. When he
was only five years of age his father, an engineer, was contracted to
work on the Mersey Tunnel, and the family moved to the respectable Liverpool seaside suburb of Hoylake. They returned to south
London, living in Peckham, when his father began work on a new
tramway system. George had a secure childhood, with all the benefits of an extended family living in relatively close proximity.
Although a spirited boy, he did well at school and stayed out of

trouble. The family moved again when he was eleven, this time to Dresden, where his father worked on the Magdeburg tramway. In Germany, George's eyes were opened to the delights of art, music, theatre and literature. In 1885 the family returned to London, where decisions had to be made about the future of sixteen-year-old George. He was a competent and diligent pupil, but the family were unable to afford university, and his later claims to have gone to Cambridge, but not to have graduated, seem to have been an affectation.

George's father decided that he should follow him into civil engineering, and he was packed off to Birmingham to learn the trade, but his heart was never in it. The lure of entertaining was irresistible, and he performed for the first time at a charity concert in Edgbaston in 1890. He was sufficiently successful for further amateur appearances to earn him a reputation for comic singing. In 1891, George returned to London, living with his family on Brixton Hill and working for an engineering firm. But – to the dismay of his parents – he began to appear onstage on a semi-professional basis. To save them embarrassment he changed his name to 'Roby', the name of an engineering firm he had known in Birmingham, but when it was mis-spelled on a bill as 'Robey', the creatively astute George preferred the look of it. So George Robey was born.

He had his first big break at an American-style 'dime museum', the Royal Aquarium in Westminster (made famous by George Leybourne in 'Lounging in the Aq'), where the arch-publicist the Great Farini was manager for a time. Despite its rather elevated title, all kinds of populist oddities were on offer at the Royal Aquarium: 'Barnum's Zulus', 'Mystic Muriel', Giovanni Succi 'the fasting man', the acrobats Zaeo and Lulu, exotic dancers from Tunisia, contortionists, illusionists and mesmerists. One semi-permanent attraction, the American mesmerist 'Professor' T.A. Kennedy, gave George an idea. Eager for professional experience and a deeper understanding of what made people laugh – a lifelong study for him – George asked to appear in the act as a stooge from the audience, to be 'mesmerised' by the professor into singing a comic song. The audience enjoyed the apparently straitlaced man being 'hypnotised' into singing, and George was soon playing different 'stooge' roles, including one as a man immune to hypnosis. In another, he had to sit impassively as a 'doctor' pushed a needle into his cheek: plainly, George was willing to suffer for his art.

George caught the eye of the manager of the Aquarium and was engaged, no longer as a stooge, but as a comic singer. Performing in a crowded room with clinking glasses and chatting diners, he concentrated on his timing and, more crucially, his diction, to capture and maintain the attention of the patrons. He became adept at altering his material and delivery to match the audience's mood.

George was keen to perform in the famous music halls, and his chance came when Charlie Brighten, the manager of the Oxford, offered him a Saturday-afternoon slot. He made his debut in June 1891, in the guise of a clergyman suffering from a marked reduction in social status: dishevelled, cassock unbuttoned, wig slipping from his bald pate, a red nose implying a sip or two too many of the altar wine, and exaggerated half-moon eyebrows showing a permanent state of surprise. He unveiled this character to an unresponsive audience, but Brighten's verdict was favourable, and he was booked to play the second house. The evening audience was more appreciative, and Brighten offered him a twelve-month contract. The future 'Prime Minister of Mirth' was on his way. George was soon being whisked between venues in a brougham as he embarked on a lucrative treadmill of several performances a night. His act developed steadily, and he always relied on his ability to read the audience, singing his comic songs with patter inserted, much as Dan Leno did. The unsteady clergyman was supplemented by a cast of characters: cantankerous landladies, henpecked husbands, bullying wives, nosey neighbours, a district nurse, a pompous mayor, a German music professor, a caretaker, a barrister and historical figures such as Richard the Lionheart. All were instantly recognisable, and were accompanied by an appropriate song from the many he purchased every week.

George Robey brought originality to his performance. While most performers simply walked to centre stage, addressed the audience and began their act, Robey made his entrance onstage as if pushed, or chased there by characters unseen. Having gained the audience's attention in this way he would pause, assessing the atmosphere, his demeanour invariably attracting a laugh. He would then shout, 'Desist, desist!' – not unlike Frankie Howerd in a later age – or 'Really, I meantersay!', immediately establishing rapport with the audience. To the accompaniment of sustained laughter, a po-faced Robey would go on to say, 'Let there be merriment by all means ... but let that merriment be tempered with dignity [remember, he would be dressed absurdly] and the reserve which is compatible with the obvious refinement of our environment.' His aura of slight pomposity and self-ridicule made for a winning formula.

Song and patter would then unfold effortlessly, with Robey taking the audience with him in all he did. The lyrics and patter of his big hits, like 'The Mayor of Mudcumdyke', 'Daisy Dillwater', 'District Nurse' or 'The Prehistoric Man', do not read well today, but in common with all great performers he was an alchemist with the ability to turn base material into performance gold. In Robey's hands, songs were performed as a series of lines punctuated with glares at the audience. A turn of the head, a gesture, an intake of breath, would embellish a performance extraordinary for its comic timing and empathy with the audience.

In 1898 Robey, by now an established favourite, married the Australian actress Ethel Haydon. There was no honeymoon, and he was onstage that night at the Canterbury. The couple settled in St John's Wood, and in 1900 a son, Edward George, was born, followed by a daughter, Eileen. The newly rich Robey relished dining with the social and financial aristocracy, glossing over his less than elevated origins and revelling in his fame.

In his private life Robey had three passions: art, antiques, especially Chinese and Japanese porcelain, and sport. He loved boxing, football, rugby, cricket, athletics, tennis and golf. With the aid of the Football Association he organised charity cup matches, and made guest appearances in charity and exhibition games for Millwall, Chelsea and Aston Villa. He was proud to play cricket with the great titan of the game, W.G. Grace, and was elected a member of the MCC in 1905.

Robey's success aroused jealousy among some of his rivals, a few of whom were openly antagonistic: one fellow comic called him 'a toffee-nosed twat'. His politics didn't help. He was politically right of centre and remained aloof from the 1907 music hall strike, which working-class colleagues like Marie Lloyd supported. Robey was unmoved, noting later: 'The man who gets to the top [in England] is almost treated like a usurper. The man who gets kicked to the ground is regarded as almost a saint. It is never suggested that both men are in places where they deserve to be. In other words we are witnessing an elaborately organised deification of inefficiency.' This observation, both poetic and prophetic, reveals a sophisticated mind, but it was an attitude that did not earn him popularity.

Like nearly all his top-of-the-bill colleagues, Robey played in pantomime each Christmas, but in his case seldom in London. His Dames graced Liverpool, Manchester and other centres in the Midlands and the north. In 1916, in the middle of the Great War, his close association with the impresario Oswald Stoll led to a musical revue based on his act, *The Bing Boys are Here*, a tale of two country bumpkins (Robey and fellow comic Alfred Lester) coming to the big city, with riotous consequences. It was a long-running engagement – which, apart from pantomime, was alien to George – and required him to learn lines and be under the instruction of a director. But £500 a week focused his mind.

The show proved to be a hit, providing Robey with one of his biggest successes. It ran for 378 performances at the Alhambra, Leicester Square, being seen by more than 600,000 people. Performances went on through Zeppelin raids: after one particularly loud bang, Robey looked up and shouted, 'Shurrup!' Not a soul left the theatre. *The Bing Boys* also left the charming legacy of Nat Ayer and Clifford Grey's 'If You Were the Only Girl (in the World)'. This beautiful, sentimental song was sung by Robey and his female lead, Violet Lorraine. The unforgettable words and melody live on today in all their life-affirming freshness and innocence:

> If you were the only girl in the world
> And I were the only boy
> Nothing else would matter in the world today
> We could go on loving in the same old way
>
> A garden of Eden just made for two
> With nothing to mar our joy
> I would say such wonderful things to you
> There would be such wonderful things to do
> If you were the only girl in the world
> And I were the only boy.

Max Pemberton wrote of what the show and Robey's performance meant to soldiers on leave from the Front: 'We at home will never understand what the name George Robey means to them out there. His jests are repeated in the silence of no-man's land ... In darkness and despair men will see visions of the great lighted house and the figures of pretty women and flowers from the gardens of England. Upon this scene comes a man who has but to look at them to banish their ills.'

One downside of *The Bing Boys'* success was the waiting between scenes. For the energetic Robey, used to dashing from hall to hall, the long gaps were tedious and dispiriting. A musical colleague made a flippant suggestion: why not take up violin-making as a hobby to pass the time? Robey did so, with some relish, and a workshop was fitted into his dressing room. Not a minute in his life was to be wasted.

The Bing Boys was followed by another revue, *Zig Zag*, and in turn by *The Bing Boys on Broadway*, which Stoll carefully timed to coincide with the American entry into the war. *The Bing Boys on Broadway* was even more successful than the original revue, and ran for 562 performances. Robey not only played the lead, but several stock American characters, including an Indian chief. Throughout the war – like Dan Leno, Vesta Tilley and Marie Lloyd – Robey used his great popularity to raise funds for the war effort. His work was rewarded with the CBE in 1919.

Post-war, the run of revues continued in 1919 with *Joy Bells*. During the first performance of this show, the success of one of his fellow acts caused the usually magnanimous Robey to put his foot down. The incident also gives us a clear sign that times, and tastes, were changing. The Original Dixie Land Jazz Band shared the stage with Robey for a section of the show, and a house packed full of patriotic American servicemen wouldn't let them leave the stage. Robey told the theatre managers that it was him or them, and the band was sacked – only to be booked the next day at the Palladium, followed by a year's tour around the country.

Robey was still the biggest name in town, and in 1920 another triumphant Stoll revue, *A Robey Salad with Musical Dressing*, illustrated his dominance. After *Sky High* in 1925 with Nellie Wallace, he produced a show himself. *Bits and Pieces* debuted in 1927, and proved so popular that he took it on tour to South Africa and Canada.

As revue began to give way to variety, Robey moved on to cinema, which was not an entirely new medium to him: he had appeared in early films made by Oswald Stoll, although none survive. *The Temperance Fete* was released in 1931, *Marry Me* the following year. In 1933 he played Sancho Panza in G.W. Pabst's *Don Quixote*, the second time he had performed this role on film. He was by now a national institution, and his fame, acting ability and crossover appeal were used to great effect in a 1935 London stage production of *Henry IV Part I*, in which he played Falstaff – a role he would reprise on film in Laurence Olivier's famous 1944 production of *Henry V*.

Success never deserted Robey, and contemporary accounts praise his ability to transcend weak material and delight audiences night after night – but his private life was less satisfactory. Fame offered him many temptations, and too often he gave in to them. He was a serial philanderer, and eventually Ethel left him in 1929 over his affair with the theatre producer Blanche Littler, sister of the impresarios Emile and Prince Littler. It was not an amicable separation. Robey took a flat on Shaftesbury Avenue, and in spite of the efforts of his barrister son and painter daughter he never saw his wife again. George and Ethel finally divorced in 1938, and he married Blanche, who remained his devoted companion and manager until he died, honoured as Sir George Robey, in 1954.

Robey's long career survived the death of music hall. As he moved into revue and then film, he must have known that each time he made another step away from the halls he was contributing to their decline. But it was music hall that secured his fame, and his legacy. A contemporary of Robey's, Harry Lauder, would tread a similar path.

Harry Lauder was a great star, and at his peak the most celebrated and highly-paid performer in the world. It is not fanciful to claim that he was the first global superstar of popular entertainment.

Lauder was born in August 1870, and no individual before or since has become more associated with the iconic identity of Scotland. Pictures of Lauder, resplendent in kilt, tufted beret and brogues, with his famous 'knobbly stick', became the very embodiment of Scottishness. Even his genes combined to make him the archetypal Caledonian – his father was a hard-working potter from the beautiful Lowlands of Lauderdale, his mother a God-fearing daughter of the Highlands. Born almost exactly a year after Robey, his early life was spent in Portobello, then a coastal resort near Edinburgh and even closer to Musselburgh, home of the oldest continuously played golf course in the world. One of Lauder's first jobs was as a caddy there.

Harry Lauder was the eldest of eight siblings, and all of them were taught the importance of thrift, hard work and personal responsibility. The family left Scotland briefly in the early 1880s when his father was offered a better-paid job in Derbyshire, but they returned less than two years later after he died of pneumonia. A small life insurance policy and a generous donation from his employer enabled his widow to pay for a funeral and move the family back to Arbroath.

Money was scarce, and almost immediately Harry Lauder, aged twelve, took a 'half timer' position at the local rope factory, earning a few shillings a week working one day in the factory followed by one day at school. At his mother's suggestion he joined the temperance society the Band of Hope, and at their weekly sing-songs he began to attract attention, consistently winning singing competitions with his performances of 'Poor, But a Gentleman Still'.

When he was fifteen the family moved to Hamilton, in the heart of the Lanarkshire coalfields, where he got a job at one of the pits. Once again he joined the local Band of Hope, and continued to win singing competitions. Audiences were hard to please – long shifts down the mines did not encourage a cheery disposition – and veered between sullen unresponsiveness and downright hostility. This was no problem to Lauder, who charmed them effortlessly and was soon being paid to perform; his first professional engagement, singing at a hall in nearby Larkhall, earned him five shillings.

Within a few years he was playing the large halls in Glasgow and touring Scotland and the north of England, usually in partnership with Mackenzie Murdock, 'the World's Greatest Fiddler'. It was a far cry from life down the pit, and Lauder must have felt he had really made it. But his career was only just beginning.

In June 1898, Denis Clark, the manager of the aptly-named Argyll Theatre, Birkenhead, was looking for new talent to entice audiences away from a circus that was in town. He had heard of an *Irish* singer, playing in Scotland, called Harry Lauder. Anything Irish was a good draw in Liverpool, and Harry was booked to appear. He scored a hit, and as the crowd cheered for an encore, Clark asked him to go back on. 'I cannae,' came the reply. 'Why not?' asked Clark. 'I havnae any moore Airish sangs ta sing.' 'What do you do in Scotland when they want an encore?' Clark asked. 'Weel, 'as different a home. A'm noon as a Scottish comedian there.' 'So sing some Scottish songs, then!' Clark pleaded. Lauder stepped back onstage and sang a Scottish song, and another, and another. He was a sensation. The house was on its feet, and the theatre was sold out for the rest of the week. Clark immediately re-engaged him, and so began an enduring friendship.

That evening was a turning point, and gave Lauder the confidence to develop an exclusively Scottish act south of Hadrian's Wall, and not to rely on extraneous material. Hungry for success, he set out to conquer London, the biggest music hall arena. On 19 March 1900 he bought a one-way ticket from Glasgow Central. Being Scottish, and remaining in character, it was a third-class ticket. He took digs in Euston, and then in Lambeth, and spent his days grinding around agents' offices, suffering rejection after rejection. Then, as so often, fate stepped in, and he picked up a 'fill in' spot at Gatti's-in-the-Road.

His songs included 'Tobermory', 'The Lass o' Killiecrankie' and 'Calligan, Call Again', the one remaining number from his Irish act. The audience loved it, and he was booked for the week. The *Era* reviewed him very favourably: 'Mr Harry Lauder, a Scotch comedian … has caused a furore with his songs.' Agents flocked to his door with contracts in hand, among them George Foster, and Lauder was soon playing Gatti's and the Tivoli.

Lauder wrote most of his songs in collaboration. At their heart were simple stories about Scotland, love, lassies, and money – especially keeping hold of it. Lauder developed a reputation for never tipping or buying a drink. He once presented the doorman of the Alhambra with a signed postcard – of himself. The music hall world was awash with stories of his legendary meanness, but many of them were invented by Lauder himself, for publicity purposes. It helped build the Lauder legend, but the Scottish people largely have him to blame for the reputation that persists today. In matters of the heart, however, there was nothing mean about Lauder. He fell in love at first sight with Annie (Nance) Vallance, the daughter of his old pit boss at Hamilton; they married in June 1891, and were devoted to one another until the day she died, thirty-seven years later. A touching illustration of that devotion, and their deep religious belief, came in 1907, when Lauder was offered the vast sum of $2,500 a week to appear in America. On tour in Liverpool at the time, he sent a telegram to Nance at home in Tooting: 'Will you come with me if this deal goes through?' The reply came by return: 'See book of Ruth, chapter one, verse sixteen – love, Nance.' Harry found a Bible, and read: '... whither thou goest, I will go; and where thou lodgest, I will lodge'.

In the event Nance did not travel to America, and their fifteen-year-old son John accompanied Harry. What happened on his first night at the New York Theatre, Times Square, has become show business legend. Understandably nervous, Lauder came onstage to cries of 'Good luck!' from a significant number of expatriate Scots in the audience. His performance was so electric that few artistes, before or since, have ever achieved such instant acclaim and fame from a single appearance. The critics were ecstatic: 'Harry Lauder, Great Artist, Captivates America', wrote one. *Variety* described him as 'a revelation in vaudeville ... a master of facial expression ... nothing short of remarkable character acting ... something vaudeville has never seen before ... perfectly self possessed. Harry Lauder is booked to remain in New York for five weeks. He could remain six months. An ovation never equalled on the variety platform was his reception. Harry Lauder, the greatest of them all.'

He was now in demand everywhere, and was soon commanding $3,000 a week, rising to $5,000 at the peak of his career in 1911–12, almost certainly making him the highest-earning act in the world. His pulling power was such that his American agent, William Morris, had to buy out his UK dates, paying $1,000 a week compensation. As well as lucrative tours of Australia, New Zealand and South Africa, Lauder would make twenty-two trips to America, undertaking punishing transcontinental tours in a special three-coach train solely for his use, with sleeping car, parlour and baggage car. He became the friend of presidents, notably Theodore Roosevelt, playing golf with William Howard Taft and Warren

Harding, and being a guest of Calvin Coolidge and Woodrow Wilson at the White House.

But a heavy touring schedule makes personal relationships very difficult, and while Harry enjoyed a warm relationship with millions of people he did not know, he had few close friends to whom he could turn. As the world's most famous Scot, it was natural that he should be drawn to his fellow countrymen, and whenever possible he made a point of seeking out members of the local Caledonian Society. Among his small number of close friends was his fellow Scot the industrialist Andrew Carnegie, with whom, although he was thirty-five years his junior, he had much in common. Both were self-made, world-famous men with similar origins in the Lowlands of Scotland. Carnegie had left the factories of Dunfermline, aged fifteen, for Allegheny, Pennsylvania. By 1900 he was producing 25 per cent of America's iron and steel. The following year he sold his interests to J.P. Morgan for $225 million. Carnegie helped Lauder's fundraising war work by writing letters of introduction to potential donors across the United States.

Henry Ford was another friend, as was the Duke of Windsor when he was Prince of Wales. The Prince would bring Lauder new 'knobbly sticks' from his travels, to augment his burgeoning collection of gnarled walking sticks, an intrinsic part of his act. The gift of a new 'knobbly stick', or as he called them 'twisted sticks', as a thank-you to Lauder when he gave a speech or made a personal appearance became something of a tradition. After his death, sixty-six of them were sold at auction for an average of £800 each (more than £20,000 today).

Lauder's friendship with music hall colleague Charlie Chaplin brought him offers of film roles, but he turned most of them down, perhaps doubtful of his ability to succeed without direct interaction with the audience. Yet he liked radio, and in 1925 he received £1,500 for his annual Christmas broadcast, the highest fee the BBC had ever paid. He also became one of the first international recording stars, selling millions of cylinders and discs during his career. It is likely that he is among the biggest-selling solo artists of all time.

To the modern ear, Lauder's performances may seem overly sentimental, a bit tame, even dull. But to Victorian and Edwardian audiences he was quite different from anyone they had seen before, his Scottish persona making him seem both exotic and authentic. He had a good singing voice, which he used well, and he learned very quickly how to captivate an audience. Outshining all his contemporaries in terms of raw box office, he combined the immediacy of Marie Lloyd, the compelling eccentricity of George Robey, the abstraction of Little Tich and the pathos of Dan Leno.

When Harry Lauder died on 26 February 1950, at the age of seventy-nine, the news of his death was flashed around the world. The *New York Times* reported his loss with a large photograph and a remarkable tribute:

So long as the world loves singing, so long will Harry Lauder live. He was a great comedian … minstrel … and entertainer. He was an artist of superlative finesse, blessed with a combination of wit and voice and personality, and an understanding of the simple thoughts and desires and emotions that make up so much of life. He was known and loved in four continents.

And never forgotten.

11

The Cross-Dressers:
Girls Who Were Boys

'Funnily enough they were always men. I never
seemed interested in impersonating women.'

HETTY KING, MALE IMPERSONATOR (1883–1972)

From the very earliest times, audiences have enjoyed the spectacle
of men dressed as women for dramatic or comic purposes. Greek,
Roman and Elizabethan dramas are full to bursting with boys playing comely girls, and men bustling about the stage as shrewish
wives or cantankerous mothers. Conversely, 'male impersonators'
were among the most popular acts on music hall bills in Britain, the
most famous of them all being Vesta Tilley.

Tilley epitomised one of the aspects of cross-dressing that is
common to nearly all the performers who chose to assume a male
persona: mocking the audience's social betters, but in her case
gently and affectionately. Her life was a mirror of her act. She would
become a part of the 'smart set' she so successfully satirised with her
Burlington Berties and Piccadilly Johnnys in their impeccable suits
and Eton collars. From humble beginnings she ascended to the very
highest levels of Edwardian society, performing before royalty and
later, as Lady de Frece, wife of Tory MP Sir Walter de Frece, attending state banquets and receptions. She amassed a huge fortune, and
retired to Monte Carlo.

In choosing to lampoon a very well understood stereotype, the swell, Tilley was following a well-trodden path that had started with a little-known artist called Annie Hindle, who enjoyed modest success around her home in the Midlands. Dressed as a man, Annie sang lions comiques-style songs about wine, women and song. By 1864, when she was seventeen, critics in Burnley were raving about her as 'the great serio-comic and male impersonator', and in the same year she was hailed as 'the Greatest Sensation in Stockton ever known since the days of man'. In hit songs like 'Racketty Jack' and 'Have You Seen My Nellie?' she lampooned the 'swell' persona. Annie's private life oddly mimicked her act. She married twice: first to British comic singer Charles Vivian in 1868; and second, using the name Charles Hindle, to Anna Ryan, her dresser, on 6 June 1886 at Grand Rapids, Michigan. She and Anna lived happily together in New Jersey, both wearing women's clothes, and ignoring social convention.

Annie's successful tour of America in 1867 inspired other female artists to dress as men. One who did so was another of her dressers, the American Ella Wesner, who was hired by Tony Pastor in 1870. Her debut was met with such an 'enthusiastic reception for her character songs, especially "The Swell of the Period"' that she was soon earning $200 a week. Wesner, like Hindle, borrowed heavily from music hall 'swell' material. Her British debut at the Oxford in 1876 was a triumph, and encouraged her manager M.B. Leavitt to write: 'her success was so pronounced that in a short period a host of imitators made their appearance'. The genre was growing.

A review of Wesner's performance at the Cambridge stated that 'in male attire she looks quite to the manner born and makes us tremble for the prerogatives of our sex'. Critics often mentioned the 'perfect fit' of her costumes, which themselves were 'a triumph of the sartorial art', and her 'flawless make-up'. Other comments suggest that she appealed to audiences' more visceral instincts: 'she dresses in male attire which becomes her very much'. It may not be fanciful to speculate that the women in her audiences were drawn to the concept of the perfect 'feminised' man, while the men were responding to the *frisson* of an attractive girl dressed in immaculate, tight-fitting men's clothes.

Two British performers, Nelly Power and Bessie Bonehill, were soon mining the same rich seam. Nelly Power performed one of her early hits, 'I'm a Jockey', dressed in male riding clothes. She was also the first to sing 'The Boy I Love is Up in the Gallery', which the young Marie Lloyd would steal and make her own. Nelly was famous for lampooning the effeminate dandies of the day with songs like 'La-di-da' and 'Tiddy Fol Lol'. Such ridicule of one's supposed betters was always popular in the halls, and Nelly, like Annie Hindle, also found success in impersonating the archetypical lion comique, George Leybourne. The *Era* described her as one of the 'warmest favourites', and enthused that her 'buoyant vivacity, intense energy and never-flagging spirits secured for her enormous popularity'. Inevitably, she went on to appear as a principal boy in pantomime, as did all of the leading male impersonators. In Gus Harris's Drury Lane production of *Sindbad** in 1883 she appeared with Arthur Roberts and Herbert Campbell.

The *Era*, despite its partiality to her, was not always complimentary to Nelly. Her material sailed close to the wind: she was criticised in 1886 for throwing nuts into the audience with too much male gusto, and was urged to 'moderate some of her impersonations'. None of this made any dent in her popularity, which was enshrined by her premature death the following year, at the age of thirty-two.

Bessie Bonehill, a Birmingham girl, was onstage at the age of six as one of the three 'Sisters Bonehill', a clog-dancing act. She graduated to a stint as a 'coon' singer, and when she began as a male impersonator in the 1870s she enjoyed immediate success. By 1881, in her mid-twenties, she was playing in New York, and eight years after that she was selling out Pastor's vaudeville theatre every night, and earning $450 a week. She used her money wisely, buying a farm on Long Island. With her cropped hair, square face and firm jaw she

---

* Promoters could not resist punning titles: *A Lad In* was another example.

was well equipped for male impersonation. She too appeared in pantomime as a principal boy, and specialised in patriotic songs such as 'Shoulder to Shoulder', written in 1882 by Edward Jonghman and Harry Adams:

> Then shoulder to shoulder, steady and true,
> Fight as your fore-fathers taught ye to do;
> Fight for your homes and the red white and blue
> And be proud that you're fighting for England ...

From the 1880s the demand for male impersonators soared, and so did the supply. Fanny Robina had a string of popular songs: 'All the Boys in Our Choir', 'Dear Mother I've Come Home to Die', 'Coming Back Home Again', 'My Little Baby Boys' and her greatest hit, 'King of the Boys'. Her life offstage was frenetic: she was married three times to fellow performers, and outlived them all. After the death of her third husband, the singer William Bint, in 1913, her career died too, and she took to running the refreshment bar in the upper circle of the Palladium in London.

Another lesser-known impersonator, Millie Hylton, had the larger-than-life and not very scrupulous Hugh Didcott as her agent, and he flooded the trade press in the late 1880s with promotional material. Millie was, he claimed, 'the Idol of both Hemispheres' and 'the Greatest Male Impersonator on either side of the Atlantic'. Vesta Tilley's agent, Walter de Frece, would not have been alone in disputing these extravagant claims, although Millie Hylton did have a number of hits – 'The Rowdy Dowdy Boys', 'The Last of the Dandies' and 'Dear Old Boy'. Didcott, on the other hand, later went on to initiate a libel action, in the course of which his lurid past as a wife-beater, adventurer and multiple bankrupt was revealed, ruining his business: in cross-examination it was said he had 'no character to clear'.

Ella Wesner was not the only American male impersonator to be acclaimed on both sides of the Atlantic. Thirty years later, Ella Shields, born in Baltimore, started as part of a sister act before travelling to England in 1904 and performing solo as 'the Southern Nightingale'. Until then impersonation had only been part of her act, but it gradually took it over. She had successful songs with 'If You Knew Susie' and 'Show Me the Way to Go Home', both of which resonate still, but her greatest success, written by her husband William Hargreaves in 1915, was 'Burlington Bertie from Bow':

> I'm Burlington Bertie, I rise at ten thirty,
> And saunter along like a toff.
> I walk down The Strand with my gloves on my hand
> Then I walk down again with them off.

The early lines suggest a typical 'swell' song, but that is deceptive. Bertie is broke and hungry:

> I'm all airs and graces, correct easy paces
> Without food so long, I've forgot where my face is
> I'm Bert, Bert, I haven't a shirt …

Nonetheless, hungry and shirtless or not, Bert has a good lineage:

> But my people are well off, you know.
> Nearly everyone knows me, from Smith to Lord
>   Roseb'ry
> I'm Burlington Bertie from Bow.

It is a song full of pathos – the well-bred, unfortunate toff, down on his luck and out of money, is a familiar figure still.

During the Great War Ella Shields had a popular success with 'Oh! It's a Lovely War', which vastly amused the troops, as it satirised their conditions in the trenches. She toured extensively after the war, visiting America and Australia several times, to great acclaim. Her private life was turbulent, with all three of her marriages ending in divorce amid charges of domestic violence and admitted extramarital affairs – none of which seems to have hurt her career. In her mid-sixties she joined Don Ross's *Thanks for the Memory* revival of music hall, earning a spot in the 1948 Royal Variety Performance. Ella Shields died in 1952, aged seventy-three, after collapsing onstage from a heart attack in front of three thousand people at a holiday camp in Morecambe Bay.

Some performers employed cross-dressing for different purposes. Lona Barrison wore men's clothes only as a prelude to stripping off to the briefest of undergarments. The *Era* covered her act in Paris in 1898, and thoroughly approved. She came onstage in white tie and tails, with an opera hat and spectacles. While singing, she slowly divested herself of her coat, waistcoat, trousers, collar and tie – leaving her dressed only in a shirt that (rather fetchingly, it was said) reached down to her knees. She then shed the shirt, which was embroidered with a coronet, leaving her stripped down to a body stocking. The *Era* reported admiringly that 'she [then] goes through a clever equestrian act, in which she sits astride. We wonder if we shall see Miss Barrison in London.'

Her act sounds rather risqué, and doubtless was, as she had been a member of the Danish/American vaudeville act the Barrison Sisters, who had played in London at the Alhambra in June 1894, to great acclaim. Provocatively billed as 'the Wickedest Girls in the World', they dressed as children, played with dolls and sang songs with highly suggestive lyrics, and achieved worldwide notoriety for their 'Kitten' routine. After asking the audience, 'Do you want to see our pussies?' they would hitch up their skirts to reveal kittens cradled in purpose-built pouches located in their groins. Few can have been surprised when, in March 1898, Lona was expelled by the German government for being a 'notoriously obnoxious person'.

There were only two 'swell' impersonators who became superstars: Vesta Tilley and Hetty King. Vesta Tilley, born Matilda Powles in Worcester in 1864, was at the top end of public regard. The second of thirteen children, she was onstage as a child, promoted by her father, Harry Powles, a painter of porcelain by trade, but also a comic singer and music hall chairman under the name of Harry

Ball. Success came almost immediately for 'the Great Little Tilley' – 'Tilley' being a diminutive of 'Matilda'. It was difficult for young performers on music hall's travelling circus to develop relationships, but Vesta and Dan Leno became lifelong friends while on the northern circuit.

Vesta's first bookings in London, as an eleven-year-old in 1875, saw her performing each night at the Canterbury, the Marylebone and Lusty's in the Mile End Road for a total of £9 a week. The motive for her adoption of male impersonation at about the age of eight is not clear. In her not always reliable memoirs she tells a story of her father hearing her sing while wearing his hat and coat. It may be as simple as that, but it is equally likely that her ambitious father was looking for a new novelty, and thought male impersonation might be a commercial success. In any event, he had an evening suit made for Vesta, and the history of show business was changed.

As Vesta grew up she developed new songs and characters: the plucky soldier, the shy suitor, the knowing son, the poor orphan boy being moved on by a policeman. In March 1878 she adopted the adult style of Vesta Tilley, and advertisements noted: 'Tilley prefers to appear in Male Attire'. In 1881, at the age of seventeen, she was appearing as principal boy in pantomime. The following year she was in Sindbad at Drury Lane understudying Nelly Power in one of Gus Harris's extravaganzas while also appearing in her own right as Captain Tra La-La.

Her father died in 1888, and two years later, aged twenty-six – much to the chagrin of Oswald Stoll, a would-be suitor – she married Walter de Frece, the son of one of music hall's foremost agents, and stayed married. No breath of scandal ever touched her, and she was idolised as much for her sweet nature and generous personality as for her many gifts as a performer.

Walter became her manager, and arranged her first tour of America – a move her late father had resisted. She was a huge success at Pastor's in New York, and soon entered into licensing agreements, endorsing Vesta Tilley boaters, waistcoats and cigars. Her earnings rocketed. She toured America six times – sometimes,

as in 1897–98, with her own touring company. She and Walter seriously considered living in America, where salaries approaching
£1,000 a week were tempting, but the lure of England, where
Walter's interests were based, was too strong. In any event, Vesta was
earning huge sums in England too.

Vesta Tilley was meticulous in performance. Nothing in her act
ever even hinted at vulgarity. Her costumes were immaculate in
every way. Her taste in men's clothes was widely copied, and her
songs were hugely popular. The sentimental ballad 'After the Ball' –
my father's favourite song – was only one of a long list that are still
remembered. Other hits were in a different tempo: the dandy songs
'Algy', 'The Piccadilly Johnny with the Little Glass Eye', 'Burlington
Bertie' (not Ella Shields' later song 'Burlington Bertie from Bow')
and 'I am Following in Father's Footsteps' were all huge successes
with music hall audiences. 'Jolly Good Luck to the Girl who Marries
a Soldier' (sometimes 'a Sailor') was both promotion of the army
and self-promotion by a serviceman seeking a girlfriend:

> Jolly good luck to the girl who loves a soldier
> Real good boys are we!
> Girls, if you'd like to love a soldier
> You can all love me.

Vesta's 1914 favourite 'The Army of Today's All Right' was used
by the War Office to encourage young men to enlist – which they
did, in large numbers. At the end of the war Walter de Frece was
knighted, and a year later entered Parliament. Vesta, by now fifty-
six, and with an eye to her husband's new career, decided to retire
from the stage. She had filled theatres all her life, and bowed out
before an emotional audience at the Coliseum – leased for the night
by her rejected suitor Oswald Stoll – and to a warm tribute from the
great actress Ellen Terry. It is hard to find an artiste more universally loved or of better repute. She was, quite simply, supreme.

In 1931 Walter, in declining health, stepped down from
Parliament and the couple moved to the more benevolent climate

of the south of France. Walter died in 1935, and Vesta seventeen years later. They are buried side by side in Putney Vale Cemetery.

Only one 'swell' impersonator came close to matching Vesta Tilley. Hetty King was born Winifred Emms into a music hall family in Cheshire in 1883. Her father, William Emms, was an itinerant comic who ran a minstrel troupe, and Hetty began her career at the age of five – like Dan Leno – as a clog dancer. Marie Lloyd's biographer Daniel Farson tells a revealing story about Hetty's life on the road as a child performer. At just ten years of age she was 'rented out' to various managers. On one occasion she was beaten for some trivial misdemeanour in the dressing room. A blonde woman putting on her make-up at the next dressing table intervened to protect her, and reassured the young Hetty: 'Stop crying, duck, and get yourself made up – no one's going to touch you while I'm here. No one.' Her protector was Marie Lloyd.

Around the turn of the century Hetty introduced imperson-ations to her act. 'Funnily enough,' she recalled in the early 1970s, 'they were always men. I never seemed interested in impersonating women.' Like Tilley, she put a lot of work into getting her imitations absolutely right. She would go down to the docks to observe sailors, to church to observe a vicar, or would study workmen in the street: 'I watched a man digging up the road, for hours on end. He was a lazy bloke. He wouldn't bend down to pick up his shovel, he stepped on the end and caught it … For a soldier, I was usually Scots Guards. My own tailor was military and every button was correct.' Her favourite compliment came from a sergeant major who informed her that he'd told his men, 'I've been drilling you lot for three months. Now go to the Empire and let a woman show you how you really do it.' Her diligence and eye for detail paid off: after being noticed by an agent when appearing in Bradford, she was soon earning £100 a week.

One of her most famous songs, 'All the Nice Girls Love a Sailor', was originally a flop when she sang it dressed as a naval officer. She changed her uniform to that of a rating, lighting a pipe and throwing away the match, and had an instant hit. 'Officers don't mean a thing to the audience,' she noted.

Impresario Don Ross believed Hetty King to be an even greater artiste than Tilley: 'Vesta Tilley ... had great charm and personality but if you are looking for a woman who really made you feel she was a man, which I assume is the ultimate in male impersonation, then I think Hetty King was much finer. Neat, precise, clean, she carried the character acting side to the greatest extent.' Ross may have been prejudiced, because Hetty King was in his *Thanks for the Memory* cast, and Vesta Tilley had retired a quarter of a century earlier, but he was not alone in his view. The author Naomi Jacob wrote: 'No one would or could deny Tilley's artistry, her finish, her grace of movement or her diction; she had great charm – more, perhaps, than Hetty King had – but, as a male impersonator, she never seemed to me to have the slightest masculinity. [Hetty King's] characters were not merely women wearing men's clothes ... they were masculine.' And yet, added Jacob, 'nowhere would you find a woman possessing more the quality of femininity than Hetty King'. While Ross might have been prejudiced in favour of Hetty, Naomi Jacob was not. She was openly a lesbian, and Hetty not only refused to meet her, but was generally unkind to all her lesbian fans. Jacob's judgement, therefore, is likely to be dispassionate. The judgement of the public was very clear: Hetty was a star. She was still entertaining in the late 1960s, when she was well over eighty years of age. Hetty King died, aged eighty-nine, in 1972.

The Great Farini (1838–1929), acrobat and tightrope walker, with his adopted son Sam Westgate, who performed as 'El Nino' Farini. In 1871 El Nino first performed to great acclaim as 'Lulu, the Beautiful Girl Acrobat', a deception sustained for several years.

Vesta Tilley (1864–1952), the best-known and best-loved exponent of one of music hall's most enduringly popular genres: male impersonation. Many of her characters were drawn from the upper classes, building on the earlier success of the 'swell' persona.

Bessie Bellwood (1856–96).
Big-hearted and volatile, with a
string of aristocratic lovers, she
could hold her own with the
toughest of audiences.

Lottie Collins (1865–1910)
made her name with 'Ta-ra-ra
Boom-de-ay' and its catchy
chorus. Her rendition was
memorably accompanied by
a provocative high-kicking
dance, meaning that her
presence on any bill would
guarantee a full house.

Dan Leno (1860–1904) as the pantomime dame in *Mother Goose* at Drury Lane in 1902. Producer Augustus Harris upset traditionalists when he brought music hall stars like Leno, Vesta Tilley and Marie Lloyd into Drury Lane pantomime in the 1880s, but the public loved the innovation, and a new tradition was born. Leno was billed as 'the funniest man in the world', and Charlie Chaplin called him 'the greatest comedian since the legendary Grimaldi' – but mental illness and depression would eventually overwhelm him.

Sheet music sold in vast numbers and acted as a 'trailer' for the singer, the song and the performance. The artwork closely allied the artiste with the song. The copyright notice is a warning against piracy and illegal performance, which was a real headache for publishers and artistes alike.

Little Tich (born Harry Relph, 1867–1928) in his famous big boots. Tich is a good example of how personal struggles pervaded the lives of so many music hall performers. Highly intelligent but very short and tubby, and born with deformed hands, he spent a lifetime trying to conquer his insecurities, while regularly topping the bill.

Marie Lloyd (1860–1922). Unchallenged 'Queen of the Halls', Marie was loved by audiences, but often censured by the morally upright. Her directness and charm delighted her fans, but her private life left her far from fulfilled.

George Robey (1869–1954).
'The Prime Minister of Mirth'
enjoyed one of the longest
and most successful careers in
music hall. As the halls began
their decline he deftly moved
into variety and revue – and
eventually film – taking his
audience with him at each step.

Harry Lauder (1870–1950).
The archetypal professional
Scot, Lauder went from the
coalfields of Lanarkshire
to become one of the most
celebrated performers on earth.

A private, rather than promotional, portrait of my father and Kitty. It is undated, but was probably taken before the First World War.

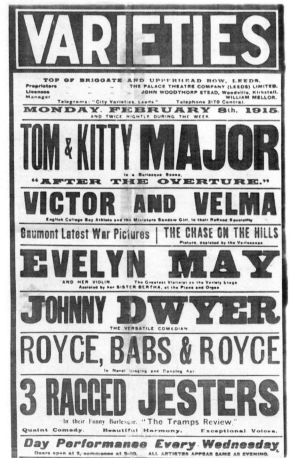

A poster from the family archives showing my father and Kitty topping the bill at the famous Leeds City Varieties in 1915.

'I'm in charge!' My father, in character, with a cast member from one of his shows.

My father and Kitty, c.1915–16, in a promotional photograph for 'After the Overture', a sketch depicting life backstage with a travelling troupe.

My father, Kitty and the cast of his revue *Special Edition*. He toured his shows all over the country, and revived them several times. This picture would have been taken in the 1920s.

A lovely picture of my father – probably in his mid-forties – clearly enjoying an anecdote.

12

Top Hats and Black Faces

'Messrs Moore and Burgess's … names are now
familiar as household words throughout the
civilised world.'

BIRMINGHAM DAILY POST, 23 DECEMBER 1872

The concept of poking fun at others is a recurring theme in entertainment. Early male impersonators lampooned the lazy, unproductive venality of the 'swells', while black-face or 'burnt-cork' minstrels lampooned Negroes, believed by the audiences to be their racial inferiors. Minstrelsy brought with it terms – notably 'nigger' and 'coon' – that are rightly regarded as offensive today, but that were in common usage in the less fastidious nineteenth century. More than 150 years later we wince at the concept of white men dressing up as caricature racial stereotypes, but minstrel shows were highly popular in both America and Britain for the best part of a century.

Black-face minstrelsy, and its offspring 'coon' singing, were born in America, but found ready appreciation in Britain from the early 1820s onwards. The concept of blacking up the face was not novel. It had long been embedded into English folk performances, and was similar to the ancient art of mumming, where performers covered their faces with masks. The origins of minstrelsy are obscure. Some argue that it began with slaves mocking the culture and behaviour of their owners. If one considers the minstrels' formal behaviour, out-of-date dress, mispronunciation, eccentric grammar and unquestioning obedience of convention, this does not seem so fanciful. Slaves would have observed white society's artificial manners and disregard of 'niggers', and may well have lampooned such conduct. It is very likely that that is what the early burnt-cork performers had seen, and copied.

In the early nineteenth century, white performers in America began to black themselves up. It proved popular, and minstrel acts became regular features of the more sophisticated theatres of New York City as well as the concert saloons and burlesques in the less salubrious setting of the Bowery in Manhattan. By the end of the 1830s minstrels were one of the staple entertainments in America, and early stars such as George Washington Dixon, Bob Farrell and George Nichols, Thomas Dartmouth (T.D.) 'Daddy' Rice – with his archetypal slave 'Jim Crow' character – and bands like Dan Emmett and his Virginia Minstrels, and the Ethiopian Serenaders, performed to packed houses across the country.

With the advent of Emmett's minstrel band, a format began to emerge. Typically, a show featured three phases: an opening of up-tempo songs, athletic dances and wisecracks; followed by an 'olio', a variety of acts performing magic tricks, acrobatics and the famous 'stump speech' full of puns and malapropisms, usually featuring the pompous 'Interlocutor', heckled by the Tambo and Bones characters known as 'end men' or 'corner men'. Finally, a popular straight play – often Shakespeare – would be lampooned or 'burlesqued' with titles like *Julius Sneezer* or *Bad Breath, The Crane of Chowder*. Later in the century, Gilbert and Sullivan's *Pirates of Penzance*, then massively popular in America, was transformed into *The Pie Rats of Pen Yan*. These performances were, quite simply, an entire variety show, and played in every kind of hall across America, from opera houses to saloons.

The classic minstrel show had three central characters: the pompous 'Interlocutor' or straight man; 'Tambo', the down-to-earth ingénue, often holding a tambourine; and the worldly, wisecracking 'Zip Coon' or 'Bones', smartly-dressed but permanently broke, who would make use of bones for percussion. Many future comic acts would trade off the minstrels' interplay of comedy: think, for example, of the Marx Brothers, Abbot and Costello or, more recently, Morecambe and Wise. It is also possible that the 'call and response' repartee in the early jazz music of King Oliver and Louis Armstrong derived from this idiom.

Minstrelsy first came to Britain as a solo act. Negro Ira Aldridge and home-grown (white) Charles Mathews, who had spent eighteen months in America, performed minstrel-inspired acts. Both were, in contemporary opinion, superb, multi-talented performers. Mathews was the young Charles Dickens' favourite actor. The sixteen-year-old Dickens saw him for the first time at Drury Lane in 1828, and subsequently at his many appearances at the Adelphi. Dickens' public readings of his own novels, decades later, owed much to the performing artistry of Mathews.

'Daddy' Rice came to Britain in July 1836, and elevated the genre to the top of the bill. His 'Jim Crow' character, with its accompanying 'Jump Jim Crow' song and dance, enchanted audiences at the Adelphi and the Surrey in Kennington. One theory about the origin of the dance is that farmers in the southern states of America regarded crows as pests, since they ate the corn in the fields. Some farmers would soak corn in moonshine and feed it to the crows. The intoxicated birds, unable to fly, would flap around, jumping up and down and getting nowhere. The farmer would then simply club them to death. Possible support for this theory is given by film shot in 1903 of the dance sensation 'the cakewalk', which shows black dancers flapping their arms in a drunken and chaotic fashion.

A typical lead-in to Rice's performance of 'Jump Jim Crow' would be:

> Come, listen, all you girls and boys, I'm just from
> Tuckahoe;
> I'm going to sing a little song, my name's Jim Crow.

CHORUS:
Wheel about, and turn about, and do just so;
Every time I wheel about, I jump Jim Crow.

I cut so many monkey shines, I dance the galoppade;
And when I'm done, I rest my head, on shovel, hoe or
     spade.

Rice apparently first heard the song in Cincinnati in 1830, and given the absurdity of its lyrics, it must have been his interpretation that gave it its power. He would also alter the lyrics to reflect current events. He dressed distinctively in very formal but ragged clothes – typical of the early minstrels – and descriptions of his dancing focus on the freewheeling exuberance of his movement. London went 'Jim Crow' mad. Fans were able to buy Jim Crow pipes, hats and figurines, and to join a Jim Crow Club. The phenomenon inspired dramatist William Moncrieff to write a burlesque specifically for Rice, *Jim Crow in London*. The *New York Spirit of the Times* described the show as enabling Rice to 'display his peculiar talent ... in the delineation of the Southern America Nigger'.

When Rice returned to America, 'Jim Crow' lived on with performers like John Dunn and Joe Cave, but the diarist and composer-singer Charles Rice was scathing about them in comparison to his namesake. 'Daddy' Rice came twice more to Britain, in 1838 and 1843.

In 1843 Dan Emmett arrived in London with his Virginia Minstrels, and the British public got their first taste of a full-blown minstrel show rather than a solo act. In a typical show, up to sixty performers would form a semi-circle, with Mr Interlocutor in the middle and the 'endmen', the 'Tambo' and 'Bones' characters, at each end. Such performances became very popular almost overnight.

The Ethiopian Serenaders first toured Britain in 1846, and boosted the appeal of the genre. This troupe featured African American dance virtuoso William Henry Luce – 'Master Juba'

– whom Dickens had seen on a visit to New York's run-down Five Points district in 1842. Dickens described him as 'a lively young negro, who is the wit of the assembly, and the greatest dancer known. He never leaves off making queer faces, and is the delight of all the rest, who grin from ear to ear incessantly.' Juba and the Ethiopian Serenaders played at Vauxhall Gardens in the summer of 1848 to ecstatic critical acclaim – Juba was marketed as 'Boz's Juba' to capitalise on Dickens' approval of his performance.* He became so popular he was commanded to dance for Queen Victoria at Buckingham Palace.

In the United States, the premier exponent of minstrelsy in the early 1840s was Edwin Christy's troupe, and its act influenced many others. The original Christy's never toured Britain, but two of its members came to England in 1857 to form J.W. Raynor and Earl Pierce's Christy Minstrels. They were an instant hit, and in 1858 played each night for over a year – an unprecedented run – at the Polygraph Hall, The Strand. In 1860 Raynor returned to America, and the troupe split into factions, each of which appeared in new bands: Wilson and Montague's Christy Minstrels, William Barton's Christy Minstrels, Christy's Coloured Comedians and Matthews Brothers' Minstrels all made their debut that year.

The British public drew clear distinctions between black performers and 'burnt-cork' white performers. The former were billed as 'Haverly's Coloured Minstrels' or, to allay any doubt at all, 'Callender's All Coloured Minstrels'. Sam Hague, a former clog dancer from Sheffield, formed the 'Great American Slave Troupe' in 1866, but it was made up of freed slaves, not entertainers, and it flopped. Some of its members were unable to deal with freedom or to provide for themselves, and died in very reduced circumstances.

The real stars of the genre were the burnt-cork minstrel bands, which toured extensively throughout the country: the Court Minstrels, Christy's Minstrels, Matthews Brothers' Minstrels, the Queen's Minstrels, even Hiscock's and Hayman's Australian Federal

* 'Boz' was Dickens' pen name in his early writing.

Minstrels. Many performed in the most elevated salons in London, and proclaimed on their promotional posters that they were 'patronised by the elite of the nobility, gentry and clergy', as well as crowned heads of Europe.

The number of minstrel performers soared in the late 1860s. In 1868 the *Era Almanack* listed 108 'Negro delineators': two years later there were 150. Minstrels differed from many music hall performers in that they totally eschewed sexual innuendo or 'coarseness'. Two home-grown troupes became very popular – the Mohawk Minstrels and the Moore & Burgess Minstrels. Both were topping bills from the early 1870s and had rival 'homes' in the capital: the Agricultural Hall, Islington, and St James's Hall, Piccadilly, respectively. Their act included 'jubilees', in effect spirituals – authentic ballads from the plantations – which had a very powerful emotional impact. In December 1872 the *Birmingham Daily Post* gushed: 'The refined and really enjoyable performances of [Moore & Burgess] have steadily increased in public estimation … their names are now familiar as household words throughout the civilised world. Wherever the English language is spoken, it would be difficult to find a household that does not possess one of the songs … rendered famous by the [Moore & Burgess] Minstrels.' W.J. MacQueen-Pope described the troupe's harmonising as 'like the tunes of an organ'.

The Mohawk Minstrels were equally popular. The *Era* in May 1886 commented: 'The celebrated band of "darkies" … had a five-week season at the Surrey Theatre [it is unclear whether this was the Surrey at Kennington or at Blackfriars] where they had a crowded pit and gallery audience. Judging by the excellence of the programme … it will be widely talked of.' Both troupes, like their American antecedents, frequently provided the whole show, a predecessor of variety entertainment years ahead of their time. The two groups remained popular until they merged in 1900.

Minstrelsy was so popular that a black face almost became shorthand for 'entertainment'. Many performers, among them the Great Vance, Harry Champion, Herbert Campbell, Little Tich, Dan

Leno, Gus Elen and even George Formby Jr started their careers with a burnt-cork act. Herbert Campbell often returned incognito to the genre when he had a free night or was in a small hall. It was in his blood.

In general terms, minstrelsy stereotyped Negroes in two ways: soft (simple, Godfearing, loving, superstitious, childlike) and hard (stupid, vain, lazy, criminal). In Britain, many of the hard stereotypes found their way into the persona of the 'coon', an extension of the earlier dandy character 'Zip Coon' – wisecracking, vain, urbanised and socially pretentious. From the mid-1870s 'coon' singers, who performed solo and almost exclusively in music halls, came to dominate, although even throughout their heyday they existed in parallel with the minstrel bands. The first to be really popular was E.W. ('the Great') Mackney, who was spotted at Evans' by Charles Morton, and booked into the Canterbury from December 1855 at £25 a week. Mackney enjoyed massive hits with 'Dixie' and 'The Whole Hog or None', which he co-wrote with George Ware.

Another hugely popular but now very little-known figure was James Unsworth. Born in Liverpool in 1821 and raised in Montreal, he joined Bryant's Minstrels, an early minstrel troupe, in New York. In 1861 he returned to Britain to escape the turmoil of the American Civil War, and was an immediate success, working with a partner, 'Eugene', a female impersonator (which was very common in early minstrel shows). He then developed a unique solo show, focusing on topical events, inspired by the Mr Interlocutor character of the black-face tradition. His catchphrase, 'Am I right, or any other man?', was eagerly anticipated by his audience. Unsworth was often described as 'the Nigger Demosthenes', and the *Era* doubted 'if there is one that can compare with Unsworth in the Minstrel line'. He performed with several minstrel troupes, most notably 'the Celebrated and Original Christy Minstrels' (aka Wilson and Montague's), throughout the 1860s. Unsworth always enjoyed separate billing as a 'Stump Orator', and his famous stump speech was praised by the press as 'one of the richest things of its kind'. By making it highly topical and relevant to the audience he was able to play the same halls for many weeks. In Dublin his performance was described as sending the audience 'beyond the bounds of reason'.

Rival performers regularly appropriated their more successful colleagues' work, and Unsworth went to some lengths to make his credentials as the pre-eminent stump orator very clear. He ran ads in the trade press using terms such as 'The Original' and reminding fellow performers that his stump speech 'or any other' was subject to copyright. He was a great favourite of Morton, and played the Oxford and the Canterbury many times from 1862 onwards.

Chance Newton was a great admirer of Unsworth, and gives us a valuable flavour of his act, which he describes as being close in tone to the then famous 'Ally Sloper' character – the lazy, red-nosed drunk in top hat and shabby tailcoat created in a comic strip in 1867, and said to have been inspired by Dickens' Wilkins Micawber:*

> Unsworth chiefly used his 'brolly' for banging his table withal, by way of punctuating certain more or less sage portions of his oration, of which the following excerpt is a fair specimen:
>
> 'My dear friends if I may call you so without risk of danger allow me to remark that we are here to-day and gone yesterday! But where are we now? (Bang with the gamp.) Am I right, or any other man? Talking of Man reminds me that all you men, except myself, are made wrong, and I will prove it, with the proofiest proof. (Bang.) The human frame, if I may call it so, is a master-piece of incongruous-gruousness-ness. We have feet, some of them two feet or more in size, and yet they tell us man is more like a monkey every day. Now what is a monkey? Is it a fish? No! Is it a fowl? By no means! Is it a good red herring? It is not. A monkey is an inhabitant of Woods and Forests. Have we not seen splendid specimens of this kind of ape? (Bang.) Am I right, or any other man?'

---

* W.C. Fields' performance as Micawber in George Cukor's 1935 film of *David Copperfield* is a carbon copy of Sloper. Unsworth's act was clearly very close to the windy ne'er-do-well persona Fields would make his own.

Unsworth's solo act was inspired nonsense – but he did not leave Eugene behind: the two continued to perform together until Unsworth died in 1875.

The star of the 'coon' genre who is most remembered today is Eugene Stratton, who learned his craft during a gruelling apprenticeship across America as an acrobat, gymnast and burnt-cork minstrel. He joined Haverly's Minstrels in 1878, and toured England with them two years later. When Haverly returned to America the following summer, Stratton stayed behind, joining Moore and Burgess's troupe, with whom he remained as the Tambo character for more than ten years. He had a natural talent for whistling, and his big solo break came when he bought a fellow minstrel's song, 'The Whistling Coon'.

Contemporary reports of Stratton's performance tell us he captured the audience's attention in a similar way to other great solo acts of music hall. He would step into a spotlight trained on the wings and then slowly, mesmerisingly, move downstage, looking up and down and across the audience. When he reached centre stage he would pause and stare at the assembled throng until he had everyone in his thrall – and only then would he begin his song. MacQueen-Pope judged him to be 'one of the finest artists who ever graced our music hall stage'.

For a while in 1892 Stratton flirted with performing out of burnt-cork, but it was a failure and he came 'back in black' with the song 'I Lub a Lubly Girl, I Do'. The first time he sang this a spotlight picked him out onstage and all the house lights were down. As he finished the song the spotlight faded, and he walked off the stage to silence, thinking he had bombed, only to hear the house erupt while he stood in the wings. In the darkness, the audience had not realised he had left the stage.

Stratton enjoyed further success with George Le Brunn's 'Dandy Coloured Coon' in 1893, and a partnership with composer Leslie Stuart produced the immortal 'Lily of Laguna' and 'Little Dolly Daydream'. Stratton, like 'Daddy' Rice, was the complete performer, with 'a natural unforced voice' and 'free, unfettered speech of the limbs' as he danced. He was also an accomplished musician with a distinctive 'theatrical' delivery. The *Era* eulogised: 'From him we have a series of portraits, sometimes quaint, sometimes romantic but always artistic and invariably clever.'

Stratton made recordings of many of his songs, and they reveal a singing style close to crooning, although his patter would be regarded as wholly unacceptable today:

> I am a bad nigger. I allus carries a razor an' a gun. There's somethin' about a razor an' a gun that people object to. For instance, yo' can walk down one side er the street with a razor an' a gun, an' that side of the street'll b'long ter you. Nobody'll bank up against yer.
>
> I hev jes bin playin' a game er cards with a lot of other niggers. An' amongs' the party there happened to be a one-eyed nigger. Now, I never did like a one-eyed nigger. There's somethin' crooked about a one-eyed nigger. I wouldn't a cared, only the one-eyed nigger was cheatin' in the game. Well I wasn't going ter let no one-eyed nigger beat me outta my good money. No, indeedy. I got right up an' declared myself in front er everybody. I say, 'Excuse me, genelmen, fer delayin' the game but there's some crooked work goin' on hyar. Now, I knows the party what's doin' the cheatin'! Now, I is too much ev a genelman ter mention any names but, if the man don' stop, I'll shoot his other eye out!'

G.H. Elliott – 'the Chocolate Coloured Coon' – continued the tradition, and left a lasting reputation. His recordings reveal a mellow, syncopated delivery rather than the exaggerated patois of the earlier 'Tambo' and 'Bones' 'stump speech' style. Elliott was a Lancastrian whose parents moved to America shortly after his birth, and he learned his stagecraft at a young age performing in Primrose and West's Minstrels. He returned to Britain in 1894, at the age of twelve, and began touring with Harry Reynolds' Minstrels four years later. He owed his opportunity for solo success to his enterprising agent Tom Pacey, who booked him to fill slots left open by the 'barring clauses' imposed on George Stratton. Contemporary opinion rated Elliott less favourably than Stratton, but he was popular for his smooth singing voice and urbane delivery. Photographs of him in costume show him to be very dapper and well-presented, in contrast to Stratton's far more extravagant persona. Elliott continued to perform until 1955, retiring after a farewell tour of theatres he had appeared in for over sixty years.

In 1958, three years after Elliott's farewell, the first of the famous *Black and White Minstrel Show*s was broadcast on BBC Television. It became a regular part of Saturday-night television for most of the next twenty years, attracting as many as eighteen million viewers a week in 1964. A stage version opened in 1960 at the Victoria Palace Theatre, and ran for ten years. Albums repeatedly reached number one in the charts and remained there for several weeks.

It was glorious entertainment, with singing and dancing of the highest quality, although to the modern eye there are many examples of demeaning racial stereotypes. Blacked-up white performers depicted black people as joyous, sexually liberated, musical, unfettered by convention, innocent, loving and unthreatening – but also as lazy, venal, socially pretentious, unintelligent, self-indulgent, childlike, feckless and never far from illegality, particularly stealing property and livestock. Although intended as innocent fun, it is easy to see how it could offend. In 1978 the BBC cancelled the show as its content came increasingly to be regarded as insensitive.

Whatever current attitudes to minstrelsy may be, it is beyond doubt that it gave many people their first appreciation of a definable black North American culture. It is intimately linked to the popularity of jazz music – the second identifiably North American cultural export – and for decades it was high entertainment for music hall.

13

The Business of Pleasure

'Go to your business, pleasure,
whilst I go to my pleasure, business.'

WILLIAM WYCHERLEY, *THE COUNTRY WIFE* (1675)

As it grew in popularity, music hall attracted gifted individuals both on and offstage. Onstage, they entertained. Offstage, hall-owners, managers, artistes, agents, songwriters and the press all jostled for a piece of the highly lucrative business. Money had begun to flow into the industry after 1870, and accelerated as the ownership of theatres became concentrated in fewer hands. The speed of change was unsettling, and by the turn of the century many performers and managers were looking back affectionately at the 'old style' proprietors. In April 1902 music hall syndicate manager Henry Tozer commented: 'They all in their youth loved and admired [the proprietor], his glossy hat, his substantial jewellery and his glowing affability, [but he has] now given way to the sharp but courteous businessman.'

Mr Tozer was viewing the past through rose-coloured spectacles. Some of the old proprietors were indeed popular, but not all. William Paul staged benefit performances in Leicester in the 1870s to raise funds for the aged, the poor and families of workers on strike, but most were not at all socially conscious. It is pure folk memory to consider them as avuncular, red-faced caricatures of 'mine host' in brightly coloured waistcoats and brimming with bonhomie. They were skilled businessmen, with a profound under- standing of how to make a profit. Success often depended upon the relationship between the proprietor and the community. If he was regarded as a pillar of local society, it was easier to obtain credit from suppliers, and support from officialdom. Outside London, audiences were more likely to attend a theatre under 'respectable' ownership. Early music hall had an unsavoury reputation, and it was commonplace for proprietors to turn to friends and family to raise capital. These 'friends' were likely to be well-heeled local figures: the reputation of the proprietor, therefore, was crucial.

So was that of the theatre manager, whose life was stressful, sometimes even hair-raising. In retirement, one veteran manager, Bill Bailey, recalled an evening at the Metropolitan when his chair- man was drunk and had to be sent home. So was his bar manager. He was sent home too. His wife, the bar manageress, followed him. Then the leader of the orchestra and the head waiter fell ill. Next, a note arrived from G.H. MacDermott, who was topping the bill, saying that he was delayed and would be late for the performance. Bailey scrambled around to find an alternative chairman and bar staff, but by the time his act was due, MacDermott had still not appeared. Bailey filled the gap himself with a soft-shoe turn. This was poorly received, and a fight started in the audience which Bailey had to calm down. At this dramatic moment, his star turn finally arrived – but Bailey's night of trial was not yet over. After midnight, a notorious local 'rough' turned up looking for a fight. Exasperated, Bailey agreed to a fight, but the rough thought better of it and left. 'After that,' Bailey said, 'we liquored up and so ended an eventful evening.'

As music hall widened its appeal, the individual proprietor was swallowed up by the growing syndicates. Edward Moss, Oswald Stoll, Richard Thornton, Tom Barrasford and George Adney Payne were building huge businesses in the 1880s. Shareholders began to replace local investors. The business of pleasure became more formal: agreements once reached with a nod, a wink, a handshake and a cheque were replaced by written contracts with legal terminology.

In the salad days of music hall Charles Morton may have been 'Master of the Halls', but in its maturity Edward Moss was Emperor. Morton's pre-eminence was confined to London, the unrivalled centre of music hall gravity, but it was Moss, and his later partners Richard Thornton and Oswald Stoll, who controlled music halls across the country. By the turn of the twentieth century the name of their circuit, Moss Empires, accurately reflected their domination.

Moss, born in Scotland on 12 April 1852, was immersed in show business from his youth. Early exposure to his father's music hall in Greenock taught him the basics of the entertainment industry. Aged seventeen, he was managing a travelling company, and eight years later he embarked on a full-time career as a proprietor, leasing the Gaiety Music Hall in Chambers Street, Edinburgh. In 1880 he added a second hall in Leith, and began to build a network eventually numbering about forty halls, the largest circuit in Britain. He started cautiously, but by the mid-1880s owned theatres across Scotland and the north-east of England. He sold one of them, in Sunderland, to a rising entrepreneur, Richard Thornton, who had built up a small circuit in South Shields. A friendship grew which in 1890 led to a joint venture, Moss and Thornton Varieties, and the construction of the Empire Theatre in Newcastle.

This Moss–Thornton partnership was the first step in the rise of Moss Empires. In a few years the syndicate would oversee the growth of variety theatre, but its first purchase looked back to the origins of music hall, with a new theatre in Newcastle on the site of an old coaching inn, the Royal Scotch Arms, that included a very popular 'singing room'. As part of the deal the site-owners insisted that Moss and Thornton kept the public house functioning, so the architects built the theatre on top of it. It was the perfect homage to the tavern-based singing-room heritage of music hall. Such a development appealed to Thornton. His early days in show business had been as a fifteen-year-old violinist playing for pennies in local pubs in South Shields. In adulthood he became a licensee, setting up singing rooms in every pub he owned, and in the mid-1880s he developed an old warehouse in South Shields into a large, plush music hall which became known as Thornton Varieties.

Thornton was pugnacious by nature, both in business and in his private life. During a holiday in Norway he was so enchanted by the wooden houses he saw there that upon his return home he built one in his extensive back garden and moved into it, renting out his own house. His neighbours, unhappy about a perceived invasion of privacy, complained. Thornton's response was to buy up the freehold to the entire terrace, and evict all those who had objected.

The Moss–Thornton partnership expanded throughout the 1890s, opening Empire theatres in Edinburgh, Birmingham, Sheffield, Liverpool, Glasgow, Hull, Leeds and Nottingham. Both men believed success depended on the comfort of their theatres as well as the quality of the entertainment offered in them – a philosophy shared by another rising entrepreneur, Oswald Stoll. Stoll, who believed that 'the ideal form of music hall entertainment is such that a father sitting next to his daughter ... would not be ashamed or embarrassed to be in the theatre', had built up a circuit based in Cardiff that was a perfect fit with the theatres owned by Moss and Thornton. The three men were brought together at the suggestion of the architect Frank Matcham, who designed theatres for all of them. Their merger in 1899 as Moss Empires made good business sense, because the scale of their joint operations would enable them to undercut rivals and monopolise the most popular talent. It was a marriage made in Mammon.

The first of the new company's many ventures was the Nottingham Empire Palace. Despite their collaboration, the three partners retained the right to invest in theatres for their sole ownership – most notably Stoll's astonishing gamble in building the gigantic Coliseum Theatre in London. As Moss Empires grew, it raised 80 per cent of its capital by floating the company on the stock exchange. This freed it of debt and financed its expansion.

Economies of scale, cheaper real estate prices and lower operating costs made it far easier for Moss Empires to expand in the provinces than for its London-based competitors to do so in the capital. And there was a further advantage: outside London, talent was cheaper.

Oswald Stoll, the younger partner, was the antithesis of a showman. Shy, taciturn and, on occasion, priggish, he was born Oswald Gray in Melbourne, Australia, in 1866. When his mother, Adelaide, was widowed she moved to Liverpool, where she married John Stoll, a waxworks exhibitor, in 1875. Stoll owned a modest music hall on the first floor of the Parthenon Assembly Rooms, and Adelaide, a former dancer with all the quick wit and charm of the Irish, inherited it upon his death in 1880. At only fourteen years of age, Oswald left Liverpool's Blue Coat School to help his mother manage her new acquisition.

Within a decade the headquarters of the 'Stoll Tour', as the circuit became known, moved to Cardiff. There is a story, perhaps apocryphal, behind the move. In his late teens Stoll, although unprepossessing in appearance, became infatuated with Vesta Tilley, a frequent and popular performer at the Parthenon. For five years he wrote songs for her: 'Oh, You Girls' (1885), 'Tablet of Fame' (1887), 'Bachelors' and 'Is Marriage a Failure?' (1889), and 'Mary and John' (1890), but his feelings were unrequited. It is possible he never declared them. In August 1890, to his dismay, she married the more dashing and self-confident Walter de Frece, whose father owned the Liverpool Tivoli, Stoll's principal rival theatre, and perhaps as a consequence Stoll moved to Cardiff. He wrote no more for Vesta Tilley, but as she lost one songwriter, she gained another. 'At the Races' (1890), 'Our Drive' and 'Brand New Millionaire' (1894) and 'The German Prince' (1896) were all written for her by her new husband. It must have been a bitter pill for the shy Stoll, but perhaps the flame never died. Many years later he lent Vesta Tilley the Coliseum for her final performance, to ensure she ended her career on the highest possible note.

Whatever the truth of the failed romance, the move to Cardiff was a rational business decision. Stoll, a precocious businessman, had bought Levine's Music Hall there in 1889, and was lavishing every penny he had on its refurbishment. It reopened as the Cardiff Empire, and when it ran into difficulties Vesta Tilley appeared at a modest fee to help. Perhaps affection, or at the least kindness, lingered on her side too.

Stoll continued to expand, opening theatres at Cardiff, Swansea and Newport. Despite his personal shyness, he was robust in business. He was one of the first to adopt the 'twice nightly' booking system, with artistes contracted to perform twice each evening – thus doubling receipts – while receiving only a small increment in wages. It was a profitable innovation, but one that, like the Moss–Thornton–Stoll merger with its taint of monopoly, caused resentment that fertilised the seeds of future controversy. It was also uncharacteristic of Stoll. His philosophy generally was that 'it does not pay managers to grind down salaries ... an intelligent man can earn money in any profession. We do not want to drive intelligent people out of the profession. We want good performances and we pay the necessary amount to get those performances.'

In 1900 Moss, Thornton and Stoll turned their attention to London. Their eyes fell on the Hippodrome in Charing Cross Road. Moss managed it personally for five years, in a pre-echo of modern practice ensuring profitability by building flats, shops and offices into the development. The safeguard was not needed, for the Hippodrome set new standards in opulence and size, and was always fully booked.

Even as it invaded London's theatreland, the new company did not ignore its core business in the fast-expanding suburbs and metropolitan centres. As working-class incomes rose, investment in theatres became more attractive. Moss Empires had emerged at one of the few times in theatrical history when building theatres was likely to be a financial success. In every season of the year music halls were packed, even when legitimate theatre struggled to attract audiences.

Taking full advantage, Moss, Thornton and Stoll built, bought or renovated halls at Holloway, Stratford and New Cross in London

– all renamed as Empires – as well as the Coliseum, Glasgow, and the Grand Theatre, Birmingham. Moss Empires opened theatres with fabulously opulent interiors and vast auditoriums capable of holding thousands of patrons. Circus acts, sometimes featuring large animals, became extremely popular, and huge stages were built to accommodate the demand for the spectacular.

There were unwelcome side-effects to such frantic expansion. Cost-effectiveness encouraged more uniformity in design, and halls became similar in style. The scale of investment pushed up the price of theatre licences, deterring competitors. And the size of the new halls enabled the syndicates to further undercut smaller owners. The independent proprietor was forced out of business as the syndicates strengthened their grip.

Some competitors, however, were not easily pushed aside: George Adney Payne in London, and Tom Barrasford in the north, provided stern competition for Moss Empires. Adney Payne, born in Ireland, the son of a pub landlord, entered show business in the late 1870s when he bought Lusby's Music Hall in London's Mile End Road, in partnership with Charles Crowder. The intention was for Crowder to run the music hall, and Payne, a wine merchant, to provide the catering. Their timing was bad: their entry into the business coincided with a fierce anti-music hall campaign waged by Frederick Charrington, estranged scion of the brewing family, which focused on the East End in general and Lusby's in particular. Charrington regarded all halls as 'dens of iniquity', and Payne and Crowder were forced to take him to the High Court to stop him harassing their audience with leaflets. They won their case, but Charrington carried on regardless. Payne and Crowder persevered, and in 1877 purchased the Canterbury from William Holland, Charles Morton's successor. When Crowder retired five years later, Payne took over both theatres.

In the 1890s Payne found a new partner in Henry Newsome-Smith, and they acquired such landmark theatres as the Tivoli, the Oxford and the Pavilion. When Newsome-Smith retired, Payne joined forces with Henry Gros to develop Palace theatres in Euston,

Chelsea, Walthamstow, Tottenham and East Ham. Although his expansion was restricted to London, Payne became a significant owner. Decisive and domineering, he earned his success, but was not universally loved, and when disputes broke out between artistes and owners in 1907 Payne's theatres were an early target.*

Another proprietor, Tom Barrasford, was an extraordinary man. Born into obscurity in 1859, he was the son of a Newcastle publican and the epitome of a Geordie street fighter, with square head, thick neck, short hair, handlebar moustache, flat nose and pugnacious expression. Nothing is known of his early life until he followed his father into the licensed trade, buying up several pubs in the 1880s and '90s. He loved sports and gambling, and as a hobby managed a black boxer, Frank Craig, known popularly as 'the Coffee House Cooler'. Barrasford owned a string of racehorses, and invented the modern starting gate, thus overcoming a long-standing problem for racecourses everywhere. He was a formidable adversary, but was never in the same financial league as Moss and his partners.

Barrasford's foray into music hall began when he refurbished an old circus building in Jarrow, and opened it as the Jarrow Palace of Varieties. He acquired the Leeds Tivoli in 1899, and by the early 1900s owned fourteen other halls in Scotland and the north of England. In common with the Moss syndicate, Barrasford spent lavishly to provide comfort for his audiences. The Liverpool Hippodrome, which he purchased in 1902, was reputed to be the best-equipped hall in the country, and the first to offer tip-up seating. He and Stoll loathed one another. Their personalities were poles apart, and mutual antipathy was inevitable. When Stoll learned that Barrasford was poaching his new talent, he banned him and his staff from all his theatres. The 'barring clauses', which prevented artistes from appearing at neighbouring theatres, often for many months after their engagement, were popular with Stoll,

---

* There may have been subliminal reasons for this. Rumours persisted that Payne was a womaniser. One story referred to a pregnant chorus girl. ''Ad any pain?' asks a friend, and the girl replies, 'Certainly not! It's my boyfriend's!' But this may simply have been malice, as I can find no firm corroboration for such stories.

but forced Barrasford to employ foreign acts. This encouraged him to expand overseas, and he bought halls in Paris, Brussels, Barcelona and Marseilles. Although outgunned financially, Barrasford was an innovative rival. In 1902 he used his own technology, the Barrascope, developed with Leeds engineer Fred Borland, to show films in his theatres.

The syndicates insisted that artistes perform under contract. Acts were no longer booked after face-to-face meetings between artiste and theatre manager. The old haphazard system had many faults. Letters were lost. Agreements were often unclear and open to dispute. Artistes were delayed while travelling. There was little or no recourse for non-performance. In one notorious example, Harry Hart, manager of the Bedford Music Hall, Camden Town, agreed a weekly fee with an artist, holding up three fingers and giving a wink. On payday the singer was offered only £2.10s., and not the £3 he had been expecting. He protested, only to be told, 'Oh my lad. Your eyesight's going. It was two fingers and a thumb – fifty bob.'

With the syndicates came contracts which ended sharp practice of the Harry Hart variety, but were still a mixed blessing for artistes. They guaranteed the level of payment, but led to protectionism, downward pressure on fees and the hated 'barring clauses'. Some contracts even specified the artiste could not ad lib: this was not only – or not primarily – to cut out coarse material, but to ensure that schedules were kept as theatres moved from one to two shows a day. This was also a factor in the demise of chairmen: they took up too much time.

In the early days of music hall, the booking of talent was piecemeal and informal. In the 1850s Harry Fox, manager of the Mogul in Drury Lane, met his fellow managers each week to share the details of out-of-town acts looking for bookings in London. By the end of the decade a more efficient system was introduced when Ambrose Maynard, a comic singer, created a register of performers. Each act paid one shilling for inclusion, and lists of artistes were circulated to all the halls. Many managers were highly sceptical of a third party inserting himself into the business of engaging performers, but they started to take greater interest when Maynard showed himself able to supply talent of good quality at short notice when gaps appeared in their bills.

Maynard's business model was simple. Acts signed up with him for an agreed period of one, two or three years at a fixed salary. A large proportion of his early clients were down-the-bill artistes, anxious to obtain whatever work they could. Maynard booked his clients into the halls for a higher rate, and took his profit from the margin. This was known as 'farming'. Both parties benefited from the arrangement, as little or no time was wasted on communications and paperwork, and a proper contract was agreed. By 1858 the far-sighted Maynard had established a system that was efficient for all concerned. For a fixed price he could book the entire bill into a theatre, thus eliminating even more paperwork. Maynard was so successful that when he died in 1889 he was a rich man.

In the early 1860s it is estimated that there were eighteen music halls in London and 119 in the provinces, employing a total of about three thousand people. Agents proliferated, and clustered together in London around the junction of York Road and Waterloo Bridge Road, a stone's throw from the Canterbury Theatre. Each Monday morning the area was thronged with booked artists seeking their itinerary for the coming week, and unbooked ones looking for 'fill-in' engagements.

Among the early agents was Charles Adolphus Roberts, who specialised in importing French acts, including the trapeze artiste Jules Léotard. Roberts also promoted the blossoming career of the comic singer George Leybourne, whom he saw at the London Music Hall in Manchester in 1864, and upon learning he had no engagement for the following week booked him into the Prince of Wales, Wolverhampton, for six nights. Soon Leybourne was earning more than £100 a week. Roberts' reputation boomed, and Herbert Campbell, Nelly Power and Bessie Bonehill were among those who joined him as clients.

By the mid-1860s a string of agencies had been formed, each with areas of special interest. J.W. Anson booked equestrian acts for circuses and music halls; George Webb & Company specialised in fêtes and galas; Parravicini & Corbyn brought over Continental acts, as did Maurin & Perrin. Some agents, like Percival Hyatt, worked for the venues themselves, as an outsourced department. Economies of scale favoured the largest agents, like Warner & Company, which booked entire troupes.

Liverpool-based Maurice de Frece was one of the first agents to operate outside London. He represented many artistes, and Jenny Hill and Bessie Bellwood were among those who got their big break in London through him. He was a theatrical polymath – agent, proprietor, troupe leader, songwriter and author. His sons Jack and Walter both followed him into show business. Jack was a variety agent, and Walter – the successful suitor of Vesta Tilley – formed his own profitable circuit of theatres before entering politics in 1920 as a Conservative Member of Parliament.

Another early agent, George Ware, started as a comic singer – either solo or as a duettist with his wife – but then worked for Ambrose Maynard in the provinces before branching out on his own. He booked the dwarf Charles Stratton, who would win international fame as 'General Tom Thumb', for P.T. Barnum, and was manager of several halls, but still found time to write songs, including massive hits such as 'The Whole Hog or None' for 'the Great' Mackney in 1855 and 'The House that Jack Built' (c.1860) for Sam Cowell. His nickname of 'Old Reliable' was richly merited. Many years later Ware gave a teenaged performer, Matilda Wood, her more familiar name of Marie Lloyd, and found time to write songs for her too, notably 'Whacky Whacky Whack!' in 1892. Ware was responsible for her first tour of America, an eight-week booking in New York in 1890 at £50 a week.

The Holy Grail for all agents was to attract the really big stars onto their books. Edward Colley represented Little Tich for many years, and Hugh Didcott, Jenny Hill's agent, was credited with giving her the soubriquet 'the Vital Spark'. Didcott, like George Ware, had been an unsuccessful singer, but was a sufficiently competent actor to have played Hamlet at Drury Lane and Othello,

Shylock and Macbeth at lesser theatres. An innovative and ruthless man, he excelled as an agent.

One of the most successful and long-serving agents was George Foster, Harry Lauder's London agent and at one time Marie Lloyd's fiancé, who was dumped after introducing her to the louche Percy Courtenay. In view of her rather rackety life, Foster may have had a lucky escape. He had entered music hall as a singer, but realised that, having only a modest voice, the life of an agent might be more lucrative. As a young man he saw show business at its most basic, being employed by Fred Albert (billed as a 'Lightning Topical Vocalist') to throw flowers at him as his act was being applauded. The purpose of this curious task was for Foster to find a seat beside, or close to, the prettiest girl in the theatre, so Albert could blow kisses to her in apparent response to the flowers.

From this modest beginning, Foster succeeded through sheer hard work and aspiration. Born in humble circumstances in Bow, he amassed a large fortune and achieved considerable social standing, being elected to the London County Council as a Conservative in 1901 and sitting on committees with the great and good of the day. He left no mark as a politician, but his skills as an agent enabled him to introduce some memorable artistes to music hall: Bransby Williams and Florrie Ford were among his discoveries.

Prior to the 1850s there was little press interest in music hall. The *Era*, founded in 1837 as a newspaper for licensed victuallers, was the first to give substantial coverage to the industry. It covered politics, sport and theatre and, given its links with the licensed trade, treated music hall as a natural topic of interest to its readers. Other specialist periodicals subsequently sprang up to cash in on the burgeoning business. The *Magnet*, the *Entr'acte* and the *Encore* joined the *Era* as interest in music hall created a thirst for information, but the *Era* remained pre-eminent. An 1856 advertisement claimed it to be 'the largest Newspaper in the World ... Operatic and Musical Intelligence, Home and Continental, is always most copious and interesting. Invaluable for reviews, news, and general theatrical information and gossip. Also of value are the assorted advertisements by and for actors and companies.'

The *Magnet*, based in Leeds, was founded in 1860 as a directory of all the halls in the provinces, and published their bills. Ten years later the *London Entr'acte* – referred to simply as the *Entr'acte* – made its debut, and featured star profiles alongside advertisements for artistes and agents. It would publish the bill at a particular hall, which would then be sold as the programme, a clever way to boost circulation and offer information to theatre-goers. In 1892 the *Encore* became yet another publication to cover music hall.

The business of pleasure was big business. The proprietors of music halls enjoyed great success. Moss was knighted in 1906 and Stoll in 1919 – although in Stoll's case it was in large part for his charity work and his generosity in donating land for a centre for disabled soldiers in 1916. George Adney Payne died in 1907 of a heart attack following a car accident, although his widow, probably with justification, blamed the stress of that year's music hall strike.

The animosity between Tom Barrasford and Oswald Stoll hurt them both in their battle for supremacy in London. In 1904 Barrasford lost out to Stoll in a costly race to see who would be the first to open a vast new West End venue: Stoll's Coliseum opened on Christmas day, and Barrasford's Lyceum on Boxing Day. Barrasford overstretched himself financially, and was forced to sell the Lyceum in 1906. Thereafter his business and his health declined. He lost control of his circuit in 1909, and died from diabetes the following year.

Despite being a founding father of Moss Empires, Richard Thornton was semi-detached from his two partners. He preferred to keep his separate but allied 'North-East Circuit' under his own control, even though most of its theatres were called 'Empires'. He died a wealthy man in 1922.

As for Stoll, his Coliseum 'victory' over Barrasford proved short-lived. His greedy insistence on four houses a day was a disaster: advance booking proved chaotic, artistes refused to rebook, and the management company collapsed in June 1906. There was a human cost too: the theatre's manager, Dundas Slater, committed suicide. Success did come for the Coliseum eventually. When Stoll relaunched it in 1907 it became *the* place to go to see the best entertainers available. Vesta Tilley, Harry Lauder, Dan Leno and George Robey – but never the uncontrollable Marie Lloyd – all performed there, as did the conductor Sir Henry Wood, Sarah Bernhardt and Serge Diaghilev's Ballets Russes. For the remainder of his life Stoll continued to show an uncanny ability to anticipate public taste. His astute business sense made him famously puritanical over issues of decency, and the theatre's dressing rooms featured a prominent sign reading 'Coarseness and vulgarity are not allowed in The Coliseum.' Stoll might have looked every inch the Victorian moraliser, with his humourless eyes, black frock-coat, top hat and pince nez, but his principal objection to vulgarity was simply that it kept audiences down – and he wanted to attract the largest possible number of people to his theatres.

Moss Empires effectively died in 1910, through a combination of shareholder pressure to change with the times and conflicts with Stoll's separately-managed circuit which included theatres in London, Manchester and Bristol. Stoll and Moss still lobbied together to set up the first ever Royal Variety Performance, in 1912. Stoll went on to become one of the first film moguls in Britain, creating a film distribution company in 1918 and a production company, Stoll Picture Productions, in 1920. He died at home in Putney in 1942.

And what of Edward Moss, who created the largest network of music halls in Europe? Despite being one of the shrewdest and most celebrated figures in show business, he was a very private man. He shunned publicity, preferring to live the life of a prosperous country gentleman in his substantial Midlothian home, Middleton Hall. His gentrification is emblematic of the route to respectability of music hall: he became a justice of the peace and Deputy Lieutenant of Midlothian. By the time of his death in 1912, music hall had completed its journey from back-room tavern to sumptuous palace, from working class to middle class, from foundry, pit and dock to drawing room, salon and theatre.

Charles Morton proclaimed 'Only one quality – the best.' Oswald Stoll banished coarseness, but Richard Thornton summed up the changes best: 'The music hall, as I remember it, was not a place where a man could take his wife. I laid down the principle that given good clean entertainment, clean people would come to see it. The man did bring his wife and that has been the secret of my success.'

14

Warp and Weft

'I'm performing because I really want, not
because I have to bring bread back home.'

YO-YO MA, CELLIST (B.1955)

The stories of George Leybourne, Dan Leno, Marie Lloyd and
Harry Lauder resonate down the years and dominate the history of
music hall. But music hall was far more than the superstars. Some
long-forgotten names, known in the business as 'wines and spirits',*
would have played at the very foot of the bill from Bristol to
Inverness, scraping a living in dreary halls and lodging in squalid
digs.

Between the stars and the 'wines and spirits' there was a broad
range of artistes who, while not as well known as the top echelon
of performers, were hugely popular with audiences. Often multi-
talented, they filled theatres all around the country and were the
'warp and weft' of the music hall loom. Among them are some
who left lasting memories – and, in the case of Harry Clifton,
expressions and sentiments still in everyday use 140 years after his
death.

* So called because the words 'Licensed to sell wines and spirits' appeared at the very
bottom of the bill.

'Handsome' Harry Clifton was the master of the 'motto song'*
and self-proclaimed author of five hundred songs in all, despite his
early death at the age of only forty-eight. Clifton's approach to song
authorship was pragmatic, and the originality of some of his songs
is dubious. Writing in 1946, Theodore Felstead was scathing: 'He
wrote the words himself – frequently nothing but gross plagiarism
of a well known ditty – and had them set to music by a hack
composer. Sometimes he didn't even bother to do that; he merely
utilised some favourite traditional air and made his "lyric" fit in.' As
Clifton was sometimes an 'improvisatore', composing songs on the
spot, this unkind criticism may be justified. Felstead compared one
of Clifton's big hits, 'Work Boys, Work and be Contented', with the
strikingly similar American Civil War anthem 'Tramp, Tramp,
Tramp, the Boys are Marching'. Another Clifton song, 'A Motto for
Every Man', was set to an existing waltz, 'The Corn Flower Waltz',
written by his publisher Charles Coote. Clifton was unabashed by
criticism. He placed an advertisement in the *Sun* in July 1867 which
read: 'Each of the songs are entirely his own composition, both
word and music … unaided he has worked against the popular
taste.' After Clifton's death in 1872, Coote observed that he himself
wrote a number of Clifton's songs, and others were collaborative
efforts.

Whatever their origins, Clifton's songs are still familiar to us
today, and some of their lyrics have passed into the language:
'Paddle Your Own Canoe', 'Put Your Shoulder to the Wheel is a
Motto for Every Man', 'Up With the Lark in the Morning', 'Where
There's a Will There's a Way' and 'Pretty Polly Perkins of Paddington
Green'. The sheet music for the first two of these, and others, credits
Martin Hobson as arranger or possibly 'hack composer'. Only he
and Clifton knew the division of labour.

The lyrics of many of Clifton's songs are simple exhortations to
conservative social conformity. 'Put Your Shoulder to the Wheel is a
Motto for Every Man' is an example:

* Motto songs had lyrics that offered advice, and often a moral.

We cannot all fight in this 'battle of life',
The weak must go to the wall.
So do to each other the thing that is right,
For there's room in this world for us all.
'Credit refuse' if you've 'money to pay',
You'll find it the wiser plan.
And 'A penny lay by for a rainy day'
Is a motto for every man.

CHORUS:
So we will sing and banish melancholy,
Trouble may come, we'll do the best we can
To drive care away, for grieving is a folly,
'Put your shoulder to the wheel'
Is a motto for every man

'Pretty Polly Perkins of Paddington Green', although not a motto song, is a classic:

I am a broken-hearted milkman, in grief I'm arrayed
Through keeping of the company of a young servant
    maid.
Who lived on board and wages, the house to keep clean
In a gentleman's family near Paddington Green.

CHORUS:
She was as beautiful as a butterfly and proud as a queen,
Was pretty little Polly Perkins of Paddington Green.

… In six months she married, this hard-hearted girl,
But it was not a Mi-lord, and it was not an earl.
It was not a Baronet, but a shade or two wuss
It was a bow-legged conductor of a tuppenny bus.

CHORUS:
She was as beautiful as a butterfly and proud as a queen,
Was pretty little Polly Perkins of Paddington Green.

Clifton sees his young love lost not to a nobleman, but to a bow-legged social equal. The moral of the song would have delighted the music hall audience. Place – both social and geographical – mattered in Victorian England, and 'pretty Polly' kept to her own.

Artistes like G.H. Chirgwin, Mark Sheridan, Herbert Campbell, Bransby Williams, George Formby Sr and Nellie Wallace were eccentric headliners who topped the bill with weird hybrids of styles, defying categorisation.

Chirgwin was one of the most eccentric of them all. In essence his was a black-face act, but his interpretation was such that he transcended the genre, creating something part eccentric and part grotesque. He wore outlandish interpretations of the traditional black-face costume, favouring a long frock-coat, tights instead of trousers, outsized shoes and a towering stovepipe hat to accentuate his already tall and lanky frame. He developed trademark white diamond make-up across his right eye, and styled himself 'the White Eyed Musical Kaffir'. Photographs show how effective his make-up and costume were. Sometimes he reversed the colour scheme, adopting white coat, tights and hat, with white make-up and a black diamond across his eye.

He was born in 1854, and by the age of six was performing with 'the Chirgwin Family'. In his teens he formed a black-face double act with his brother, and until the mid-1870s toured successfully as one half of 'the Brothers Chirgwin'. Advertisements stressed their musical versatility: they played the banjo, piccolo, bagpipes, Japanese fiddle, flute, violin, cello and guitar, all accompanied by 'eccentric dances'.

Chirgwin's career took a decisive turn after a mishap at one of the de Frece halls in Liverpool in 1877, when his brother failed to appear – probably because he was drunk. His brother had form in this respect: he had been part of a double act with another performer, called Dignan. They split up, and an advertisement in the *Era* informed readers that Dignan was seeking another collaborator – 'teetotaller preferred'.

In the absence of his brother, Chirgwin went onstage and pretended there was no problem. Nor was there an apology. Instead, he informed the audience of hardbitten Scousers, in the style of banter that became his stock in trade, that there was no mistake in the billing: he had been christened 'Brothers' Chirgwin because his mother had been expecting twins. Chirgwin was soon advertising a solo act as 'the White Eyed Musical Nigger'. The white diamond motif had come about by accident. Just before going onstage in black-face at a fête in Gloucestershire, he had wiped a bit of dust from his eye, revealing the skin beneath, and performed his act unaware of the white smudge. It was an immediate comic success. Recognising a gimmick that made him distinctive, he adopted it as a fundamental part of his act. Chirgwin would come onstage with his face covered by one of his many bizarre top hats, then jerk his head back to reveal the shape on his face. The crowd – awaiting the gesture – would go into ecstasies at this simple device, with cries of 'Good old George!!!'

Chirgwin's switch to a solo act, combined with joining forces with the shrewd agent Hugh Didcott, sent his career into orbit. In less than twelve months he rose from the relative obscurity of provincial houses to performing three times a night in the biggest halls in London. Critics and managers were extravagant in their praise. R.G. Goldsmith, general manager of the Museum Concert Hall, Birmingham, gives us a flavour of Chirgwin's act, which included impromptu banter with the audience, songs and stylised dancing: 'Screams of laughter greet his comic business, and then absolute silence his beautiful solos on several musical instruments. The indescribable hat and eye movement is immensely funny.' Chirgwin was consistently praised as grotesque, spontaneous, witty, droll, versatile, clever, eccentric, original – and 'never vulgar'.

Two songs became indelibly linked to him: 'My Fiddle is My Sweetheart' and 'The Blind Boy' (written by British minstrels Harry

Hunter and G.W. Moore respectively). Both were sung in his distinctive falsetto voice, and he would be constantly interrupted by cries of 'Give us the blind'un!' or 'The fiddle! The fiddle!' until he sang them, sometimes repeatedly.

Chirgwin was popular on the Continent as well: unusually for an English music hall artiste, he appeared in France, Spain and Germany to equal acclaim. He remained popular at home until his retirement, when he traded the halls for running a pub. He claimed to be a teetotaller, but he died in 1922 from cirrhosis of the liver. Drink was, perhaps, a family failing for both the Brothers Chirgwin.

'Jolly' John Nash was another artiste who was never a shrinking violet: he appropriated the Greek god of humour and satire into his billing as 'the Merry Son of Momus of Side-Splitting Notoriety'. He learned his trade in his native Midlands, singing comic songs in the evening while working in local foundries by day. He came to London in the 1850s, and was an early headliner at the new South London, appearing even above George Leybourne on the bill. His songs projected a personality that could best be summed up as 'jolly' – a convivial, back-slapping 'good fellow' – and most, if not all, of them involved him laughing along with the lyrics. He often included 'comic walking songs' to show off a humorous walking style, much as Max Wall was to do half a century later. His big hits were 'Sister Mary Walks Like That', 'Racketty Jack', 'I Couldn't Help Laughing, it Tickled Me So', 'Little Brown Jug' and 'The Merry Topper', which featured his infectious laughing skills.

Nash was a contemporary of Arthur Lloyd and Alfred Vance, and appeared with them in 1868 when they became the first music hall artistes to perform before royalty at a party organised by Lord Carrington for the Prince of Wales. The young Prince was vastly amused by Nash's songs, and 'Jolly' John was soon singing in smart London drawing rooms as well as music halls. He performed for the Prince on many occasions, but one evening, in an excess of exuberance, he unwisely slapped him on the back: the association ended.

Like G.H. Chirgwin, Mark Sheridan was a visually striking performer. He dressed in a trademark outfit of towering bowler hat, tight-fitting raincoat flared at the waist, 'ratcatcher' trousers tied at the knee with string, which flared out over outsized shoes. Accentuated eyebrows and a bulbous umbrella completed the picture. Sheridan was born Frederick Shaw in County Durham in 1864, and made his reputation touring his native north-east in a double act. In 1892 he and his partner were enticed to Australia by Harry Rickards, and he returned three years later as a solo artist. In the early twentieth century he had a string of hits with very catchy chorus songs such as 'Here We Are, Here, Here We Are, Here We Are Again', 'All the Little Ducks Went Quack Quack Quack' and 'You Can Do a Lot of Things at the Seaside You Can't Do in Town'. Two of his songs, 'I Do Like to be Beside the Seaside' and 'Who Were You With Last Night?', which he co-wrote with Fred Godfrey, remain familiar today. Sheridan's story has a tragic ending. In 1918 he took his touring revue to the Coliseum at Glasgow. The show was poorly received, and he overheard someone calling him a 'has-been'. For a man already suffering from depression this proved too much, and he shot himself in Kelvin Grove Park.

A similar fate befell T.E. Dunville, another eccentric dresser, long, lean and a little loony, who made a speciality of nonsense songs such as 'Bunk-a-Doodle-I-Do', 'Umpi-Doodle-Dum' and 'Pop-Pop-Popperty-Pop'. Dunville was popular for over a quarter of a century, but depression overcame him. Playing the Clapham Grand in 1924, he overheard a member of the audience describe him as a 'fallen star', and a few days later drowned himself in the Thames.

Dialect comedian Harry Liston appears to have had no such problems of self-belief. Scarcely a week passed without an announcement in the press from the self-styled 'Comic Pet of the Public', 'Star Comique', 'London Lion' and 'Dancing Swell'. Liston was born in Manchester in 1843, and when not on tour lived there most of his life. He developed a two-hour one-man show called *The Stage Struck Hero*, which showcased his talents and in which he was billed as 'mimic, vocalist, ventriloquist and instrumentalist'. In 1865 he arrived in London, and was a big hit at the larger halls, especially the Metropolitan. The *Era* paid him a back-handed compliment: 'Mr. Liston has not been long at The Metropolitan but he has become exceedingly popular, as he deserves to be if only on the score of originality.' Liston's reputation was made by 'The Tin-Pot Band', which he sang with tin pans and saucepan lids draped from his costume, and wearing a saucepan for a helmet. He had several hit songs, including 'The Heavy Swell of the Sea' and 'When Johnny Comes Marching Home'. Liston toured extensively throughout his career, initially as a solo act, then with Arthur Lloyd in 1866, and finally with his own company, Merry Moments, in 1869. The troupe was advertised as 'Fun without Vulgarity', and toured until at least 1915.

Many performers were eccentric, but by any measure Nellie Wallace stands out. Born in Glasgow in 1870, she was a child clog dancer, part of a sister act. Her big break came in 1895 when she understudied Ada Reeve in *Jack and Jill*, the annual pantomime at the Comedy Theatre, Manchester. When the ballooning Reeve had to rest Nellie took over, to great acclaim. In a profession that worshipped female glamour the skinny Nellie was at best plain, so she turned her looks to advantage, coming to embody the accident-prone, lovelorn spinster in songs like 'I've Been Jilted by the Baker, Mr. White', 'Under the Bed (My Mother Said)' and 'I Lost Georgie in the Park':

> I've lost Georgie in Trafalgar Square
> Going on my honeymoon, but I don't care,
> I've lost him in the fog
> But I'll bet anybody a bob
> He won't enjoy his honeymoon if I'm not there.

Nellie was often described as a 'grotesque'. Her onstage persona was as chaotic as the lives of the characters in her songs, and not to everyone's taste. She wore garish, ill-fitting dresses and shawls, had a beaky nose and protruding teeth, and sang with a snuffle. But the public found her hilarious. She enjoyed a long career, which came to an end when she collapsed after performing in the Royal Variety Performance at the Palladium in 1948. She died soon afterwards.

Less eccentric, but equally hard to categorise, was Bransby Williams. Handsome, elegant and with glossy black hair, he was born Bransby William Pharez in Hackney in 1870, worked for a time as a tea taster and wallpaper designer, but became famous as an impersonator. After a spell in black-face he began to impersonate Dan Leno, Gus Elen and other familiar stars in small-time halls on a semi-professional basis. He developed his act to include monologues from Shakespeare, Dickens and Henry Fielding among others. The leading classical actors of the day, Herbert Beerbohm Tree, Henry Irving and Fred Terry among them, also provided him with material for impersonation. He brought a pastiche of legitimate theatre to the masses in a package anybody could enjoy – 'classic lite' for the halls. In the absence of television or radio, the only entertainment on offer to the vast majority of people was to be found at their local music hall. Given that Leno, Beerbohm Tree or a touring production of *Hamlet* was not likely to be on offer in, say, Sunderland on a weekly basis, Bransby Williams supplied the next best thing.

His monologue 'Stage Door Keeper' can be heard today on a scratchy recording, made in 1916, that gives us a flavour of his act. In it, he plays a theatre worker who wants the boss to give him a turn onstage to do impersonations. In the course of the monologue he imitates the theatrical giants George Alexander, Johnston Forbes-Robertson and Sarah Bernhardt, as well as music hall favourites G.H. Chirgwin, R.G. Knowles and George Formby Sr – the latter playing Hamlet, an impersonation within an impersonation.

Williams appealed to audiences by flattering them with 'culture'. He was fond of interpreting Dickens' characters, especially Sydney Carton, the flawed hero of *A Tale of Two Cities*, who speaks the immortal line: 'It is a far, far better thing that I do, than I have ever done; it is a far, far better rest that I go to, than I have ever known.' He had the chameleon-like ability to bring Fagin, Bill Sikes and Little Nell's grandfather to life onstage. He would turn from the audience as Ebenezer Scrooge and, with a touch of make-up from his table, turn back to them as the fawning, cringing Uriah Heep. Melodrama and sentimentality were always popular, and Williams supplied them nightly. My father loved his act, and with the slightest encouragement would recite from 'The Green Eye of the Little Yellow God', written by J. Milton Hayes in 1911 especially for Williams:

> There's a one-eyed yellow idol to the north of
>   Kathmandu,
> There's a little marble cross below the town;
> There's a broken-hearted woman tends the grave of Mad
>   Carew,
> And the Yellow God forever gazes down ...

By 1897 Bransby Williams was sharing top billing with the source of his original inspiration, Dan Leno, at the London Pavilion, and was signed up by the Empire for a three-year contract. Managers looking to attract more affluent punters liked his elevated act. It was different fare from that offered by any of his contemporaries – civilised and 'improving', with quick costume changes and plenty of humour. The ultimate accolade for any performer seeking respectability came to Williams when he was asked to perform at Sandringham before King Edward VII in 1903. Like so many before and after him, Williams made and lost a great deal of money during his career. His earnings were eroded by over-ambitious international tours which failed to earn enough to cover their costs. But, unlike most of his contemporaries from the halls, Williams lived a long life, dying in 1961 at the age of ninety-one.

Two other class acts who were much in demand were Marie Loftus and her daughter Cissie. Marie came to London from Glasgow in 1874, at the age of seventeen, and had an early success with the song 'I'm So Shy'. She toured America and South Africa, becoming revered as 'the Sarah Bernhardt of the Halls'. Cissie was a talented impersonator of theatrical celebrities, especially Yvette

Guilbert but also Noël Coward, Harry Lauder, Beatrice Lillie, and even the great tenor Enrico Caruso. She became a star in her teens after a debut triumph at the Oxford, and her talent and beauty not only mesmerised audiences but attracted the admiration of literati like Max Beerbohm and artists like Toulouse-Lautrec.

As an eighteen-year-old, Cissie eloped and married – and later divorced – a man sixteen years her senior. It was a minor scandal, but it did her no harm with her public. In 1901, during one of her many US tours, she was spotted at the Knickerbocker Theater, New York, by the great actor-manager Sir Henry Irving, who asked her to join his company. She accepted, and successfully mixed 'legitimate' acting with music hall, although the latter remained prominent, not least because it was far better paid. Despite a liking for drink and drugs, her career continued until the middle of the Second World War.

Another of my father's favourite memories was the classic 'little girl lost' serio, Gertie Gitana. Eight years younger than my father, she was born Gertrude Astbury in Staffordshire, in 1887 or 1888. She was onstage as a child in a troupe called Tomlinson's Royal Gypsy Children, and, adopting the Spanish word for gypsy, was billed as 'Little Gitana'. She came to London in 1900 and carved out a career singing a selection of highly sentimental songs including the still popular 'Nellie Dean', 'Never Mind', 'Silver Bell' and 'The Star Who Never Fails to Shine', which remained a big favourite with audiences throughout her career. In the 1940s, at the behest of her husband, impresario Don Ross, she joined Hetty King and others as part of the music hall revival show *Thanks for the Memory*. In 1957 she died in her sleep in Brixton, half a mile from the Empress Theatre where *Thanks for the Memory* finally closed. My father had tears in his eyes when he heard the news. Her obituary in the *Stage* reported that she had banked £40,000, which implies prudence as well as success.

Herbert Campbell put impersonation at the centre of his act. By his own admission he weighed in at nineteen stone, and all his characters – whether boys, girls, aunts, uncles, kings, queens, wives or mothers-in-law – were always fat. Campbell was truly a giant figure in his day, and with Dan Leno and Harry Randall became the ultimate Edwardian pantomime performer.

He was born Herbert Story in Kennington in 1844, in lowly circumstances, and was employed for a time as an office boy at the *Sun* newspaper. He later worked at Woolwich Arsenal, where he started a semi-professional black-face troupe, a typical apprenticeship for budding music hall artistes. He was attracted to black-face after delivering the *Sun* one day to the Polygraphic Hall, where he saw J.W. Raynor's Christy Minstrels, the troupe that launched a thousand minstrel bands. He began to earn a reputation for himself as a 'Bones' cornerman, and became a popular singer and comedian. At the height of his career he was playing six halls a night in London, and taking lucrative bookings across the country. One of his early successes was a wicked parody of G.H. MacDermott's 'Jingo Song':

> I don't want to fight, I'll be slaughtered if I do,
> I'll change my togs, I'll sell my kit and pop my rifle too.
> I don't like the war, I ain't a 'Briton true',
> And I'll let the Russians have Constantinople.

Campbell flirted also with music hall ownership: he, Leno and Harry Randall ran several London halls, including the Clapham Grand and the Granville in Fulham, but lost money in the face of heavy competition (and barring clauses) from the syndicates that paid their wages as performers.

But Campbell will forever be associated with pantomime. He made his first pantomime appearance at the Theatre Royal, Liverpool, in 1871, playing King Autumn in *King Winter: or the Four Seasons*. He was re-engaged the following year by the Theatre Royal, then moved to London for five seasons at the Grecian, followed by two at Gatti's.

For many years British pantomime had followed a time-honoured format based on *commedia dell'arte*'s centuries-old Harlequin and Colombine love story. By the time Augustus Harris took over Drury Lane in 1879 the format was becoming tired, and to breathe fresh life into pantomime's dwindling popularity he began to employ crowd-pulling music hall artistes. At first they appeared 'front of curtain' to keep the audience amused between scene changes, but they were rapidly incorporated into the performance. Traditionalist critics complained that 'vulgar' artistes from the halls were ignoring tradition by using their own songs and patter. The review in the *Theatre* was apocalyptic: in its view there was an invasion of filth emanating from the fetid halls of south and east London:

> I object to the inclusion of [music hall artists] into the domain of Pantomime … They bring with them not only their songs which, when offensive in their wording, are sometimes made doubly dangerous by their tunefulness – not only their dances, which are usually vulgar, when they are not inane, but their style and manners and 'gags', which are generally the most deplorable of all. The objection to the music hall artists on the stage is … that they have the effect of familiarising audiences, and children especially, with a style and a kind of singing, dancing and 'business', which, however it may be relished by a certain class of the population, ought steadily to be confined to its original habitat.

The *Theatre* believed music hall to be crude, and many agreed. Nevertheless, the uncomfortable truth for the traditionalists was that their form of pantomime was less appealing to the public than Harris's music hall version. Audiences flocked to hear the interlopers, who built a new tradition, still honoured every Christmas in many parts of the world.

Herbert Campbell played twenty-two seasons of pantomime at the Theatre Royal, Drury Lane, from 1882 onwards, sharing the stage with the biggest names in the business: Marie Lloyd, Vesta Tilley and, most famously, his friend Dan Leno, with whom he often alternated the role of the dame. Sadly, Leno and Campbell both died in 1904, within three months of each other. Campbell died after a bizarre accident. It was his habit to return home between shows, and stepping down from his brougham outside his house one night he barked his pick-up time to his coachman. For some reason, perhaps due to his powerful voice, one of the horses was startled, and reared up. Campbell was knocked over, and died from a resulting brain haemorrhage. The lovable fat man was only fifty-nine.

George Formby Sr began life in Ashton-under-Lyne in 1875 as James Booth, the illegitimate son of an alcoholic teenage girl. Young James had to fend for himself from the earliest age, and was frequently left to sleep on his doorstep while his mother lay drunk inside. His parents did marry, but his father was abusive, and their union made life harder, not easier, for the young boy. He went to work in iron foundries in Wigan, which, coupled with the hardships of his childhood, left him with lifelong tuberculosis. But ill health could not quell his ambition.

He started singing in pubs at the age of thirteen, having formed a double act, 'the Brothers Glenray, the Song Birds of the Music Halls'. The act faltered when the partners' voices broke, so James struck out on his own as 'George Formby', taking his name from the seaside town north of Liverpool. Appearing in the trade press for the first time playing the Tivoli in his home town of Ashton in July 1897, he developed a comic patter/song act that drew heavily on his own background, creating the character of John Willie, a classic hapless northerner. He was spotted by hall-owners, and was soon playing the larger halls in the north of England, coming to London in 1900 when George Robey recommended him to the manager of the Pavilion.

Despite his constant ill-health, Formby soon became one of the biggest acts in the country. He hid his tubercular cough by incorporating it into his act. 'Ee,' he'd say, 'that's champion coughing tonight,' or 'I'll cough anybody 'ere for five shillin's. And I'll give'em five coughs up to start with.' The audience lapped it up, little knowing the genuine distress he was in.

Formby made many recordings, including the 'John Willie' songs 'Send for John Willie', 'John Willie's Ragtime Band' and 'John Willie's Jazz Band', and an amusing parody of the sentimental 'My Grandfather's Clock'. They reveal that, unlike many music hall stars, including even Dan Leno and Marie Lloyd, he instinctively understood how to sing in a studio in the absence of an audience. Divorced from the life-giving energy of their public, Leno and Lloyd's studio recordings sound distant and cold. Formby's, by contrast, are warm and intimate, reflecting his highly engaging act – he would often get down from the stage during a performance and chat to members of the audience as if talking to them in a bar.

There are obvious similarities between 'John Willie', Formby's philosophical, downtrodden but ultimately unbowed victim of life's ups and downs, dressed in shabby, oversized tailcoat and ill-fitting bowler hat, and Charlie Chaplin's everyman 'Tramp'. It is beyond question that Chaplin would have seen Formby perform, as he did Little Tich, and it is not difficult to imagine the great clown incorporating the essence of their appeal into his own act. In so doing he carried their magic to cinema audiences calculated in tens of millions around the world.

Formby's chronic illness finally took its toll: he collapsed onstage during a pantomime in Newcastle in 1921, after bursting a blood vessel. He died a few days later – his diary fully booked for the next five years – at the age of forty-five, leaving a teenaged son, George Formby Jr, who would become the ukulele-playing embodiment of Lancastrian humour.

15

The Exotic and the Bizarre

'Who are you going to believe,
me or your own eyes?'

GROUCHO MARX (1890–1977)

As music hall became more popular, the appetite grew for more and better performers. New acts were booked from Europe and North America. Many of them were unusual. Some were bizarre. Some left a lasting legacy, others were soon forgotten.

The advance guard of the French invasion was the tightrope-walker Charles Blondin, whose extraordinary skill and bravery had made him an international celebrity. On 30 June 1859 he astonished the world by crossing Niagara Falls, 160 feet above the raging torrent. One slip would have meant certain death, but he enthralled thousands of onlookers by turning a somersault on the rope and then lying full-length along it. He repeated this performance a month later, blindfolded and bearing a man on his back – a feat so astounding that many refused to believe it could be true, thinking it must be a hoax. Blondin silenced the doubters with another cross-ing, this time on stilts. In 1860, during a royal tour of Canada the Prince of Wales watched one of his performances, following which Blondin cheekily offered to carry the Prince on his back. Unsurprisingly, this offer was wisely declined on the Prince's behalf.

William Holland brought Blondin to England to appear at Crystal Palace in 1861, followed by a provincial tour and bookings at the Canterbury and the Alhambra. At Crystal Palace he was paid £100 a performance, and embellished his reputation by playing the violin while dancing on the rope and cooking an omelette in mid-air. His feats appalled Charles Dickens, who attacked the 'morbid curiosity' of the crowds who came to gape.

At the Alhambra, patrons paid £5 to be carried on Blondin's back as he walked along the tightrope high above the heads of the audience. At Sheffield he pushed a lion cub in a barrow. After the Oxford burned down in 1868, Charles Morton arranged a benefit at the Crystal Palace for the staff who had lost their livelihood. Blondin wished to string his rope up at the fifth – and highest – level, but was forbidden to do so by the owners, who insisted he could not go above the third level. Blondin was insulted, not least since he had performed on the fifth level in 1861, and believed his reputation would be damaged if the height was reduced. Angrily, he withdrew from the benefit. Morton replaced him with another tightrope walker and acrobat, the Great Farini, who – dressed up to resemble Blondin – walked across a rope strung between the balconies of the centre transept bearing his nine-year-old adopted son on his back. No one realised it was not Blondin – nor, apparently, did anyone attempt to prevent the child being exposed to such danger.

Farini was not as lastingly famous as Blondin, despite his comparable skill. Born William Leonard Hunt in New York State in 1838, he arrived in Britain in 1866 with a huge reputation, having repeated some of Blondin's most daring feats. After Blondin walked across Niagara Falls, so did the Great Farini. Successive crossings became more risky. Blondin wore baskets on his feet. Farini did handstands mid-crossing. After Blondin carried a stove and stopped halfway over to cook an omelette, Farini crossed with a washtub, lowered a bucket into the torrent and washed some handkerchiefs.

Farini retired in 1869. His adopted son Sam Westgate, whom he had borne on his back at the Crystal Palace, had been incorporated into his act as 'El Nino' Farini, but in 1871 he was reincarnated at the Concert Hall, Cremorne, as 'Lulu, the Beautiful Girl Acrobat'. Under his father's management Sam, in the guise of 'Lulu', performed to great acclaim, especially from admiring male critics. 'Lulu' was excellent box-office, not least since his acrobatic feats seemed even more remarkable when being performed by a woman. In August 1876 'Lulu' was injured in an accident at Hengler's Hall in Dublin, and was out of action for nearly two years. 'Her' comeback in August 1878 was soon followed by the revelation that 'she' was a boy. Instead of being embarrassed, Sam's father used this brilliantly to generate additional interest, running advertisements presenting Sam to the public as a new 'exotic'.

It is not hard to imagine how Farini and Sam fooled audiences for so long. Pictures of 'Lulu' are convincing, and 'she' even inspired female rivals like 'Lolo – Prettiest of all Lady Gymnasts'. It is harder to understand how Sam sustained the deception backstage and outside the theatre. There is no doubt that Farini, who protected his investment in 'Lulu' with widespread threats of litigation, was an imaginative showman with a keen eye for marketing.

Farini has one further claim to fame: he invented a large coiled-spring mechanism that allowed a performer to be shot from a cannon. It was used for the first time at the Royal Aquarium in 1877, with a fourteen-year-old girl, Rossa Matilda Richter, who appeared as 'Zazel', as the human cannonball. To add to the spectacle, the cannon used gunpowder in small doses to create smoke and a convincing 'explosion'. Inevitably, Farini was Zazel's manager.

Against the expectations of many, Blondin and Farini lived full lives, dying in their beds aged seventy-two and ninety respectively. Another French sensation, Jules Léotard, did not. Léotard, the original 'daring young man on the flying trapeze' (the title of the song about him sung by George Leybourne), entranced London from his first appearance, inevitably at the Alhambra, on Whit Monday, 1861, when he swung over the audience while they ate and drank at their tables. Brave and talented, Léotard was immune to fear – but not to smallpox. He died of the disease in 1870, aged only twenty-eight.

Another French import saw the Alhambra fall foul of official-dom in 1870. The Alhambra had specialised for years in dance and ballet, and its management believed that a new dance – a highlight of the ballet *Les Nations* and performed by the dancing troupe Colonna – would be a money-spinner. It was the 'can-can'. Although new to London, the dance was familiar to Parisians, having first been performed in the working-class area of Montparnasse thirty years earlier. It had caused a fuss, but was never banned. In London, some people were not ready for provocative high kicks and flounced petticoats. Those who wished to be shocked – and there were many prepared to be shocked to the core – reacted violently. There was a great row, and the Alhambra lost its licence and closed. Music hall was denounced, once again, for its low tone.

The Alhambra was unfortunate: three years earlier, W.S. Gilbert's pantomime *Harlequin Cock Robin and Jenny Wren* at the Lyceum had featured a can-can performed by the French dancer Finette, which had been hailed by the press and created no contro-versy at all. Finette had a scandalous past, with numerous lovers and as a *poses plastiques* model. which, to those who were aware of it, may well have added a *frisson* to her performance. The *Pall Mall Gazette* commented that 'The characteristic immodesty of the Can Can is certainly toned down in Mlle. Finette's version, but her capers are, nevertheless, such as no woman should witness and no man applaud.' Colonna had also performed the can-can at the Oxford without adverse comment – Charles Morton had even introduced opera glasses, available for sixpence and fitted to clips on the back of the seats, for his audiences' greater enjoyment. It was fourteen years before the Alhambra's music hall licence was restored; in the interim it staged dramatic ballet under a theatre licence.

Colonna's lead dancer was Sarah Wright, known as 'Wiry Sal', and the daughter of one of the waiters at the Oxford. Emily Soldene, the rather stately resident soprano, was amazed by her athleticism: '[She] had shorter skirts and longer legs than most girls – to the great delight and satisfaction of herself and London – [and] kicked up her agile heels a little higher than had previously been deemed possible.' It was Wiry Sal's high kicks, in which her heels rose above her head, that had so excited the authorities that they closed the Alhambra.

The fuss over the morality of the can-can highlighted once again the inadequacies of the law. While the Middlesex magistrates clamped down savagely on the Alhambra, the can-can was soon being performed nightly in a 'condensed' opera at the Philharmonica, Islington, with no action taken by the Lord Chamberlain. As the can-can spread around the country, its opponents simmered with rage. In 1871 the *Penny Illustrated Paper* demanded that 'the pest of Can-canism must be stamped out', and urged the Lord Chamberlain to take action. But the Lord Chamberlain sat it out, and the can-can danced on.

In 1876 Soldene, then running her own show, took Colonna to America, to the dismay of the *Boston Globe*: 'How any man who respects a woman can take her to witness one of these performances surpasses understanding.' No doubt the many thousands who paid to see the show would have been able to tell him. So could Soldene, who described Colonna as 'human, healthy, handsome girls and a female [Wiry Sal] who kicks in a style unparalleled in the annals of gymnastic experience'.

Some music hall acts were bizarre, some tasteless, and some both: Miss Nellie Gertine, the Lady Baritone; Felix, the Mind-Reading Duck; Prago, the Missing Link; Fred Bithill's Performing Crows; The Dancing Quakers; Succi, the Fasting Man; Daisy Squelch and her Big Brass Six; the Beautiful Jessica, Queen of the Slack Wire – all entertained in their turn. So did numerous ventriloquists, salamanders (fire-eaters), knife-throwers, siffleurs (whistlers), dentalists (acrobats who hung by their teeth) – nothing, in the life of music hall, was beyond imagination.

Among the acts that qualify as both tasteless and bizarre were the 'water spouters', an art form – mercifully lost today – that was born in Jacobean times. The most celebrated '*fartiste*', Joseph Pujol, better known as 'Le Pétomane', could blow out candles and perform music in many different sharps and flats as well as spout water on demand from the same lower orifice. This turn caused much hilarity at the Moulin Rouge, and for a time Pujol was the toast of Paris, rumoured to earn twice as much as Sarah Bernhardt. However, his 'art' did not attract support in Britain, and he was never engaged to appear in even the most obscure theatre.

One fascination for nineteenth-century audiences was physically challenged performers – often cruelly called 'freaks'. Barnum & Bailey's Circus routinely advertised 'human curiosities of every description'. The unfortunate Hermann Unthan was born in Prussia in 1848 without arms, yet, as the South London Music Hall assured its patrons, he was able to 'sharpen pens, shoot accurately, play the violin and cornet, play cards and offer a glass of wine' – all with his feet. He appeared in all parts of the country for over thirty years, even topping the bill at the Edinburgh Empress in April 1897. Yet he was essentially a public 'freak' at whom people came to gawp. In private, during the First World War, without publicity, he taught wounded German ex-servicemen how to cope with their disabilities. He refused a captain's pay, believing it would undermine his work with the maimed soldiers, but he did accept the honorary rank of 'High Military Official in Civilian Clothes'.

A 'freak' of a different sort was John Bottle, who had an uncanny ability to commit to memory an extraordinary volume of information on any subject. He entered music hall by a fluke. While employed at the Anerley Gas Works in Crystal Palace, he interrupted a discussion between workmates to correct some facts about the famous court case of Arthur Orton, the Tichborne Claimant. In the ensuing conversation he was asked about other matters, and to everyone's surprise he invariably knew the answers, and had a formidable recollection of significant dates. Bottle was invited to display his powers of memory to the manager of the Standard, Pimlico, and was on stage the same evening. Thereafter, he appeared at the Palace Theatre, performing under the stage name 'Datas'. After answering a question from a member of the audience he would sign off with the enquiry, 'Is that right, sir?' 'Datas' became the model for 'Mr Memory' in Alfred Hitchcock's 1935 film of John Buchan's classic tale *The Thirty-Nine Steps*, and the scenes of 'Mr Memory' onstage faithfully reproduce Bottle's act and the atmosphere of the theatre.

Illusionists and conjurors had been a feature of travelling fairs and shows for centuries, and remained popular in music hall. Many were talented. Some were charlatans. Washington Bishop was both. He astounded audiences by finding pins that had been hidden by others, and identifying the serial numbers on banknotes he had not previously seen. Like all mind-readers, his act was based on a sophisticated analysis of facial expression and involuntary muscular movement. Offstage, Bishop was married several times, sometimes without the benefit of divorce from his previous wife, and was forced to flee Britain after losing a libel case in 1885 and being ordered to pay £10,000 in damages. In 1889 he collapsed after a private performance, and doctors pronounced him dead. An autopsy was held during which, in accordance with his previously expressed wishes, his brain was removed for medical science. It was then learned that Bishop normally carried a note stating that he suffered from blackouts, and that no autopsy should be performed without the consent of his family or his lawyers. No such note, however, was – or ever has been – found. The following day his mother viewed the body and accused the doctors of murder. An inquiry was held and a further autopsy was carried out, during which, bizarrely, Bishop's brain was discovered in his chest cavity. Despite repeated attempts by his mother to have the doctors charged, they were cleared of all blame.

Greater talents than Bishop had more conventional lives. The French illusionist Jean Eugène Robert-Houdin toured Britain in 1848 with a pioneering levitation act in which his son 'slept' in mid-air supported only by a walking stick – this was advertised as being possible due to the gravity-defying properties of ether. Imitators soon followed: the Scottish illusionist 'Professor Anderson, Wizard of the North', credited levitation to 'Superman Chloroform'. Sometimes the illusion was a straightforward trick. Robert-Houdin would place a box weighing only a few pounds on the floor of the stage, and invite burly members of the audience to pick it up. After they had failed, he would lift it with his little finger. The deception was simple: the box was magnetised and then demagnetised, but to the audience it was a mystery.

Among the many illusionists and conjurors on the music hall stage, two of the most popular and accomplished were John Nevil Maskelyne and George Cooke. Maskelyne had been a watchmaker and his friend Cooke a cabinet-maker, and their technical skills enabled them to construct mechanical illusions. In effect, their act was a series of tricks dramatised into a short play. The plot was merely a peg to showcase eye-popping levitations, plate-spinning, vanishing ladies, appearances and disappearances from apparently secure cages and boxes, and apparent decapitation: Maskelyne walked around the stage with Cooke's disembodied head tucked under his arm. Singers, dancers, jugglers and quick-change artistes joined the act to spice it up and conjure mayhem.

As men whose act was based on technical skills, Maskelyne and Cooke were keen to distance themselves from a superstitious belief in supernatural powers. They billed themselves as 'illusionists and anti-spiritualists', which brought them into conflict with fellow performers. Maskelyne was one of the sceptics to expose Washington Bishop's false claims to possess psychic powers – indeed, it was he who sued Bishop for libel and was awarded £10,000 by the court.* In 1865 Maskelyne debunked the American illusionists the Davenport Brothers, who ascribed their powers to spiritualism, by repeating their tricks without any claim of otherworldly aid. In doing so he had a young assistant, John Brodribb, later rather better known as Sir Henry Irving, the legendary Victorian actor-manager.

When not in battle with his fellow performers, Maskelyne was an inventor – the mechanism for the penny-in-the-slot lavatory was his, as were many self-designed automatons. He was also a

---

* Bishop had accused Maskelyne of colluding with another man to discredit his mind-reading act.

musician, a talent sometimes incorporated in his act. In May 1873 he became the lessee of the suitably exotic- and ethereal-sounding Egyptian Hall in Piccadilly. The building had been used to house curiosities since 1811, and got its name from its façade, which featured a temple-like entrance adorned with all manner of hiero-glyphics and sphinxes. Initially, Maskelyne took out a lease for three months, but he ended up using it as his base for the next thirty years, while continuing to tour around the country. It was here, at 'England's Home of Mystery', that his music-playing, portrait-drawing and card-dealing automatons were housed.

When the Egyptian Hall was scheduled for demolition in 1904, Maskelyne moved the whole operation to St George's Hall, Langham Place, calling it 'Maskelyne's New Home of Magic'. He died of pneumonia in May 1917, but 'Maskelyne's Mysteries' contin-ued to perform on the same site until 1933, when the BBC took over the building and turned it into a radio studio, until it was destroyed by bombs during the Second World War.

Maskelyne was very supportive of new talent, and many of those he encouraged became big stars. Among them was David Devant. Devant started out as an illusionist at the age of eighteen, and by the early 1890s was playing some of the biggest halls across the country with his 'Delightful Delusions'. His break into the big time came when he invited Maskelyne to see him perform in 1893 – an invitation many aspiring illusionists offered – in the hope that he would be asked to join the great man's ensemble.

Although Devant had considerable technical skill, it was his witty banter and engagement with the audience that underpinned his success. Little-known today outside theatrical circles, he was hugely influential, and the epitome of the dapper magician, an image still familiar to us. Wearing immaculate evening dress with white tie, he would perform his tricks effortlessly, while telling amusing anecdotes and gently teasing his onstage victims, much to the delight of the audience.

Following George Cooke's death in 1905, Devant became Maskelyne's business associate. After Maskelyne's death he

– together with the Maskelyne family – ran both the London and the touring operations, as well as continuing to perform as the pre-eminent illusionist in the country. He was instrumental in establishing the Magic Circle, the society for the conjuring profession, which still exists today, and was appointed its first president in 1905. Sadly, hard work took its toll: Devant suffered so badly from nervous exhaustion that he often had to take lengthy periods of rest. He was forced to retire as a performer in 1920, but remained a mentor to others until his death in 1941.

Another giant of the halls who is little remembered today was 'the Great Lafayette'. A talented illusionist and a genuine eccentric, he started life in Munich as Sigmund Neuberger, and moved with his family to the USA in his teens. He cut his teeth with a magic show that toured the hard-living mining camps of the California gold rush in the 1890s. In the closing years of the century he travelled to England, where he enjoyed instant success. Always flamboyant, he was never separated from his beloved, diamond-festooned terrier 'Beauty' (a gift from Houdini), who travelled in her own train compartment with porcelain bath and all the comforts of home, including five-course meals and specially made sofas.

Lafayette's own home was extraordinary. It was the outward expression of the man, with lavish furnishings, and painted throughout in stripes of different colours. The entrance bore the words 'The More I See of Men, the More I Love My Dog'. His cheques were specially printed with a picture of Beauty and a sack of gold. Underneath were the words 'My Two Best Friends'.

Despite his eccentricities, this 'Man of Mystery' was phenomenally successful, and was believed to be the highest-paid act on the music hall stage at the time. After his London debut he packed halls all over the country with his spectacular shows featuring lions, horses and a cast of forty. His brilliantly staged illusions were a magnet for audiences and guaranteed box office for managers.

In May 1911, four days after burying his beloved dog at Piershill Cemetery, Edinburgh, Lafayette was performing at the Edinburgh Empire. A fire started onstage after a light exploded. At first the audience thought it was part of the act, and didn't move. The fire spread rapidly. The elaborate set went up in minutes, and Lafayette was burned to death when he returned to the stage to rescue one of the horses. Ten other performers also lost their lives, and the theatre burned to the ground.* Remains believed to be the Great Lafayette's were taken away for burial, but a few days later workers clearing the ruins found another body which proved to be his: the earlier one had been that of his double, identically dressed for the performance of some of the tricks. There is one touching ending to this tragedy: Lafayette was buried in the same grave as Beauty – something Edinburgh City Council had insisted on as a condition of allowing the dog to be buried in Piershill. Thus the two of them were reunited for eternity.

Maskelyne, Devant and Lafayette all used technology onstage, but some illusionists used science to take their acts to a completely new level. In the early 1900s Dr Walford Bodie MD (in reality Samuel Brodie, and not a doctor of medicine, or indeed of anything else) – who, among other superlatives, styled himself immodestly as 'the Rage of London' and 'the Greatest Novelty Act on Earth' – made the new miracle of electricity the heart of his act. Many thought him a charlatan, but he held audiences spellbound with spectacular, but entirely harmless, displays of static electricity. Audiences thrilled as blue flashes arced across terminals, and electrical elements made exotic liquids boil and bubble in jars. Bodie's onstage presence – with pointed, waxed moustache, glaring eyes, full evening dress bearing unearned medals – was an impressive concoction. If challenged about his non-existent medical qualifications, he laughed off his 'MD' as meaning that he was a 'merry devil'.

As part of his act, Bodie invited members of the audience onstage and encouraged them to hold electrodes while 'thousands of volts' appeared to pass through them. Couples were asked to kiss

* It was for this reason that the first Royal Command Performance, which had been intended to take place at the Empire, Edward Moss's favourite theatre, was instead held at the Palace Theatre in London the following year.

one another, and the audience gasped as bolts of electricity flashed between them. In fact it was all perfectly safe: the electricity bypassed the volunteers, and was controlled by switches Bodie operated with his feet. The effect, however, was striking to an audience unfamiliar with this new source of power.

Bodie's claims became ever more absurd. 'Bring me your cripples!' he cried, and claimed he could heal the sick with 'bloodless surgery'. A memoir of his appearance at the Britannia Theatre, Hoxton, records that sick people were examined onstage; Bodie 'discovered' the ailment, manipulated it to the accompaniment of sparks flying from his fingers and – lo and behold – the patient would be cured. The gullible were amazed, but the more worldlywise were affronted and sceptical, and Bodie slipped further and further down the bill. He died in 1939, aged seventy, after a season at Blackpool.

The music hall stage was often a scene of illusion, but few conjurors were more convincing than Chung Ling Soo. Promotional posters show him as a quintessential inscrutable Chinaman, complete with shaved forehead, long Mandarin-style pigtail, baggy silk tunic, pantaloons and platformed slippers. In fact he was born in New York of Scottish parents, and baptised William Ellsworth Robinson. His true ethnicity was repeatedly exposed in the press, but the public preferred to continue to regard him as a Chinaman. On 23 March 1918 Chung Ling Soo was performing his famous 'gun trick', in which he 'magically' caught a bullet fired at him, at the Wood Green Empire. Unfortunately, the mechanism of the gun malfunctioned and a real bullet was fired into his chest. He died shortly afterwards, widely lamented and long remembered.

The greatest of all stage illusionists was born Erich Weisz in Budapest in 1874. When he was twelve his family moved to New York, where his name was changed to Weiss, and after training as a locksmith he began his stage career as an acrobat and then a card trickster, before he and his younger brother Theo turned to escapology in 1892. After a couple of years they split up, and Theo was replaced in the act by Erich's wife, Bess.

Before the 1890s, escapology was generally just one part of a 'séance' or 'medium' act. The Davenport Brothers, old foes of Maskelyne, extricated themselves from bonds and shackles with the pretence that the escape was in some way supernatural. Erich Weiss changed all that, and turned escapology into an art form. In homage to the French illusionist Robert-Houdin he changed his name to Harry Houdini.

My father knew Houdini, and greatly admired his charm as a man and his skill as an artiste. The diminutive escapologist was fearless, I was told, and quite simply the best. His amazing ability to free himself from straitjackets, handcuffs, locked trunks and water tanks became legendary. Strangely, he was not an immediate success in America, and used his savings to come to London, where he made his debut in 1900. Soon he was spicing up his reputation by performing escapes where failure would mean death. Charles Dickens would not have approved of the huge crowds that flocked to see an act that could end with a fatality. Houdini encouraged this morbid anticipation. 'Failure means a drowning death' was the legend fixed to the milk churn in which he was locked before it was filled with water.

He jumped into rivers from high bridges, while shackled and manacled with heavy chains. One of the lasting images of Houdini is of him hanging suspended from a crane while freeing himself from a straitjacket. This was a sensational feat, but another amazing escape made it seem pedestrian. Houdini's feet were locked into mahogany 'stocks', and in full sight of the audience he was lowered upside down into a locked, steel-reinforced glass tank filled with water. It took him only thirty seconds to extricate himself from his 'water torture cell'. It seemed a miracle.

Like Maskelyne, Houdini campaigned against spiritualists, and for the same reason: both wished to be admired for their technical skill and ingenuity, and not for some 'otherworldly' power, which they scorned. Houdini's mockery of spiritualism led to a very public and painful row with his close friend Sir Arthur Conan Doyle. Conan Doyle, despite having created Sherlock Holmes, the supreme master of logic and deduction, had a firm belief in spiritualism. This grew into an obsession after the deaths of his son Kingsley and his younger brother Innes. Houdini believed all spiritualists to be unscrupulous frauds, preying on the gullibility of the bereaved, but even when he exposed the deceits they used to conjure up ghostly hands and voices, he could not persuade Conan Doyle that spiritualism was bogus. The great author needed the comfort of believing in an afterlife, and would not be swayed.

Despite their opposing views, they remained friends until Conan Doyle held a séance at which he claimed to have contacted Houdini's late mother. In 1924 Houdini published *A Magician Among the Spirits*, in which he publicly ridiculed Conan Doyle's beliefs, and the two men never spoke again.

Two years later, on 22 October 1926, Houdini was performing at the Palace Theatre, Montreal. He was visited in his dressing room by a student, who asked him if it were true that if he was punched, he felt no pain. Houdini replied that he had heard that had been reported, whereupon the student punched him – several times. Having had no time to brace his body, Houdini fell to the floor. He died just over a week later, at the age of fifty-two. It was an ironic end for a man who risked death daily. In 1929 Conan Doyle, still a believer, wrote to Houdini's biographer: 'I have no more doubt he used physic power than I have that I am dictating this letter.' One is left to wonder what Sherlock Holmes would have made of this disregard of facts.

All these extraordinary performers had one thing in common: spectacle. The acrobats, conjurors, mind readers, escapologists and limbless violinists gave music hall audiences a display of virtuosity to make them marvel – and then to return to the theatre again and again.

16

Amusement of the People

'People mutht be amuthed. They can't be alwath
a learning ... they an't made for it.'

MR SLEARY, IN CHARLES DICKENS,
HARD TIMES (1854)

In the second half of the nineteenth century, music hall, despite its
phenomenal growth and popularity, had to take its place alongside
many other new recreational activities. Up until mid-century, most
people had worked longer hours for less money, and were less
mobile. Except for the fortunate few, life offered little opportunity
for leisure.

But as free time, a little spare money and wider access to travel
became a reality, there were more opportunities for simple pleasures to be enjoyed. Many chose music hall, but others preferred
recreational sports like football, cricket, horseracing and bicycling.
Some even opted to use their newly acquired literacy to read for
pleasure during their time away from work.

In the two decades after its rules were agreed in 1848, football
blossomed from a public-school hobby to a Saturday-afternoon
obsession for millions. The Football Association, established in
1863, was initially dominated by patrician teams like Old
Carthusians and Old Etonians, but working-class teams grew out of
their own social networks. Famous clubs like Aston Villa and Derby

County grew out of sporting clubs or pub teams, while West Bromwich Albion, West Ham and Arsenal were originally founded as teams representing workplaces.

In a vignette of classless competition, the two opposite demographic spheres came together in the 1883 FA Cup final. Working-class Blackburn Olympic beat the Old Etonians 2–1. Their victory was a catalyst for clubs across the country to join the Football Association. Shortly after that, in 1888, the Football League was created, initially as a mechanism for organising club fixtures in the Midlands and the north.

In many ways, football, as a spectator sport, offered a very similar appeal to music hall: it was cheap, it was local and it was an escape from drudgery. Moreover, stardom was open to anyone of talent.

Cricket also had a powerful hold on public sentiment, and during the Victorian era was more popular than football. In 1892 an impressive 34,000 people, from all walks of life, watched the first day of a mere County match between Surrey and Nottinghamshire. But football was catching up: the following year an estimated 60,000 spectators saw Wolverhampton Wanderers beat Everton 1–0 to win the FA Cup at Fallowfield Stadium in Manchester.

Another diversion, gambling, had strong links with music hall. Betting on horses became more accessible as the nineteenth century progressed. Until the 1840s, bets had mainly been between wealthy individuals or through so-called 'legs', the runners for early bookmakers. One notable pioneer was William 'Leviathan' Davis, who in the 1840s pinned up his lists of odds in pubs near The Strand. Such list-making continued until 1853, when social campaigners persuaded Parliament to ban the practice. This legislation inevitably drove the trade underground, and led to far greater abuses than those it sought to solve. After 'lists' were banned, Charles Morton, who had posted them at his India House pub in the City, moved to sweepstakes and advertised them heavily in the trade press. The

scale of advertising implies that sweepstakes made a serious contribution to his profits.

Horseracing, as a leisure activity, was becoming better organised, better publicised and very popular. Vast numbers of people
crammed onto trains from Liverpool, Manchester and London to
enjoy the huge meetings held at Aintree and Epsom, which was the
course of choice for working-class Londoners. The Derby meeting
there in 1823 attracted an estimated crowd of 23,000, which as prosperity, leisure time and the railways grew, swelled to 250,000 by 1851.

There were no stands and no rails at Epsom, and the whole site
would have been alive with the ballyhoo of a funfair offering all
manner of innocent and salacious amusements: pickpockets, prostitutes, crooked bookmakers, gypsy fortune-tellers, jugglers,
gymnasts, swindlers, card sharps, cockfighting pits and bare-
knuckle fights. All Victorian life was there.

The social reformers, who disapproved so much of music hall,
disliked racing also, and in the 1890s distributed pamphlets urging
the working classes to dissociate themselves from 'the degraded
mob, the blasphemers, greedy, obscene, Bohemianism that revels on
Epsom Downs'. The 'degraded mob' was unpersuaded, and attended
in force, intent on fun. Parliament was unlikely to restrain them,
because every year since 1848 both the Lords and the Commons had
adjourned for the day to attend the Derby.

Not all new sporting pursuits were competitive. In the mid-1880s
John Stanley began mass-producing an affordable 'safety' bicycle,
and in 1887 a Belfast vet, John Dunlop, invented a new pneumatic
tyre to improve the comfort of his small son's tricycle. The tyre was
a success, and had obvious commercial potential. Its application to
adult bicycles gave the appeal of leisure bicycling a huge boost.
Bicycling became big business.

In 1895, more than 750,000 bicycles were manufactured in
England alone, and organisations were formed to cater for the
craze. One of them, the Cyclists' Touring Club, had its own uniform
of grey jacket and knickerbockers, with a Stanley helmet with a

small peak. Clubs proliferated, some with extraordinary names: the Up-to-Date Female's Emancipation Society Cycling Club, the Woman's Rights Federation Cycling Club, and the very catchy New Swindon Street Congregational Church Young Men's Bible Class Amateur Cycling Club.

Music hall was full of all these activities, and inevitably songwriters followed the public tastes. Mark Sheridan sang 'At the Football Match Last Saturday', pronouncing the last word 'Saterrrdy' to make it scan better. Tom Maclagan sang 'The Cricketer' in 1869, and W.G Grace featured in 'The Song of the "Centuries"' in 1895. Marie Lloyd sang 'Salute My Bicycle' with appropriately saucy lyrics, 'I'll Never Ride Any More on a Bike' was a popular hit for Vesta Victoria, and of course there was the memorable hit 'Daisy Bell'.

There were also acts that were *all* about bicycles: 'Verno and Voyce – the Singing Bicyclists' and 'The Seven Musical Savonas' magically mixed cycling with singing and the playing of instruments. Music hall stars enjoyed the new attractions as much as anyone. George Robey was a fanatical football and cricket fan throughout his life, and old photographs show Gus Elen, and Dan Leno and family, as enthusiastic cyclists.

Higher wages encouraged leisure, as did public and paid holidays, and together these revolutionised people's attitudes to 'spare' time. By the late nineteenth century the 'Wakes Weeks' of the Yorkshire and Lancashire mill towns had grown from patchily observed religious festivals into the mass exodus of the entire working population of the town.

While money and free time offered greater opportunities for leisure, so did education. A succession of enlightened pieces of legislation, especially the Elementary Education Act of 1870, led to reading becoming a significant leisure activity. The government encouraged this trend as taxes fell on advertising, newspaper and newsprint.

And there was plenty to read. Periodicals were enormously successful, and hundreds of thousands of readers were served up a regular diet of scandal, murder and popular science through titles such as *Reynolds' Weekly Newspaper* and *Lloyd's Weekly*, both of which sold for a mere tuppence. By 1890 *Lloyd's* was selling a million copies each week.

Another hugely popular publication, *Tit-bits*, first published in 1881, was the brainchild of George Newnes, a travelling haberdashery salesman. Its full title, *Tit-bits From All the Interesting Books, Periodicals and Newspapers of the World*, shows it to have been an amalgam of snippets from many sources. Newnes had much in common with the music hall owners in wanting the widest possible readership to buy his publications, and he censored them himself to remove any smut or innuendo. He was also the guiding hand behind the *Strand Magazine*, which brought Sherlock Holmes, the greatest single creation in Victorian fiction, to households of every class and income. It was an immediate success: its first edition, in January 1891, sold 300,000 copies, and it was soon enjoying a circulation of half a million copies a month.

Increased literacy was a great victory for the famous Victorian reforming zeal, but that zeal would soon turn its gaze upon music hall. The ensuing conflict would bring about a titanic clash between two conflicting Victorian values: morality and free trade.

Its unlikely battleground would be the Promenade of the Empire, Leicester Square.

17

The Literati and the Artists

'I regard the theatre as the greatest of all art
forms, the most immediate way in which a human
being can share with another the sense of what it
is to be a human being.'

OSCAR WILDE (1854–1900)

Decades after its demise, it is not easy to see music hall clearly; to cut through the rosy glow of sentimental memories and hagiographic biographies on one side, and on the other the dismissal of music hall as tawdry and meretricious. There are recordings of performers after 1890, a few of which can be seen on early film, but they are mostly a disappointment: music hall artistes thrived on audience contact, and the primitive recording and film technology of the time provided only a pale reflection of the real thing.

Contemporary reports and reviews do help to bring music hall alive. There is also a window on this lost world – incomplete, but illuminating – from the pens of literary figures and the brushes of contemporary artists. From the 1880s onward a number of influential artists, writers, critics and poets recognised the social significance of music hall. Walter Sickert, Max Beerbohm, William Archer, Arthur Symons, Rudyard Kipling and

T.S. Eliot are among those who gave enduring life to the performers and their public.

Walter Sickert, one of the greatest of all British artists, was obsessed with all facets of music hall, and produced countless sketches and paintings of theatre interiors, performers and audiences. His work is alive with detail, and gives us some of the most vivid images of the heyday of music hall in the last two decades of the nineteenth century.

Born in Munich in 1860, Sickert led an early life that was the near definition of that of the avant-garde aesthete. After flirting with the civil service he became an actor, and toured for a short time with several companies in 1879, meeting figures such as Oscar Wilde and actor-manager Johnston Forbes-Robertson. In 1881 he gave up acting to study at the Slade School of Fine Art, but dropped out after a few months to become a pupil of James McNeill Whistler – 'The only painter alive,' he wrote, 'who has … immense genius.' It was through Whistler that Sickert met Degas, who was to have a strong influence on his work. In Paris in 1883 Sickert saw some of Degas' completed and half-finished works, including *Café Concert* (1876), *Café Concert at Les Ambassadeurs* (1876), *Café Concert Singer* (1878) and *Singer at a Café Concert* (1878), as well as numerous paintings of ballet dancers, with whom Degas was captivated.

Manet too was an early influence. Sickert was invited to his studio, where it is likely he saw studies for *The Beer Drinkers* (1878), *Café-concert* (1878) and *Singer at a Café-Concert* (1879). He certainly saw the finished *Bar at the Folies Bergère* (1881–82), Manet's last major work. Manet's use of the mirror in this famous painting was a device Sickert was to employ to great effect in his music hall pictures.

In his debut solo show in London, at the end of 1886, Sickert exhibited his first theatrical painting, *Rehearsal: The End of the Act*, later to be renamed *The Acting Manager*. It is in fact a portrait of Helen Couper-Black, general manager of the D'Oyly Carte Opera Company and soon to be the second Mrs D'Oyly Carte. In April

1887 he showed *The Lion Comique*, generally agreed to be his first music hall painting, the subject of which was the 'swell' vocalist Fred Albert, at the Marylebone Theatre. The perspective is from a seat in the stalls looking directly up at the stage over the heads of the orchestra. The figure of Albert is starkly lit in front of the drab, one-dimensional backdrop. In *Bonnet and Claque, Ada Lundberg at the Marylebone Music Hall,* also from 1887, he turns his focus onto the audience, which he had already made the subject of many etchings. The mask-like faces of the claque – rowdy dowdy boys, shouting their approval – dominate the picture rather more than Ada, or her bonnet.

That same year, Sickert began work on *Gatti's Hungerford Palace of Varieties: Second Turn of Miss Katie Lawrence,* which was exhibited at the New English Art Club the following April to a storm of hostility. The painting offended on several fronts, one of which was Sickert's choice of setting. Gatti's had a bad reputation. It was situated in Villiers Street, just off The Strand and a stone's throw from Hungerford Bridge, a favourite haunt of prostitutes, from where they could solicit men going to and from Charing Cross and Waterloo stations. One contemporary critic derided the work as 'tawdry, vulgar and the sentiment of the lowest Music Hall'. Another referred to it as the embodiment of 'the aggressive squalor which pervades to a greater or lesser extent the whole of modern existence'. For some, the outrage was as much stylistic as moral. Sickert's impressionist style was unfamiliar, and the subject matter he chose to commit to canvas was considered deeply unsuitable. One critic complained that he had rendered Lawrence as 'a hideously malformed creature', and called the picture a 'dirty smear, as vulgar in execution as choice of subject'. Another said it was 'the lowest degradation of which the art of painting is capable'.

Lawrence, a serio comic who gave wings to Harry Dacre's song 'A Bicycle Made for Two', was then at the height of her fame. In the picture she stands alone on the stage in a primrose-yellow frock that is altogether too short and too low-cut for contemporary standards of decency. Sickert gives the impression that she is performing for an audience of single men and one unaccompanied woman, in an extravagant hat, who is suggestive of the loose women believed to frequent the halls. Katie Lawrence herself disliked the painting. When offered another full-length portrait of herself she is reputed to have said, 'What! That thing? Not even to keep the draught from under the scullery door!'

Today, it is difficult to understand the outrage critics expressed, but the reasons for it were twofold. Firstly, performers like Katie Lawrence and Marie Lloyd did nothing to dispel the impression that the music halls were colluding to degrade public morals. What to them and their audiences was mere nudge-and-wink suggestiveness was regarded by a large swathe of public opinion as representing a complete lack of morals. Secondly, although for some time the music halls had been attracting a respectable middle-class audience, there were still many who believed them to be dens of iniquity where drink, prostitution and all manner of licentiousness were freely available. Their outrage was multiplied by what was implied, rather than depicted, in the picture. Katie Lawrence, and her formidable agent George Ware made the most of the controversy. There must have been a namesake, because he ran advertisements advising managers to book 'the right Katie Lawrence'.

Notwithstanding the furore surrounding *Gatti's Hungerford Palace of Varieties*, Sickert was entering a productive phase, with music hall paintings coming in rapid succession. *Little Dot Hetherington at the Bedford Music Hall* (1888–89) was the first of many depicting the interior of an old-style hall of the kind that was soon to give way to the larger variety theatres. The Old Bedford, in Camden High Street, was close to where Sickert lived, and was built in 1861 – six years before Gatti's-under-the-Arches and only nine years after the New Canterbury. *Little Dot* is one of the most significant of Sickert's paintings. By using a mirror, similar to that in Manet's *Bar at the Folies Bergère*, he simultaneously captures all aspects of the hall: the performer, in the shape of Little Dot, and the boy in the gallery to whom she addresses her song; the apparently all-male audience from several walks of life; the symbolic unaccompanied woman; the chairman who cranes his neck to see what is going on behind him; a patron in the stage box and the somewhat sinister figure of a woman dressed in black watching from the wings – parent, chaperon, agent, perhaps?

At the time Little Dot was possibly as young as eight, and at the beginning of her career. She clearly had talent, and had already earned approving reviews: 'very clever and graceful, this little girl … a wonderful little protean artist … a versatile Little American with bright and characteristic impersonations. She appeared in ten characters and changed her costumes so rapidly and neatly as to win enthusiastic tokens of approval.' Little Dot was in fact English, not American – the reviewer was probably misled because she was appearing with the American Moore & Burgess Minstrels.

Little Dot, dressed in a voluminous white smock, stands on stage singing 'The Boy I Love …' She points to the gallery, as the words of the song require, but with some pathos. Her expression, from what we can make out, is resigned. Many music hall performers – Marie Lloyd, Ada Reeve, Vesta Tilley, Hetty King, Bessie Bellwood and Minnie Cunningham among them – started as children, and frequently sang adult songs, but Little Dot was exceedingly young to be singing about adult love to a predominantly male audience. Fortunately, the painting did not stall her career. She was soon touring with Vesta Tilley, and by the mid-1890s was playing Cinderella in pantomime. Sickert stayed with the subject of child performers with *The Sisters Lloyd* (1889) – probably Marie's sister Rosie, then aged ten, and her twelve-year-old cousin Bella Orchard. Legislation passed that year prohibited children under seven from being employed in the theatre, and required those under ten to be licensed.

Sickert visited Gatti's-under-the-Arches and other halls on a regular basis. His studio was strewn with sketches, sheet music, trade papers and pictures of music hall stars, and he was friendly with many of the performers, including Katie Lawrence, Queenie Lawrence (no relation), Bessie Bellwood and Minnie Cunningham. Minnie Cunningham was much admired by the literati, especially by another devotee of music hall, the writer and poet Arthur Symons, who introduced her to Sickert. Sickert first painted her in 1889, and in 1892 he completed a picture of her which was more a portrait than a music hall painting *per se*. Though the backcloth is thought to be that of the Tivoli, where Sickert first saw her perform, it is possible that she posed for him in his studio. When the picture was exhibited at the New English Art Club, the critic Frederick Wedmore wrote of 'the agile and expressive Cunningham whom painters approve of, and men of letters encourage'. Sickert subtitled the portrait '*I'm an old hand at love, though I'm young in years*', a line from Cunningham's own composition 'The Art of Making Love'. She is depicted in a brilliant red dress, which hardly suggests the feigned innocence of her typical ingenue serio-comic material. Cunningham was a talented dancer as well as singer, and after a quick change out of children's dress she would dance for the audience in a more suggestive way. She clearly inspired creativity in some of her audience: Symons, as music hall critic for the *Star*, wrote a review of one of her dances in the form of a poem, and Sickert wrote a sonnet to her.

Sickert's painting of another serio, *The Stage Box – Vesta Victoria at the Old Bedford* (1890), is notable because he chose it for exhibition at the Royal Academy in 1898. It is probable that he saw this picture, in which he again uses the mirror to reflect several aspects of the hall, as an especially fine example of his work.

Around 1890, Sickert began to paint landscapes of Venice and Dieppe, portraits of the famous, and nudes of the not so famous, but when he returned to music hall the emphasis was on the boys in the gallery. The Old Bedford was on his doorstep, and he painted numerous studies of it in which the mirror was integral to the perspective. Of one of them, subtitled *The Boy I Love is Up in the Gallery* – a companion to *Little Dot* – George Moore, then the art critic of the *Speaker*, wrote: 'For its very rare beauty of tone I admire Mr Walter Sickert's picture representing the gallery of a music hall. I like it because of its beauty of tone, colour and composition ... The great mirror in which vague shadows are reflected, is it not a triumph.' This collection of paintings shows the gallery boys crammed into the cheap seats aloft, their working-class clothing in stark contrast to the top hats of the patrons in the stalls featured in Sickert's earlier paintings. Ten years later, Sickert would visit the Old Mo – the Middlesex Music Hall in Drury Lane – night after night. 'I am night and day absorbed in two magnificent Mogul Tavern pictures,' he wrote to a friend. In fact there would be three, and he regarded the first of them, *Noctes Ambrosianae*, as one of his best works. It is an atmospheric painting of the theatre audience crouched high up in the cheapest seats – 'the gods' – and craning their necks to look down at the performers on the stage.

The Old Bedford had burnt down in 1896, and lamenting 'the dear old Bedford in the days beyond recall', Sickert embarked in 1914 on an ambitious three-panel commission of its replacement, the New Bedford, which he never completed. In 1920 he made studies of two theatres in Shoreditch, the Empire and the Standard, where music hall was clinging on. His painting *That Old-Fashioned Mother of Mine* features Talbot O'Farrell, the dapper Scot who sang Irish ballads and made the song famous. He also revisited an old haunt with *Percy Honri at the Oxford*, a hall he had previously painted in 1888, in which the distant figure on the stage is presumed to be Marie Lloyd.

What was Sickert's motivation in choosing music hall as such a frequent subject? Clearly Degas and Manet gave him inspiration, but beyond that there was a deeper intent: he was trying to capture one aspect of the urban life that was exploding all around him in London. This is suggested by his reaction to a review of his painting of *Sam Collins' Music Hall* when it was shown in 1889. The critic of the *Scotsman* noted a French influence in the choice of subject, and Sickert responded robustly: 'It is surely unnecessary to go as far afield as Paris to find an explanation of the fact that a Londoner should seek to render on canvas a familiar and striking scene in the midst of the town in which he lives … I found myself one night in a little hall off Islington Green. At a given moment I was intensely impressed by the pictorial beauty of the scene, created by the coin-cidence of a number of fortuitous elements of form and colour … [that is] sufficient explanation of his motive for painting it.' In the preface to the catalogue for the London Impressionist Exhibition the same year he wrote: 'for those who live in the most wonderful and complex city in the world, the most fruitful course of study lies in the persistent effort to render the magic and poetry which they daily see around them'.

Sickert had become a respected and influential voice at the heart of cultural life in London, and was not alone in his interest in music hall. It was shared by many in literary and artistic circles, although their attitude to it was sometimes more equivocal than his. There were, however, those who could find neither magic nor poetry in it. The satirical magazine the *Tomahawk* in 1867 was typical: 'We have endeavoured to point out the utter stupidity and worthlessness of the entertainments which are to be heard at these places all over London, and it remains for the public to contribute its quota towards a general reformation, so that, in time, the Music Hall may really furnish a home for music, instead of being, as at present, an insult to the art from which it has filched its name.'

But music hall was a buoyant art form, and as it boomed in the 1880s serious critics began to look at it more positively. Walter Frith was a regular contributor to the influential literary journal the *Cornhill*, and in common with many of his literary colleagues he had mixed feelings about music hall. He was scathing about its humble origins: 'sprung from the old free and easy behind the public bar … discomfort, drink, dirt, debt, all these demons reign in the music hall menage'. Nor was he charitable about the perfor-mances: 'the humour is the humour of the gutter' – or the perform-ers: 'The music hall stage will often be a resting place for those who are going up and coming down in the theatrical world.' Nonetheless, he recognised, 'unhappy the nation that has no appreciation of hopeless vulgarity! Woe to the country that has no love for senseless laughter! The day when England echoes no longer with an utterly foolish and inexplicably popular comic chant will be the day when the knell of her decadence will most surely have struck.'

While Frith was brimming over with anti-music hall prejudice, he could not fail to notice that the halls were packed and profitable, whereas the legitimate stage was not. This posed an intellectual dilemma for him. Why should an entertainment he thought so inferior be so popular? His explanation was nonsense: 'Let it be remembered that these audiences, mainly composed of honest tradesmen and their women whose lives are full of order, duty, labour and self-denial are not laughing with the artistes – but at them.'

A fellow art critic, the American Elizabeth Robins Pennell, had less difficulty rationalising the phenomenon. In an 1893 article, 'The Pedigree of the Music Hall', she warns her fellow writers against being too dismissive of music hall, especially at a time when straight theatre is struggling:* 'legitimate theatre be dead in England, the reign of *Tit-Bits* has been inaugurated on the stage as in literature, and, at last, the theatrical ideals of the great English public have been adequately realised'. She defies the critics to explain why plays are art with 'a big "A", and music hall is art with a small "a" … music hall offers variety; the theatre monotony; variety the people prefer and always have preferred. No other reason is needed to account for the permanent success of London's 189 music halls and the varying fortunes of its 43 theatres. If the music hall be a modern institution the entertainment it provides is the heirloom of centuries.'

In her defence of music hall, Mrs Pennell drew no distinction between the travelling actors portrayed in high art and Marie Lloyd driving in her carriage each night from hall to hall. Why, she asks, criticise something simply because it is entertaining? After all, she argued, 'Have not playgoers for centuries shed tears over Hamlet one night and laughed at a puppet show the next?' Notwithstanding

---

* One reason for the success of music hall by comparison with the legitimate theatre was that it paid much better than the theatre, and many of the greatest talents turned to the halls to increase their income. As E.T. Smith, the manager of Drury Lane, told a House of Commons Select Committee in 1866: 'A man can go and get £6 a week from a music hall … take his brougham … and get four or five turns a night, and earn £20 or £30 a week!' Salaries in the legitimate theatre were paltry in comparison.

the attractions of music hall, she offered a prescient warning about its demise: 'Evidently, music hall's days are numbered. When too late, when it is no longer to be studied first hand, the scholar will learn its value.'

The writer Max Beerbohm, half-brother to the famous actor-manager Herbert Beerbohm Tree and an influential opinion-former, mourned the passing of authentic music hall. As early as 1898 he was casting his mind back five years to a golden age when he could 'bask in the glow of my own superiority' and revel in 'the joyous vulgarity' of the halls. While he enjoyed slumming it, he recognised that – in some ways – the audience was slumming it too. His was a very patronising view: 'The aim of the music hall is to cheer up the lower classes by showing them a life uglier and more sordid than their own.'

Five years later, in 'Demos's Mirror', an examination of music hall's popularity, Beerbohm wrote: 'The entertainments in the Music Hall have grown, feature for feature, from the public's taste. They are things which the public itself has created for its own pleasure.' He drew a contrast between music hall's connection with its audience, and 'legitimate' theatre, which has loftier aspirations: 'Every "turn" has but one aim: to please the public in the quickest and most obvious way ... There is no nonsense in the Halls, no pretence. The mirror is held up, and in it the face of Demos is reflected, whole and unblurred. The Hall is nearer to life. The Hall is preferable to the theatre. The average song, maybe does not distort life less than the ordinary play; but, at least, it distorts life exactly as the public like to see life distorted ... An intelligent foreigner will learn more about the soul of the English people in one visit to say The Tivoli than a hundred excursions to this or that "typical" locality.' Despite this praise of the performers, Beerbohm is very critical of his fellow spectators. He frequently describes their reactions as 'stupid', compares the lower classes to 'philistines' and even calls them 'grotesque'.

William Archer found it harder than Beerbohm to find any redeeming features in music hall. One of the leading drama critics of the 1890s, he was instrumental in bringing the plays of Ibsen to the English stage. In the essay 'Theatre and Music Hall' (1895) he questioned the fashion for calling music hall 'art', comparing it rather to a barrel organ: 'Insert a fresh strip of perforated paper and turn the handle ... The art of music hall is elaborate ugliness, blatant vulgarity, alcoholic humour and rancid sentiment. It does not really mirror or interpret any side of life whatsoever. It exhibits the life of the rich as one long rowdy swagger, the life of the poor as a larky, beery, maudlin Bank Holiday.' He ascribes the motives of those, like Beerbohm, who are apologists for music hall to a sort of snobbery: 'The vulgarity of other people, besides being often amusing in itself, ministers to our sense of superiority ... and it is a love of physical comfort and mental idleness that draws them to the music hall. There is far more art – far more skilled and intelligent adaptation of means to an end – in acting of ordinary competence than in the cleverest performances the English music hall stage can show.' Nor did he like music hall songs, commenting that 'not one song, one verse, one line ... has passed into the common language' and dismissing examples such as G.W. Hunt's 'By Jingo' as momentary flashes of public taste. His hostility is clear, but his assertions, as time has shown, were wrong.

Another leading drama critic, Percy Fitzgerald, took a more balanced view. In a semi-satirical monograph written in 1890, he speculates about a foreign country called 'Music Hall Land'.* He sees it as the epitome of working-class aspiration – or pretension, depending on which aspects and which performers you look at. The protagonists are the swells like George Leybourne and 'The Chairman', whose affectations to gentility provide the perfect illustration of this aspiration. Fitzgerald identifies certain acts, Herbert Campbell and Charles Coborn in particular, as 'great men' at the peak of their art: 'The Thing – such as it is – could not be better done. Everything "tells".' He also singles out the black-face act G.H. Chirgwin for his eccentricity, and the French singer Paulus for his

---

* Subtitle: 'An Account of the Natives, Male and Female, Pastimes, Songs, Antics and General Oddities of that Strange Country'.

deft professionalism, but mocks the self-delusion of those who, Cinderella-like, have dressed up in all their finery, 'transient dream though it be, to end on their return to the garret'.

Rudyard Kipling was more enthusiastic, and was typically straightforward in his view of music hall. In the autumn of 1898 he had lodgings in Villiers Street, opposite Gatti's-under-the-Arches, and in his posthumously published autobiography *Something of Myself* (1937) he gives a telling cameo of life in the inner city. Short of money, he had to make every penny count. His rooms were above Harris the Sausage King, and for tuppence he was able to buy all the sausage and mash he could eat. A further tuppence bought him half an ounce of tobacco, and fourpence got him a seat at Gatti's with a 'pewter of beer or porter' thrown in. It was at Gatti's, 'in the company of an elderly, but upright, barmaid from a nearby pub, that I listened to the observed and compelling songs of the Lion and Mammoth Comique, and to the shriller strain – but equally "observed" – of the Bessies and Bellas whom I could hear arguing beneath my window with their cab drivers as they sped from hall to hall.' Of performers, he wrote: 'I could never hope to rival [them], but the smoke, the roar, and the good natured fellow-ship of relaxed humanity at Gatti's "set" the scene for certain sorts of song.' Those certain sorts of song were to be emulated in his famous 'Barrack Room Ballads'. His muse, the barmaid, inspired the first of them when she told him about 'a friend o'mine 'oo was mistook in 'er man', which became 'Mary, Pity Women'. Yet Kipling was looking at a rapidly setting sun. By the early twentieth century the way the halls were built and organised had radically changed – notably with the introduction of rows of seating – and the behaviour of the audience was more sedate. Performance had become more important than audience participation.

As music hall critic of the *Star* and the more upmarket *Fortnightly Review*, Arthur Symons was among the first to take music hall seriously as an art form, and to give its talented performers proper critical appreciation. A self-confessed 'aficionado', he made such a special study of the genre, and those who patronised it, that his friend W.B Yeats referred to him as 'a scholar of music hall'. 'Music hall,' wrote Symons, 'amuses me, and I'm always gratified to anyone, or anything, that amuses me.'

Another literary figure who, like Max Beerbohm, saw poignancy in the passing of authentic music hall was T.S. Eliot. Like Beerbohm, Eliot saw the interaction between performer and audience as fundamental: 'The working man who went to the music hall ... and joined in the chorus was himself performing part of the act; he was engaged in that collaboration of the audience and the artist which is necessary in all art and most obviously in dramatic art.'

Despite the interest in music hall of many members of the literary set, very few authors attempted to explore the genre in novel form. Thackeray gave vignettes of song and supper rooms in *The Newcomes* and *Pendennis*, but I can trace only three novels and one series of short stories that are essentially about music hall.

The social reformer Walter Besant's *Dorothy Wallis* (1882) takes the form of the autobiography of an East End woman who aspires to become an actress. Throughout the novel Besant focuses on the hard work and dedication needed for a career onstage or in the halls. He later published an essay, 'At the Music Hall', also written in the character of Dorothy Wallis, that highlights the hardship of life in an overcrowded profession. His fictional actresses complain about lack of money and opportunity, too much competition for work, and the marital stress faced by women performers. One of them explains her husband's irritation with the stage: 'He wants to know why I can't give up going on in the halls and stay at home in the evening till he gets back; but I'm so dull and miserable by myself, all night, I can't. I'd do a great business to get on the halls, but he just can't say "no" to me, when I've really made up my mind to a thing. So I went and learnt dancing and all, and used to shut myself up in a room trying to do the American twist and the Rocks, and clean forgot meals and everything else.' Besant's intention was to discourage women from entering music hall.

The popular novelist Hall Caine's *The Christian* (1897) was a bestseller in its day. It is a cautionary tale about the conflict between a young woman trying to live an independent life, and society's perception of women's rightful place. Glory Quayle, the beautiful daughter of a Manx clergyman, 'goes over to the enemy' and becomes a star of music hall. As success enables her to rise in the social sphere, John Storm, an Anglican minister who believes the halls degrade the poor, drifts away from his aristocratic origins to become a charity worker. The novel paints a depressing picture of London's East End, and Max Beerbohm described it as 'a false garish farrago' of London life. In the book, Glory defends her choice of career: 'There are not many ways a woman can succeed – that's the cruelty of things. But there are a few, and I've chosen the one I'm fit for ... I shan't give up my profession. The idea of such a thing! It's ridiculous! Think of Glory in a convent! Or back serving up sewing at a mothers' meeting! Give it up! Indeed, I won't.' In this, she spoke for many female music hall performers.

Henry Nevinson wrote about a character called 'Little Scotty' in a collection of short stories, *Neighbours of Ours*, set in the London slums of 1895. Little Scotty, a working-class boy with a natural talent for mimicry, takes to the halls, and Nevinson gives a graphic account of an evening of music hall entertainment complete with acrobats, conjurors and minstrelsy, with Scotty at the top of the bill stealing the show as the 'uncrowned heir apparent of serio-comics'. Like Hall Caine, Nevinson paints an unflattering portrait of working-class life. Scotty's repertoire includes 'Annie Laurie' and 'Comin' Through the Rye', but in one of his songs he appears to revel in violence:

> For there's Neligan a-sayin' as Macarthy's self wants
>   flayin',
> And 'e's doin' business on 'im as'll cost ten pound;
> Then there's blue-eyed flaxen Lily as is knockin' Susan
> silly,
> And there's Jemmy Green just leavin' off from stampin'
>   on 'is wife ...

The most surprising author of a music hall novel, *Sellcuts'*
Manager, is Laura Ormiston Chant, who in 1894 opposed the
licence renewal of the Empire Theatre for encouraging prostitution.
The story itself is unremarkable, but some of the instincts and
sentiments of the author are in stark contrast to the image of her
that history has passed down to us. It is striking that her hero, Peter
Blake, is a music hall manager, and after his theatre is burned down
and rebuilt he says: 'We have called it the Palace of Amusements ...
The word theatre is still an offence to a great many excellent people,
whom we can enlist on our side if we concede a little to their not
always unreasonable prejudices; also we are departing from some of
the traditions of the music hall of old; and while we shall still have
variety performances they will not be night after night as formerly,
but ballad concerts, drama, opera, and oratorio will each have their
evening in due course.' This suggests that the abuse heaped upon
Mrs Ormiston Chant during the Empire campaign may have been
misplaced.

By way of contrast to writing about music hall, Sidonie-
Gabrielle Colette, prolific French author of the 'Claudine' series of
novels at the turn of the century, and later of the equally celebrated
Chéri and *Gigi*, made her name as a music hall artiste at the turn of
the century. After leaving her husband, who had taken the credit –
and the profit – for her novels, she took to the halls as a dancer and
mime artiste. She had no special talent for either, but went on to
appear topless at the Moulin Rouge and continued to tread the
boards well into her fifties, while her writing drew extensively on
her experience on the stage.

Other writers about music hall tended to be campaigners who
considered it a focus for depravity. Some, like the contributors to
Tempted London (1888), a collection of articles that first appeared in
the Christian journal *British Weekly*, went to extraordinary lengths
to warn the innocent of the evils of the entertainment on offer in
the capital, of which music hall was considered by far the most
pernicious. It paints a lurid picture of life in the city for the young
men stepping off trains from the country and coming face to face

for the first time with 'wickedness in its most seductive form'. Drink is regarded as 'the latchkey to everything that is vicious' – crime, disorderliness, profligacy, gambling and, of course, prostitution. Pubs in Charing Cross, Oxford Street and Islington, known to be frequented by women of bad character, are to be avoided at all costs. Music halls, to which young men are attracted because they can smoke, drink, 'ogle' girls, and contribute to a performance by joining in the chorus without overtaxing their intelligence, are regarded as particularly iniquitous. The author of one article admits that 'there is no great, particular, terrible blot upon them', but 'their atmosphere is replete with all that is noxious, demoralising, debilitating, destructive of energy and intelligence'. The contributor does, however, concede that, when isolated for inspection, the evils are 'apt to seem almost harmless'.

Tempted London describes a chairman, 'whose idea of wit is obscenity and whose enjoyment is summed up in the most expressive meaning that can be attached to the lower forms of sensuality', introducing the first turn of an evening's entertainment: 'Mr Poppy John – we have invented the name, which we hope is as meaningless and stupid as the majority of names taken by music hall artists'. Mr Poppy John is followed by 'the Evergreen Tottie, the irresistible male impersonator'; a child singer who is unable to make herself heard; 'a nigger minstrel'; and a pair of Irish comics. There are many young girls in the audience, although every song 'has something objectionable in it. When it is not absolutely indelicate it is absurdly inane, and when it is not vulgar it is without feature at all. The women accompany their efforts with movement and motions that offend the taste and that arouse the laughter of young men already fuddled with smoke and spirits'. Then there are the prostitutes, 'the loosest women in town'. One hall – not named, but almost certainly Gatti's-under-the-Arches, the haunt of Sickert, Katie Lawrence and Kipling – is singled out as having problems of this type which are a threat to its licence. Their presence is good for business, so resourceful hall-owners, while banning entry to unaccompanied women, issue them with free passes. Having obtained these, the women congregate outside, and accost every man who comes up to allow them entry in his company: 'This sort of thing goes on in some halls and young men find it difficult to refuse such a trifling request.'

It is easy to disparage *Tempted London*, but those behind it had honourable aims. They shared their bleak view of the moral degeneracy of music hall with another group of writers with very different motives – pornographers. Together, the reformers (for worthy, if misguided reasons) and the pornographers (for unworthy reasons) promoted the commonly held belief that all women associated with music hall had loose morals. A racy example of this perspective is the anonymous *Crissie: A Music Hall Sketch of Today*, published in 1899. In it a theatrical agent, Edward Piddlewick, spends as much time 'interviewing' comely maidens in his private office, or lining them up as escorts for the great and the good – a landowner, a Cabinet Minister and a member of the London County Council sitting on the Theatres and Music Hall Committee – as he does booking them into the halls.

The reader is assured by the author that 'no attempt will be made to hide the lustful depravity or shameless licentiousness of those grades of society'. Nor is it. Within the first ten pages a young woman looking for work as a singer accommodates Piddlewick on the casting couch, while in another room a singing duo pleasures the dissolute character Sir William Pixton. On the flimsiest of pretexts, Piddlewick and Pixton go to the Pandora Palace of Varieties, Leicester Square, to watch the dress rehearsal of *Cleopatra*. During their visit five different men have their way with the lead dancer – the Crissie of the title – in the same room, in the space of about thirty minutes.

The assumption throughout the book is that any woman involved in music hall is never more than a heartbeat away from sexual activity of the most salacious kind – thus reinforcing much of what the anti-music hall moralists were so concerned about. *Crissie* may have been a crude caricature for pornographic purposes, but for the reputation of music hall it was a caricature made damaging because it contained an element of truth. Little Dot Hetherington and her underaged sisters did sing songs totally inappropriate to their age, to a large adult audience. Moreover, music hall did titillate, and a minority of performers came close to prostitution, in fact if not in name. In 1894 the halls' perceived immorality would lead to one of the most serious attacks they ever faced.

18

Enterprise and Outrage

'Music Halls are the one great incubus that sits
on the souls of young and old England.'

SIR WILLIAM HARDMAN, BARRISTER,
JOURNALIST AND DIARIST (1828–90)

One evening in early 1894, two American tourists went to the music
hall performance at the Empire, Leicester Square. Like many
members of the audience they relaxed on the promenade, a semi-
circular walkway that divided the foyer from the dress circle. It was
a popular meeting place for the colonial officials, bohemians,
'enlightened' clergy, civil servants, young bloods and aristocrats,
many in evening dress and top hats, who formed the upmarket
clientèle of the theatre. There were tables and chairs, and liveried
waiters, resplendent in black, blue or gold, serving the new craze
from across the Atlantic – cocktails. It was an evening similar to any
other, but it became significant when the two men were propositioned by some women, and later complained about it to an English
friend.

Unfortunately for the Empire, that friend was the prominent
campaigner for women's rights and social reformer Mrs Laura
Ormiston Chant. She would not have been surprised at the incident. Six years earlier she had written reports on music halls for the
house magazine of the National Vigilance Association (NVA),

which she edited. She knew that many of them attracted prostitutes, and the relatively well-to-do clientèle of the Empire would have been seen as an enticing market. Mrs Ormiston Chant brooded over the complaint, but took no action. Then, in the summer, after adverse publicity about nearly-naked women (they would have been wearing flesh-coloured tights) featured in *tableaux vivants* at the Empire, she saw an opportunity to attack the seedy elements of music hall. It is likely that her intention was to reveal the extent to which theatres tolerated – and, she believed, encouraged – prostitution to boost their attendances and profits.

In 1894 the palatial Empire, with its rich decor, deep carpets, expensive hangings and general air of luxury, was *the* place to go for music hall. The biggest stars performed there: that year Marie Lloyd, Gus Elen, Yvette Guilbert, Eugene Stratton and Charles Coborn all appeared. Tickets were priced between sixpence for the gallery and three guineas for a box. Typically, the first half of the show featured popular music hall acts, while the second generally comprised an elegantly staged and beautifully danced ballet.

In the company of her friend the social reformer Lady Henry Somerset, leader of the Women's Christian Temperance Union, Mrs Ormiston Chant made five visits to the Empire in July and August, and satisfied herself that prostitutes regularly solicited on the promenade. She noted that when the near-naked *tableau vivant* displays were shown at 9 p.m., the promenade became flooded with women 'more or less gaudily dressed'. Both ladies witnessed these new arrivals approach men, accept drinks, and then depart with them in hansom cabs. They drew the obvious conclusion. In September the owners and managers of the Empire were preparing their annual application for the renewal of their Music and Dancing Licence when they received a letter from the NVA, signed by its leading members, including Mrs Ormiston Chant, informing them that they would be attending the hearing in October. The stage was set for a struggle between two classic Victorian instincts: the right of libertarian free trade and moral indignation.

Formed in 1885 after a 'national purity campaign' launched by the Salvation Army, the NVA was a formidable body containing many notable religious and moral crusaders, and could not safely be ignored. It was at the forefront of the war on vice in London, and had trenchant views on censorship, prostitution and alcohol. The music hall was a prime target.

The Empire had reason to worry. The London County Council (LCC), set up in 1889, was responsible for licensing halls, and it had proved much tougher than the magistrates: in its first two years it refused 93 per cent of licence applications from saloons. Reformers, Fabians, New Liberals and non-conformists were keen to purge London of 'drink and moral corruption', which they saw as the root of social unrest. These liberal-radicals, who could be relied upon to support the NVA, formed a majority of the Theatre and Music Hall Committee, which had already formed a sub-committee to examine the probity of the halls. Even more ominously for the Empire, the hardliners of the LCC saw music hall as a legitimate target. An LCC pamphlet, *Three Years' Good Work for the People*, had a section on 'Temperance Reform'. It boasted that the Council had 'prohibited drinking in the auditorium of theatres and music halls. It is not a pleasant arrangement for the audience that there should be a bar at the back of the pit.' The Empire was not facing an impartial judge.

The NVA was blunt in setting out its opposition to renewal of the Empire's licence: 'The place at night is the habitual resort of prostitutes in pursuit of their traffic, and that portions of the entertainment were objectionable, obnoxious and against the best interests of the community at large.' One dilemma for the Empire was that many accepted the caricature of the music halls' depravity without question. Less than twenty years before, an encyclopaedia had described music halls as 'cheap-priced places of entertainment' that were 'with few exceptions of an inferior and often of a vulgar type'.

Theatre-owners were used to receiving complaints: Marie Lloyd routinely attracted controversy, and *tableau vivant* displays were regarded with contempt by early feminists. But the NVA objected not only to the promenade's unofficial commerce, but to the content of the Empire's shows, by implication an attack on the management of the theatre.

George Edwardes, the managing director of the Empire, was no pushover. He ran the largest hall in the country – the Empire was so profitable that an enormous 75 per cent dividend had been paid to shareholders. In 1887 he had headed the syndicate that took it over. The theatre was his life, and his halls had glittered with entertainment of the highest quality. He was an extrovert, a *bon viveur*, a lover of horse-racing and gambling, and a man of many passions, with a fondness for women which may explain why he turned a blind eye to soliciting on the promenade. But Mrs Ormiston Chant was not daunted. To her, Edwardes was simply a publican with loose morals, a man who sold alcohol, staged immoral shows and harboured prostitutes. It was clear from the outset that no amicable compromise could be reached.

The Empire was fighting for its existence. The NVA regarded the promenade as facilitating prostitution, while the show onstage tacitly encouraged it. Superficially, the habitual presence of prostitutes soliciting theatre-goers seems indefensible, but it appears things were not entirely clear-cut. Winston Churchill wrote innocently in *My Early Life* (1930) that he and his Sandhurst friends used to visit the promenade twice a month, and 'were scandalised by Mrs. Chant's charges and insinuations', as they never saw 'anything to complain of in the behaviour of either sex' – except for the rough manner of the 'enormous' uniformed commissionaires whose duties included throwing out unruly cadets. Churchill's criticism was to be a significant factor in the hostility that history has heaped on Mrs Ormiston Chant.

But others saw what the young Churchill did not. No one denied that prostitutes regularly plied their trade on the Empire's promenade, as they did elsewhere, but the prominence of the Empire encouraged the NVA to single them out as an example. But these were not, it seems, the grubby, coarse girls of the streets. They were well-dressed, well-groomed and well-mannered. Their approaches were discreet, which may explain why Churchill and his young friends did not notice them. They didn't look out of place on the promenade, but seemed a natural part of it, adding glamour and no doubt a certain *frisson* to the largely male gathering. The music hall historian W.J. MacQueen-Pope described them as 'the aristocrats of their profession', and noted that 'some of them ... made good wives and mothers and married men they met on the Promenade'. In 1894 the Empire girls even featured in one of Marie Lloyd's songs, 'The Barmaid' by E.W. Rogers:

> For she's so gay, the men all say
> Awf'lly jolly girl, don't you think so?
> Tol-loll, then Poll, until tonight!
> The Empire? See you there? All right
> I never saw a lady wink so.

One curiosity of the NVA's campaign was that it focused only on the Empire's expensive second tier promenade, and not on the rent boys who solicited in the pit promenade and at the nearby Alhambra. It was boys recruited from these two halls who contributed to the conviction and imprisonment of Oscar Wilde for 'gross indecency' by testifying against him. They were less numerous than the girls, so it is possible, if unlikely, that the NVA was unaware of them; in any event, it ignored male prostitution in its opposition to the renewal of the Empire's licence.

The NVA's case against the Empire attracted a great deal of publicity. At the public hearing of the LCC Licensing Committee on Wednesday, 10 October 1894, the galleries were packed with supporters of both sides, members of the public and the press. The complaint against renewal – supported by the Salvation Army, bishops and other lobby groups – alleged that the Empire was 'the habitual resort of prostitutes ... and that portions of the entertainment were ... against the moral wellbeing of the community at large'. This line of attack was familiar. A decade earlier Frederick

Charrington had wanted to close down music halls, regarding their 'indecent dances and filthy songs' as the road to hell.

The NVA's argument was that prostitutes were admitted to the Empire's promenade without an entrance fee, and that this amounted to official endorsement of their presence. It may have been in the Empire's commercial interest to turn a blind eye, but there was no actual evidence of connivance by the management. It is more likely that doormen were tipped (or bribed) by the regular girls for giving them free entry to the promenade and auditorium.

Mrs Ormiston Chant spoke for the NVA, and put its case clearly and without undue emotion. Other witnesses were less effective. Mr Collins, a tea merchant, claimed to have visited the Empire twenty times in three months, and to have counted about 180 women of dubious character. How did he know their characters were dubious? And if he found them so objectionable, why did he keep returning? We can only guess.

Counsel for the Empire, Charles Gill, pursued three lines of argument. He began by painting the NVA as 'well meaning' but with 'violent and extreme' views. He then appealed to the commercial instinct of LCC members. The Empire, he said, was a legitimate investment that was hugely successful. How could it be against the moral well-being of the community when it was filled each night by members of that very community, who paid to enter? The subtext was that it was these very people who elected the LCC. His final strand appealed to populist sentiment: the campaigners were seeking to censure society as a whole, and should be resisted.

Having left the aggression to his legal representative, George Edwardes was sweet reason itself. He didn't deny that there were prostitutes at the Empire – that would not have been credible – but claimed that the theatre did all it could to observe propriety: it employed a former police inspector and several sergeants, some of whom kept a close watch on the promenade; and it did not tolerate prostitution. The girls who were soliciting, he said, had paid to get in like every other theatregoer: they were certainly not encouraged by the management.

It is doubtful if the advocacy of either side changed the view of any of the sixteen members of the Licensing Committee who were present. Opinions were fixed, and probably unchangeable. But the decision to favour enterprise or outrage was politically tricky, and it was no surprise when the committee's ruling was a classic fudge, that offered something for both sides. To the initial delight of Edwardes, the committee voted narrowly to renew the licence – but that renewal was made conditional upon the promenade being closed, and no more alcohol being served in the auditorium. The following day Edwardes gave notice of an appeal to the court, on the grounds that the LCC had no power to attach conditions to a licence renewal, and that some of the committee members had an undeclared conflict of interest. He then announced that if the Empire could not sell alcohol it would mean ruin, and the closure of the theatre. Days later, in order to ramp up the pressure on the LCC and to hammer home the threat, Edwardes gave fourteen days' formal notice of dismissal to 670 employees.

A debate raged. The unions, fearful of job losses, pitched in, with George Shipton, Secretary of the London Trades Council, calling the Licensing Committee decision 'a wanton piece of meddlesome cruelty'. Organised labour was united in backing the Empire, and was joined by liberal clergy such as Selwyn Image, who wrote to the *Pall Mall Gazette* warning of 'imminent disaster for the families of hundreds of hard-working men and women' put out of work. George Edwardes' threat of job losses was an emotive weapon in securing support. It was addressed to the public, not the court, but he had no doubt it would influence their decision.

The press backed the Empire all the way. The *Daily Telegraph*, after a patronising nod to the 'well-meaning ladies' of the NVA, argued that free association was an important issue, to be tampered with at peril. The campaigners were, it wrote, foolish to think they could 'suppress public thirst by forbidding wine and beer in a music hall, rebuke beauty and grace by lengthening skirts or eradicate the ancient and universal social evil by persecution and driving those who minister to it to seclusion and despair'.

On 13 October the *Telegraph*'s letters page featured some lively views, under the headline 'Prudes on the Prowl'. One correspondent saw the campaign against the Empire as 'tyranny of the worst, lowest and vilest description ... a vicious intolerance of personal liberty'. Another asked, none too innocently, 'whether every public space, railway station, place of worship need to be shut down, as that is where women congregated'. A 'Publican and Sinner' questioned the composition of the LCC Committee. So did 'A.B.' and 'Anglo-Indian', the latter urging electors to 'throw them out' in favour of 'a sensible set of men who know the world and human nature'. 'Anti-Humbug' noted that he had seen prostitutes in church, and wondered if churches ought to be shut down. 'Honi Soit' said he 'had taken his wife to the promenade and not been accosted', while 'C.V.H.' claimed to have been propositioned fifteen times. He should perhaps have taken his wife. 'Loather of Humbug' felt that anyone objecting to the *tableaux vivants* was guilty of 'hopeless and ignorant fanaticism'. His argument was that since these establishments were tolerated, why pick on the Empire? 'M.F.' reminded readers of the notorious 'semi-tolerated brothels' that posed as nightclubs, and noted: 'Within a hundred yards of The Empire Theatre ... there exist a dozen of these night hells ... at these dens the licensing laws are openly defied ... the lowest form of human scum gather.' The *Telegraph* pitched in with an editorial on 15 October telling its readers that closing the Empire would mean the West End would once more become 'a howling wilderness of brazen faced women'. It was not clear why this would be so, but in defending the Empire hyperbole was in fashion.

The National Vigilance Association had its supporters, but if they wrote to the popular press, few of their letters were published. Nonetheless, their arguments were well represented in letters to the LCC and their own in-house publications. Peter Thompson, chairman of the Wesleyan East End Mission, had seen at first hand the effect of prostitution, and compared the alluring girls at the Empire with their older sisters, 'forced on to the streets as [their] only promenade', the older women abandoned to become 'the hopeless,

homeless, houseless hags of Whitechapel': no doubt he had in mind
Jack the Ripper's reign of terror only six years earlier. Thompson
then turned to an issue largely ignored by the press, but of crucial
concern to George Edwardes – the profits of the Empire. He
dismissed Edwardes' actions in giving notice to his employees as 'a
hollow farce', argued that tolerance of prostitutes was about profit,
not personal liberty, and claimed that the famous 75 per cent dividend paid to the Empire's shareholders 'depends solely not on the
excellence and interest in the entertainment but upon the
Promenade with women and wine'. He overstated his case, as did
nearly everyone involved, but his arguments united the critics of
the theatre.

Although many of her opponents lampooned Mrs Ormiston
Chant as a self-righteous, narrow-minded prude, her strongly held
views were based not on abstract notions of propriety, but on her
own life experience. Born in 1848, Laura Ormiston formed the
ambition to become a missionary nurse, rather than follow the
conventional path of a young woman of her time and background.
This so upset her strong-willed father that he banned her from the
family home. Over the next few years she worked as a nurse at the
London Hospital, Whitechapel, and thereafter as a matron at a
lunatic asylum. These experiences strengthened her determination
to improve the lot of the disadvantaged.

In 1877 her marriage to Thomas Chant, a surgeon she had met
at the London Hospital, gave her the freedom to pursue her convic-
tions more fully. She joined groups campaigning for social reform,
pressed for amendments to the criminal law and was active in
efforts to curb the spread of venereal disease. Her opposition to
prostitution was based not only on moral outrage but on public
health and a desire to counter the abuse of women. A forceful
speaker, she was a delegate at the first International Council for
Women in 1888. Whether Mrs Ormiston Chant was right or wrong
in her campaign against the Empire, her case was far more substantial than her detractors allowed, and she deserves to be remembered
more positively than as a mere killjoy. Many sneered and scoffed,

but none of them addressed the wider concerns she represented. She was a principled and strong-willed woman, with the courage not to be deterred.

The controversy over the Empire produced some interesting subtexts. After the NVA activist and white slave trade reformer W.A. Coote tried to draw a distinction between nudes in art (uplifting) and the *tableaux vivants* (depraving), George Bernard Shaw defended the *tableaux vivants* in the *Saturday Review* as 'living' and 'human'. He went on: 'Human nature and the human body are to [Coote] nasty things. Sex is a scourge. Woman is a walking temptation which should be covered up as much as possible.' Coote, concluded Shaw, was wrong to make nudity, or semi-nudity, the criterion of indecency.

A great deal of personal scorn was directed at Mrs Ormiston Chant. *Punch* lampooned her as 'Prowlina Pry', and Arthur Roberts, starring in the burlesque *Claude du Val* at the Prince of Wales Theatre, sang:

> Prudes on the prowl, boys! Down with their cant!
> Down with the sneak who has eyes but won't see!
> Let us march onwards with this for a Chant!
> Let them be Puritans! We will be free!

He was not alone. In the song 'New Women', the normally affable Herbert Campbell, cruelly dressed in deliberately mannish costume, mocked:

> Oh! A woman is an artful card
> If she mayn't promenade
> If Mrs. Ormiston has to chant
> Let her chant in her own back yard.

She did – but not always to good effect. In an interview with the hostile *Pall Mall Gazette* she so overestimated the likely earnings of prostitution that George Bernard Shaw observed that it would create 'more prostitutes in a week than [the *tableaux*] in ten years'. She was on firmer ground in the *Daily Telegraph* on 18 October in remarking that the controversy over *tableaux* would be resolved swiftly if men, not women, were on display.

The LCC Main Committee met on Friday, 26 October, and endorsed the decision of the subcommittee, passing by a two-to-one majority, but with many abstentions, the banning of alcohol and the closure of the promenade. George Edwardes, knowing the support he had among opinion-formers and influential habitués of the Empire, reacted boldly, delivering a dramatic speech to a packed theatre in which he declared he had been laid low by progressive moralists – cries of 'Foul bigots!' and 'Shame!' erupted from the audience – and was closing the theatre from 27 October to 3 November, presumably so he could erect trellis screens to block the view of the stage from the promenade.

On 8 November the High Court rejected the Empire's appeal in every particular, but Winston Churchill recalls in *My Early Life* that on the night it reopened following alterations, the trellis screens were soon demolished by vigorous kicks from enraged supporters of the theatre: Churchill claimed to have made his 'maiden speech' from atop the wreckage, after which the crowd dispersed into the streets, bearing fragments of the screens as souvenirs. The bars of the Empire were closed, and brass railings replaced the screens.

Public reaction against Mrs Ormiston Chant was very strong, and she acknowledged that many saw her as 'an imperious, sour-visaged, unhappy, wretched, miserable Puritan'. If such frankness was an attempt to capture hearts and minds, it failed: on Guy Fawkes' Night 1894 hers was the effigy most commonly burned.

Sometimes what she said – and how she said it – did not help either her or her cause. A year after the hearing she published a justification of the NVA's campaign in a pamphlet, *Why we Attacked the Empire*, which did her much harm: 'The Secretary of the London Trades Council placed himself and his supporters on the side of the money men, the greedy capitalist, the monopolist, the heartless, fashionable ruffian who employs the pimp and the procuress ... and all the conscienceless crew ...'

This was simply not true. The Council had supported the Empire because it feared for the jobs of its members, not to protect the dividends of investors. Mrs Ormiston Chant should have understood this. She asserted that she was not trying to close music halls down, but to put a stop to a double standard: 'We have no right to sanction on stage that which, if done on the street, would compel a policeman to lock the offender up.' It was a trite point, and far from the best she could have made. Her case had merit, but her *post-hoc* justifications were defensive and weak, and explain some of the hostility she attracted. In an absurd and objectionable speech to the Playgoers' Club she said: 'The music hall supplies a class of entertainment to suit people who, out of sheer tiredness of brain or want of a superior education, could hardly appreciate a play ... The music hall caters for people who have a small proportion of brains.' This was received with laughter and cries of 'No!'; one magazine described the speech as 'a Sunday Night farce, the all-pervading motive of which was self-advertisement'. In the summer of 1895 Mrs Ormiston Chant sailed to America on a speaking tour, encouraged on her way with the bitter comment of the *Pall Mall Gazette* that she left England amid 'the jeers of its inhabitants'. She never forgave the *Gazette* for that remark.

On 25 October 1895, while she was still overseas, the LCC retreated fully from its earlier policy, permitting the Empire to reopen the promenade with no restrictions, on the fatuous grounds that as behaviour had not improved, they might just as well be lifted. On 3 December the LCC permitted the alterations to the promenade to be reversed, and within weeks all trace of them had gone. The ladies of the promenade returned in force. One reason for the *volte face* was that at the LCC elections of March 1895 many of the opponents of music hall had lost their seats. The *Era* scoffed: 'The Music Hall proprietors have a very strong ally in the public whose opinion ... was expressed in no uncertain voice at the County Council elections.' The NVA continued its campaigns: in

1896 the Oxford was its target, but its case had lost much of its force.

Throughout the rest of her life, Mrs Ormiston Chant remained an active campaigner for temperance, women's suffrage and – far ahead of her time – for the ordination of women. She had four children, and died at home in Oxfordshire in 1923, aged seventy-four.

Music hall had seen off a dangerous threat, but as it did so it failed to anticipate its real nemesis. Ironically, the very next year the Empire screened 'moving pictures' to fill in the time between acts, and to demonstrate that it was fully up to date with every novelty in entertainment. No one realised that these innocent-looking, flickering black-and-white images would one day help to bring about the death of music hall.

19

Overseas Music Hall

'Every crowd has a silver lining.'

PHINEAS T. BARNUM (1810–91)

The image of music hall is as a phenomenon of Victorian Britain: home-grown, inward-looking, boisterous and rowdy, and blossoming outwards from the East End of London. This cosy picture has some merit, but is far from the whole truth. The essential elements of music hall were copied overseas, refined and re-imported. Other aspects were born in France and the United States. This interchange of ideas and talent accelerated as long-distance travel became easier, and artistes, styles of entertainment and even business models crossed the Channel and the Atlantic. Entrepreneurs and performers learned that what worked in London was likely to be well received in Paris and New York. American black-faced minstrels, from T. D. 'Daddy' Rice, who created the 'Jim Crow' character, onwards enjoyed huge success in England, while British stars such as Annie Adams, Little Tich, Alice Lloyd, Lottie Collins and, above all, Harry Lauder played across continents, winning huge acclaim and lavish salaries. This cross-pollination influenced new forms of entertainment out of which would spring revues, vaudeville and styles of performance that survive today.

*

Café concerts, immortalised in paint by Monet and Degas, were an indigenous French entertainment that were music hall in all but name. Degas' *Café Concert at Les Ambassadeurs* (1876) depicts the performers in evening dress, with a backdrop of pretty girls in lieu of scenery and costume. The first cafés concerts were open-air cafés chantants that offered singing as entertainment. By 1870 a number had become well-known: Le Pavilion, l'Horloge, Eldorado, Le Bataclan, La Scala and, most famous of all, Les Folies Bergère, which began in 1869 as a large café with a small stage at 32, rue Richer in Paris, and adopted aspects of music hall from the outset. Its sexually adventurous spectacles like the can-can were more racy than British music hall, and soon attracted the young bachelors whose successors still flock to it today. The cafés concerts' inexpensive food and drink, light-hearted entertainment and conviviality were in the classic music hall tradition. Ticket prices were a modest two and a half francs for the larger and better establishments.

The cafés concerts sprang from the earlier tradition of cafés dansants, that featured dancing, or cafés chantants. There is evidence that the original idea for cafés dansants was the brainchild of an Englishman, a Mr Tinkson, who set up a small garden and bar in Montparnasse – then a small village to the south of Paris – in 1793. Tinkson was probably trying to replicate the success of English pleasure gardens such as Vauxhall and Ranelagh. He offered a semi-rural idyll with a suitably rustic name: La Chaumière, a thatched cottage. La Chaumière was a summer venue only, where bourgeois and working-class customers could drink and dance in attractive surroundings and enjoy cheap and informal entertainment. Such establishments spread, and became known as *guinguettes* after the cheap local white wine that was served. Tax on food and drink was lower on the outskirts of Paris, and hundreds of *guinguettes* flourished as city dwellers deserted the centre of the capital for an inexpensive day or evening in the countryside. Both Renoir and Van Gogh painted pictures of the relaxing pleasures they offered.

After the success of La Chaumière, other cafés dansants began to open, some of which offered all-year-round entertainment indoors rather than *al fresco*. The Prado, established near Notre Dame in 1810, led the way, and was followed by many imitators. By 1850, *guinguettes* were common in Paris. Among the better-known were Le Jardin Mabrille and Le Château des Fleurs, which offered dancing and drinking in the summer, and Le Casino Cadet, which was open in winter and featured two orchestras, a smoking room, galleries, bars and a promenade which was a frequent abode of prostitutes. Charles Morton would have approved – except, perhaps, for the promenade.

At about this time, cafés chantants began to become more popular than their *dansant* rivals. One of the first was Le Café des Aveugles, which was named after its resident blind band, but also featured singers, comedians and magicians. It was an instant hit with chic Parisians. A similar but less fashionable venue was l'Estaminet Lyrique, where a young tenor, Darcier, sang his own songs and became a city favourite. Paris was soon alive with cafés chantants. The public were able to enter without an admission charge, but were expected to order food and drink without delay before settling down to enjoy the likes of Darcier, or comic singers such as Emma Valadon – immortalised in paint by Degas – and Anne Judic, who was famous for *double-entendres* made more shocking by her youthful and innocent appearance. Such artistes were supported by a variety of comics, jugglers, acrobats and conjurers.

In these early pre-café concert days the performers were not paid by the management, but earned their fees from their audience, who contributed to a collecting tin that circulated after each act. It was a precarious existence even for the better-known performers. The managers soon learned how to maximise profits: the audience were expected to eat and drink continually, or leave, and the most popular acts were held back until late in the evening.

Mirroring Britain, the cafés chantants fused with an earlier tradition of '*caveaux*', which were very similar to the catch and glee clubs that merged into music hall. These had been popular among the professional and mercantile classes of Paris since the 1740s, and folded easily into the newly popular *chantants* to create the soon-to-be-famous cafés concerts.

Café concert shows were often raw and, to judge by an entry in Edmund Goncourt's journal, very similar to early music hall. Goncourt paints a vivid picture of a visit to the Eldorado in 1865:

> [It was] dazzlingly lit by chandeliers, with a café in the middle, the men's black hats, working-class women in their bonnets, soldiers, schoolboys, with peaked caps, a few hats worn by tarts accompanying shopmen; the visible breath of all this crowd, a dusty cloud of tobacco smoke. At the back of the hall, a stage with footlights; on it a comic in evening dress. He sang … interrupted by clucking … in a farmyard – the St. Vitus dance of an idiot. In the hall, delirious enthusiasm.

With not-so-gentle prodding from the ever-vigilant authorities, the cafés concerts soon became gentrified, while an earthier version of their entertainment became popular with the working classes. Raucous and raunchy, '*gogettes*', as they were known, were often highly political, and would cruelly lampoon authority with ribald lyrics set to popular tunes. The authorities resented this impertinence, and after the *coup d'état* in 1851 Napoleon III's government was swift to protect its dignity whenever an artiste went too far. It was particularly severe on vulgarity, although this was generally tolerated on the legitimate stage, with its more sophisticated audiences. An article in the British stage periodical the *Era* in December 1872 is indicative of contemporary attitudes:

> [*Gogettes*] are now in hot water with the police authorities, and a new and stringent code of rules has been forced upon them. The songs had approached the highest pitch of immorality, no sacred or refined subjects being free from the ruthless attacks of the writers … The programme … has to be submitted each day to a comptroller, and once approved, must be rigorously adhered to. All the double entendre songs … are ruthlessly tabooed … these

merry and improper ballads can be allowed only in a Theatre, because the Music Halls are frequented by loose characters, and the entertainments presented should aim at elevating their minds and not try to debase them still more by pampering to their depraved tastes.

All of this was absurdly patronising: in short, the riff-raff must be protected from themselves. It was, however, a convenient stick with which the authorities could beat the *gogettes* and gradually shut them down. But they left a legacy. In the hands of the bohemian artist Rodolphe Salis they would be transmuted into 'cabaret' (the term is derived from a word for a kind of informal tavern) at his club Le Chat Noir, which opened in 1881. Le Chat Noir was part bar, part gallery, part club and part music hall, and these attributes, together with its iconic poster art, all contributed to making it a fashionable spot.

By the mid-1870s, sumptuous new versions of the cafés concerts were, to all intents and purposes, music halls. From the 1880s onwards many of the most popular French performers, like the singers Paulus and Eugénie Buffet, or the mime specialist Felicia Mallet, imitated the stridency of British music hall. Others, especially in the larger theatres, focused on everyday subjects familiar to their audience, such as the new-fangled railways, telegraphs and the Eiffel Tower: their style was wistful and romantic rather than satirical or ribald. This too mirrored British music hall.

In 1886 a new format was unveiled at Les Folies Bergère. Called the 'Revue à Grand Spectacle', it was probably inspired by developments in New York theatre. It was effectively 'variety theatre', with lavish sets and huge casts, and was soon copied at other large theatres like the La Scala, Eldorado, Le Nouveau Cirque, l'Olympia and the Alhambra, set up by British impresario Tom Barrasford, who was trying to avoid being squeezed out by the Stoll and Moss syndicates in England. Most of these spectacles, which borrowed the concept of a chairman-like compère from England, were simple stories played against extravagant sets, with various acts slotted rather unconvincingly into the drama. The French managers had expansive ideas, staging fights between cowboys and Indians, introducing sumptuous backdrops and flooding their stages with water. This new genre did not last long. As in Britain, fire and safety regulations, planning requirements and customer demands for wider aisles and more comfortable seats ate into profitability. The result was that many venues disappeared or became cabarets, backstreet dance halls or, in the early decades of the twentieth century, cinemas.

In Paris, public taste was moving towards more intimate theatre, and one feature of the new Revue à Grand Spectacle took root: nudity. It began with the Bal de Quat'z Arts at the Moulin Rouge dance hall, but did not transfer to either Britain or America, where a more puritan ethic held sway. Shows which had formerly featured 'tasteful' *tableaux vivants*, long familiar to British audiences in some of the sleazier halls, began to show female artistes 'Taking a Bath', 'Going to the Doctor' and 'Getting Ready for Bed'. One performer, Augèle Hérard, performed 'The Flea', which involved her searching *very* thoroughly for the cause of her itch. By the First World War nudity was a staple of the bill at the Folies Bergère and other big theatres, and it has remained so ever since.

Despite the decline of cafés concerts and 'big spectacles', France produced a stream of stars over many years who became internationally famous. The singer, actor and raconteur Maurice Chevalier was a popular compère, and Yvette Guilbert charmed audiences everywhere, while Mistinguett, Madame Mealy and La Belle Otero were among the many others who were successful.

Max Linder, a modest French music hall performer, wrote, directed and starred in over two hundred silent films, and gave Maurice Chevalier his first role. He was famous for his hopeless hobo routine, which Charlie Chaplin saw in Paris in the early 1900s. So similar were their acts that when Chaplin left Essanay Studios in 1916, Linder was signed as a replacement. Sadly, he was not a success, and committed suicide in Paris.

If Chaplin appropriated the mannerisms of other performers, he wasn't alone. Britain, France and America were united in their love of Lottie Collins' risqué interpretation of the song and dance 'Ta-ra-ra Boom-de-ay'. Collins heard the song in America, and embroidered it with a new can-can-like dance during the chorus. It became a huge hit. Telling the story of a 'nice' young girl who prefers 'boom-de-ay' with nice young men to the company of her staid parents or grammar lessons, it clearly struck a chord across continents, although in Paris the chorus was changed to 'Tha-ma-ra boom-di-hé'. The lyrics of the French version had the girl preferring to dance the '*chahut*', a wildly popular can-can performed at the Moulin Rouge.

In America, brilliant showmen took elements of their own home-grown popular entertainments, melded them with elements of other traditions like music hall, and gave birth to a form of variety shows that became known as vaudeville. The source of the term is obscure: it could be derived from *voix de ville* (voice of the city), but no one really knows. It was used in the United States in the 1830s, but only became widespread forty years later, after the formation of a troupe called 'Sargent's Great Vaudeville Company' in Kentucky in the early 1870s. Vaudeville spawned stars of the calibre of W.C. Fields, the Marx Brothers, Bob Hope, Charlie Chaplin, Stan Laurel, Fred Astaire, Al Jolson, Irving Berlin and Eddie Cantor – and that list is far from exhaustive.

Modern vaudeville sprang from concert saloons, dime museums, burlesque, freak shows, minstrel shows and British music hall, and crystallised in New York from the middle of the nineteenth century. Concert saloons in the city catered to a working-class male audience mainly clustered in the Irish and German immigrant areas around the notorious Bowery, on the Lower East Side of Manhattan. Its near neighbours were Chinatown and Little Italy, which suffered a reputation for gang violence and lawlessness.

Concert saloons were part bar, part theatre, often part brothel, very rowdy, and at the heart of the prelude to vaudeville. They were the equivalent of the boisterous tavern theatres that preceded music hall in Britain. They employed 'waiter girls', often off-duty dancers seeking to boost their income, encouraging the customers to buy drinks and cigars while enjoying the comics, magicians, acrobats and dancers and, if the girls were willing, more basic pleasures too. The performers battled against the bustle and noise, with the comics poking fun at Irish and German stereotypes. Their efforts were often in vain, for the entertainment was merely a backcloth to the drinking.

Another popular, and sleazy, form of entertainment was the dime museums, which flourished in towns and cities across America for thirty years after 1840. These palaces of bad taste charged ten cents (a dime) for entrance, and were a mixture of self-improvement, light entertainment and ghoulish voyeurism. Most offered lectures and entertainment in small auditoriums. They also had rooms full of jars of pickled animals and body parts, and live animals such as monkeys. The tasteless displays of the dime museums would become the appalling freak shows that exhibited the deformed, the odd and the sad. They must have been pitiful spectacles. Many of the exhibits were fakes, but the public flocked to gape and laugh at bearded ladies, hermaphrodites, conjoined twins and three-legged people.

Despite the success of this cruel entertainment, the American middle classes were essentially conservative by nature, and smart managers saw that the greatest potential for profit lay in good, clean, family entertainment, perhaps with a bit of self-improvement thrown in. The man who most clearly saw the future was Phineas T. Barnum, self-styled 'Greatest Showman of All Time', and the future he saw included no alcoholic drinks, no waiter girls, no fist fights and no crude and salacious displays.

The displays that Barnum envisaged were of natural wonders with singing, dancing, magicians, acrobats, comics with family appeal and, Barnum being Barnum, anything else that attracted the crowds. His two great gifts were his legendary flair for publicity and his raw business acumen. Like Charles Morton in England, he spotted that the saloon-bar model of business excluded families, and planned to extract entrance fees from men, women and their children. By doing so he would also avoid the attentions of the authorities, whose disapproval of waiter girls was growing.

Barnum began in 1841 by buying Scudder's, a failing New York dime museum, and converting it to his new idea. It was phenomenally successful, with over a million customers a year paying twenty-five cents admission. In the promotion of his performers Barnum dealt only in superlatives. One of his first triumphs was the Swedish singer Jenny Lind, who, he proclaimed, had 'vocal powers never approached by any other human being'. Bowing to God and the American way, he added that her character was 'charity, simplicity and goodness personified'. Since her voice more than lived up to expectation, queues stretched around the block to hear this extraordinary talent.

In 1864 and 1872 legislation, in the form of Concert Bills, sought to curb the activities of the concert saloons. Only two of alcohol, staged performances or waiter girls were permitted in the same establishment. Although the restrictions were ignored at first, they eventually took root, and forced most of the concert saloons out of business after a crackdown in 1886. This left many managers facing a choice that greatly boosted vaudeville. Legitimate theatre was expensive, with tickets at $15 a show, which priced most people out of attending. Dime museums were cheap, but were becoming passé. The gap was filled by vaudeville, for which tickets were modestly priced. Moreover, catering for a mixed-gender audience in halls that did not offer alcohol, and from which bawdy material was generally barred, it was popular among the middle classes.

Vaudeville grew rapidly in New York as the city's population boomed. Its story is littered with charlatans, crooks and self-publicists. It created fortunes for some and ruin for others. During its lifespan, America developed from a frontier nation to an unrivalled industrial giant. It catered for a wide range of tastes, with a typical bill including up to a dozen acts. Comedians and vocalists, often operatic singers, were standard fare, as were dancers, acrobats and jugglers. Acts that failed were given short shrift. 'Burk and Andreus and Their Trained Mule' did not go down well at the Temple

Theatre, Detroit, in December 1902, and the manager's report to his circuit office was blunt: 'This act, if it can be so classed, was closed after the evening performance.' Perhaps the mule was not house-trained – we will never know.

The 'fathers' of vaudeville were the impresarios Edward Albee (adoptive grandfather of the playwright), Benjamin Keith, John Koster, Albert Bial and Tony Pastor. Pastor is credited with inventing vaudeville in 1881, at his 14th Street Theatre in the heart of New York, close to Union Square. As with Morton and music hall, it is an attractive myth, but is not to be taken too seriously. Many of the trailblazers had worked for Barnum, and they pioneered a sanitised, family-friendly version of the concert saloons. The entertainment was similar in nature to that of British music hall, but the experience was packaged to maximise profit and minimise official interference: no alcohol was permitted in the auditorium, and there were continuous performances throughout the day, an innovation Stoll would try unsuccessfully to introduce at the Coliseum twenty years later. As one show ended another began: five or six performances a day was normal.

The schedule of acts was planned to maximise continuity. Shows opened with visual, non-speaking performers – acrobats, jugglers or animal acts – while the audience were taking their seats, and closed with the poorest acts, which were most likely to encourage the audience to leave. Smartly dressed bouncers were on hand to quell any hint of rowdiness. Tickets were inexpensive: most of the smaller houses kept to the familiar 'dime' for entrance. The larger houses had bigger audiences and bigger stars, but even so, entrance was only a modest $1.50. This was the origin of the phrases 'small time' and 'big time', and Tony Pastor was the king of big time. Fashionable New York attended his shows, and he is immortalised in Jerry Herman and Michael Stewart's 1964 musical *Hello, Dolly!* with the line 'We'll join the Astors at Tony Pastor's'.

Like Charles Morton, Pastor was very popular with performers because he treated them well and paid them generously. As vaudeville grew, he was one of the larger-than-life managers who dominated American show business: Oscar Hammerstein (grand-father of one of the world's most successful librettists), F.F. Proctor, Sylvester Poli and M.B. Leavitt all challenged Pastor, Keith and Koster and Bial for supremacy. To attract custom, many theatres included well-appointed lounges and bars (separate, of course, from the auditorium), restaurants and bowling alleys. While Pastor focused on quality and stayed in New York, a number of his rivals spread their activities across the country. They set up the Vaudeville Managers' Association, a cartel dominated by Benjamin Keith and Edward Albee, and rotated performers around vast theatre circuits to keep programmes fresh and attractive. The crowds rolled in.

The search for talent was relentless. Much of it was imported from Britain – the singers Annie Adams and Marie Loftus led the way, but a host of others soon followed. Oscar Hammerstein booked Dan Leno, who loved the experience but never repeated it. On his heels came Vesta Tilley, Vesta Victoria, Albert Chevalier, Lottie Collins, Little Tich, Marie Lloyd and her sister Alice, who was more successful than her risqué sibling, whose act was rather too raunchy for American tastes. Charlie Chaplin came over as a member of Fred Karno's troupe, little knowing the fame America would one day offer him.

The Chinese illusionist Ching Ling Foo was a popular visitor, and France contributed Yvette Guilbert and later Maurice Chevalier. There was also plenty of home-grown talent: Harry Houdini, Fanny Brice, the Three Keatons, Bill 'Bojangles' Robinson, Jimmy Durante, William and Walker (absurdly made up in 'black-face', as they were African-Americans). While home-grown acts were expected to be squeaky clean, French and British imports were given more licence. The Americans thought degeneracy was a European disease – in the case of some of the Parisian performers, not without cause. All performers in Benjamin Keith's theatres were left in no doubt what was acceptable: 'Don't be a slob', 'son of a gun' and 'holy gee' were among the innocuous phrases that earned instant dismissal if used onstage, and a Notice to Performers warned: 'If [performers] utter anything sacrilegious or even suggestive, [they] will be immediately

closed and will never again be allowed in a theatre where Mr. Keith
is in authority.' Nor was Keith the fiercest Puritan. F.F. Proctor, who
liked to call his productions 'polite vaudeville', sacked performers
for swearing offstage, or if they were caught drinking off-duty in a
saloon. If such strictures had applied in Britain, many of the greatest stars would soon have disappeared into oblivion.

Vaudeville's lifespan was a mere half-century. Its high noon was
shorter than that of music hall, and its decline was hastened by one
of Britain's greatest exports. Harry Lauder was wildly popular in
America as a result of recordings of songs in the early 1890s that
had preceded him across the Atlantic. On his New York debut he
overran his scheduled act by an hour as the audience demanded
more. Their enthusiasm never waned, and Lauder would tour
America more than twenty times, making him a very rich man.

As gramophone recordings and inexpensive radio receivers
became more widely available, the appeal of live performances
diminished. These were not the only factors contributing to the
decline of vaudeville. By 1905 costs had soared, and ticket prices
were spiralling beyond the reach of the mass audience. New and
inexpensive alternatives were explored, and penny arcades with slot
machines and nickelodeons (the slot version of motion pictures)
began to take root. They were followed by the arrival of the cinema,
and by 1915 the brief golden age of vaudeville was over. It lingered
on in an ever-decreasing number of theatres in the big cities, but as
its stars committed their acts to celluloid, they hastened its end.
Vaudeville was finally laid to rest in November 1932, when New
York's famous Palace Theatre, the heart of vaudeville, was converted
to a cinema.

It was as if the whole vaudeville establishment simply decamped
to films. In 1920 Marcus Loew, 'the king of small time', bought
Metro Pictures, and four years later joined Samuel Goldwyn
(formerly Goldfish) and Louis B. Mayer to create Metro Goldwyn
Mayer. Loews' old partner Adolf Zukor joined up with Sam
Goldwyn's brother-in-law Jesse Lasky and then a distribution
company to form Paramount. In 1913 vaudeville entrepreneur

William Fox bought a chain of theatres from Sylvester Poli to screen movies, and two years later went into production with Fox Film Corporation. Within a decade he had joined Twentieth Century Films to form Twentieth Century-Fox. Keith and Albee's failing vaudeville chain re-emerged as Radio-Keith-Orpheum Pictures, better known as RKO. The new company went on to epitomise Hollywood glamour with a string of hits in the 1930s starring the popular vaudeville act Fred Astaire with his new partner, Ginger Rogers. Many more of the new movie sensations – Buster Keaton, Roscoe ('Fatty') Arbuckle, Rudolph Valentino, Mae West and Lon Chaney – came from vaudeville.

One young British music hall artiste epitomised the exodus from live variety to film. Charles Spencer Chaplin was born in London on 16 April 1889. He began his music hall career at the age of five, by being pushed onto the stage from the wings at the Alexandra Music Hall, Aldershot, when his mother was booed off it. Ill health stifled her career, but her gift for mimicry was passed on to her son, who had a taste for the theatre, and a talent for comedy.

Chaplin came from a music hall family, and from the age of nine was given a unique schooling in popular performance art thanks to family friend William Jackson and his 'Eight Lancashire Lads' clog-dancing troupe. For two and a half years Chaplin toured with Jackson, playing most of the significant halls in London and the provinces. In the process he shared the bill with the biggest stars of the day. Night after night he was able to observe these acts at very close quarters, much as Little Tich had done. He saw for himself how the likes of G.H. Chirgwin, George Robey, Dan Leno, Bransby Williams – and Tich himself – cast their spell over audiences wherever they played.

Chaplin soon put his scholarship to work. After stints in various troupes, he settled on Will Murray's 'Casey's Circus', which he later described as 'low vulgar comedy in dirty fourth rate houses'. Murray wanted to lampoon other performers, and asked Chaplin to impersonate the fake mesmerist Dr Walford Bodie. Chaplin spent hours rehearsing Bodie's mannerisms, to the point that he had the act perfectly honed. 'The more serious I was, the funnier it struck the audience. I had made a hit,' he recalled later.

Casey's circus folded in 1907, and soon afterwards Chaplin joined his brother in Fred Karno's 'Speechless Comedians' company. He took part in several sketches, one of which was 'The Mumming Birds', a music hall act within a music hall act: for Chaplin, this would prove to be a life-changing performance. In the sketch, a music hall audience endures a truly awful bill of dire performers. Within the 'audience', Chaplin played 'an inebriated swell', stumbling around while taking his seat, lighting cigarettes, and eventually falling out of his box. Company member Stan Laurel called it 'one of the most fantastically funny acts ever known'. In this instance we are lucky, in that most of the sketch can still be seen today, in the 1925 film *A Night in the Show*.

In 1909 Karno's company would be in Paris, and the following year in America, where it toured the show until 1912. It was during the US tour that Mack Sennett saw 'The Mumming Birds' (or 'A Night in an English Music Hall', as it was called in America). He loved Chaplin's performance, and in 1913 signed him up for $150 a week. They made their first film together, *Making a Living*, in January 1914, followed swiftly by many more.

Some have seen Chaplin as something of an unwitting 'praying mantis' of music hall, using every aspect of it to forge his own career, only to play a central role in its death. It is easy to see why that impression was created: born into the profession, he went from street performer to Leno-esque clog dancer, to Tich-esque performance scholar, to Bransby Williams-esque impersonator (of a music hall artiste), to a classic music hall persona: the drunken 'swell'. He then went into film – the medium that took the heart out of the halls – only to play that same drunken swell in a film about music hall ...

Be that as it may, no one would deny that he was – and remains – one of the greatest comedy talents of all time, and cinema's first global superstar.

20

Music Hall War

'Elephants or pictures? Elephants?'
'Yes! Yes! Yes!'
'Very well, we will put on the elephants again.'

THE MANAGER OF THE SOUTH LONDON MUSIC HALL TO THE
AUDIENCE AS THE 1907 STRIKE BEGINS TO BITE

Music hall performers worked long and unsocial hours for pay which, for most of them, was not very high. They did so because they were dedicated to their chosen career, even though onstage frivolity often concealed a hard life. The grim reality was a constant battle for jobs, for new material, for better slots on the bill and, when touring, the hard slog of uncomfortable travel and modest lodgings. Despite these hardships, most artistes lived for applause, and were content to settle for a small wage, rather than no wage at all.

Often they had little choice. Theatre-owners like Oswald Stoll, Walter Gibbons, George Adney Payne and Frank McNaughton were hard taskmasters who were economically astute and brooked no opposition. It was they who decided the level of pay, the length of the contract, and even imposed restrictions on lifestyle: no drinking, no bad language, no misbehaviour.

Not every artiste was at a disadvantage. Crowd-pullers like Lloyd and Leno, Little Tich, Robey and Tilley were able to dictate terms, but down-the-bill performers struggled for a fair wage in a business relentlessly focused on profit. Managers would only pay the minimum, and since the implied threat of choosing someone else for a given slot was potent, the minimum was sufficient. After all, hard-nosed managers reasoned, if Little Tich topped the bill, who came to see the supporting acts?

Many performers lived on hope as much as money. In 1900, at the lower end of the spectrum, an act might earn £3–5 a week, broadly similar to the wage of a skilled lower-middle-class artisan. Middle-ranking acts, rising up the bill or falling from the top, could expect £10–40 a week, while the top-of-the-bill headliners could earn in excess – sometimes well in excess – of £100 a week.

The performer's pound had to go a long way: it had to pay for lodgings, food, rates, clothes, costumes and possibly family expenses. Budgets were tight for the unsuccessful: they did receive help with travel costs, but only after the Music Hall Artistes' Railway Association lobbied the railway companies for discounted fares in the late 1890s.

In the heyday of music hall most acts were booked on a weekly basis, which offered minimal job security, and even for this short time contracts were impossible to enforce. If a booking was arbitrarily cancelled, there was no redress. If additional performances were demanded, there was little choice but to comply: artistes who refused or asked for extra pay were not rebooked. If they were badly treated, they couldn't afford to go to court. In June 1887 Gus Elen wrote to the *Era* detailing a long-standing contract that had been cancelled with a telegram: 'Shall not expect you; Business bad.' Elen received no compensation.

But the old order was gradually changing. On 18 February 1906 the underprivileged toilers of music hall banded together to form their own union, the Variety Artists' Federation (VAF), registered as Trade Union No. 1378. The first member to pay his shilling fee – immediately thereafter increased to half a crown – was the Irish comic singer and dancer Joe O'Gorman. Within a year the membership of the VAF had risen to 3,799, and music hall was bracing itself for its first full-scale strike.

The showdown was foreshadowed by small but vigorous skirmishes. In late 1906 Walter Gibbons, owner of the Brixton Empress, bought the nearby Brixton Theatre. To boost his profits he pressed the cast of the Empress to appear at both theatres every evening, with no increase in salary. The artistes refused, and went on strike, but with no wider effect. Soon, that would change.

Prior to 1900, music hall entertainers had enjoyed flexible working arrangements with theatre-owners, but as competition grew they became more restrictive. Many contracts had clauses barring performers from appearing at any nearby theatre, which cut their income and was against all precedent. Such clauses were also used to force rival theatres out of business, a ruthless tactic made possible by the growing power of the big syndicates: Moss Empires alone controlled over forty halls, all in prime locations. The harsh facts of life for down-at-heel performers were that if they did not dance to the tune of the syndicates, they were not likely to dance at all – and if they did not dance, they did not eat. Alone, they were powerless; collectively they hoped they were not.

The spark for the 1907 dispute came when some theatre-owners began demanding that artistes perform up to six matinées a week, for no extra pay. The multi-talented Percy Honri outlined the unfairness of the situation:

> Rule Britannia, Britannia rules the waves,
> Two shows every night and six matinées …

The VAF decided to act, joining forces with bodies representing stage hands and musicians to form a National Alliance which presented a Charter for fairer treatment. It proposed basic levels of pay, contract guarantees, a modification of barring clauses, arbitration to resolve disputes, and pro-rata payment for matinées. The Charter was presented to three owners: Frank MacNaughton, who agreed to it, and George Adney Payne and his son-in-law Walter

Gibbons, who did not. Gibbons offered a verbal assurance, but would not put his name to an agreement. It was not enough. He was targeted for the initial action and given until 4 p.m. on Monday, 21 January 1907 to comply. After consulting with other owners, he decided to call the bluff of the VAF – but it then called his. The strike began at the Holborn Empire: all Gibbons was able to offer his audience was a film show about the Alps and some songs from an elderly, semi-retired lady accompanied by a pianist.

Within days, the strike spread to the larger circuits, with performers, musicians and stage hands walking out. At the South London Theatre the manager offered a film and a troupe of elephants. It was poor fare, and the show soon came to an end. The audience were asked which act they wished to see again, and they chose the elephants, only to heckle them with good-natured shouts of 'Blackleg!' It was the first public indication of support for the strike.

The dispute spread throughout the syndicated halls, and was headline news across the country. A further twenty-two London theatres were affected, and at its peak about three hundred artistes, over two hundred musicians and ninety stage hands were on strike. Fellow performers, political activists and hundreds of supporters joined the picket lines. But the profession was not united. While top-of-the-bill stars such as Arthur Roberts, Joe Elvin, Marie Lloyd, Little Tich and Gus Elen were vocal and active in support of the strike, others held back, causing great bitterness. The press was sceptical about the sincerity of the highly paid stars. *Punch* published a spoof letter: 'My blood boils for the poor downtrodden colleagues who are starving in order that popular artistes like myself may roll in motors on a salary of £7,500. Cruel, cruel managers. (Signed) Arthur Elvin Lloyd Tich.'

The trade's weekly paper the *Performer*, naturally pro-strike, 'named and shamed' strike-breakers, including 'Datas the Memory Man' – and the 'blackleg' elephants. Poor 'Datas', nervous and fearful, had caved in because he was being sued for breach of contract, and bigger names than him would give ground to the threat of legal action before the dispute was over.

Some top-of-the-bill stars were lukewarm. Vesta Tilley merely remarked that she 'has no grievance, nor had any of the leading artistes, but she knew of the grievances of those who were in less demand'. George Robey remained detached, but comments made after the strike suggest he may have disapproved of it: 'I have never failed to do my night's turn. No manager has ever let me down and ... I have never let them down ... My employers pay me, and the public pays my employers, and there you are.'

Alec Hurley, by contrast, had no doubts: 'What we are fighting ... is a music hall trust. An average artiste is at the mercy of the manager. He has to sign a contract for six nights and he is not allowed to perform at any other hall in the neighbourhood for twelve months thereafter ... it practically means ruin.' Harry Randall agreed: 'This agitation has been underground for ten years and will not be allowed to rest until a substantial change has been secured.'

Such views were anathema to the syndicate theatre managers. Oswald Stoll thought barring clauses were essential: '[They] are the very foundation of the variety super-structure. It means managers pay a large salary for the exclusive services of an artiste. Performers who appear everywhere soon tire the public, but when they play at one place alone, they speedily assert their true value.' This was nonsense. For many years performers had appeared at several theatres in the same locality on the same night. Stoll would not even acknowledge that less popular performers should be exempt from the restriction, nor that they were poorly paid: 'every performer with an iota of real entertaining power is getting ... a handsome living'. This, too, was nonsense. An Emergency Relief Fund set up by Little Tich, Arthur Roberts and Joe Elvin attracted widespread donations. Marie Lloyd pumped up the supportive publicity, telling the *Daily Mirror*: 'Our demands are just. We stand together as a profession. We want to see that everyone concerned with Music Hall receives a living wage. The Labour Party is with us' – as indeed it was, notably Ben Tillett, the radical dockers' leader, and the Party Chairman, the iconic Keir Hardie – 'and we shall win.'

Marie Lloyd's devotion to the cause went far beyond inter-
views – and prudence. Standing on the picket line in her open car,
swathed in furs against the chill, she enlivened the evenings by singing to fellow pickets and onlookers. It must have been a colourful
scene – pickets, placards, crowds gawping at famous faces they
usually had to pay to see onstage, and Marie Lloyd giving an
impromptu concert in streets lit by gaslight.

One evening she was picketing a theatre when she recognised an
old adversary, Belle Elmore, trying to enter it. Lloyd shouted, 'Let
her through, girls, she'll close the hall faster than we can!' It was a
spiteful barb, and one she may have regretted. Three years later,
Belle Elmore had a tragic claim to fame – she had become the
second wife of the notorious Dr Crippen, and after her remains
were discovered buried under the cellar of their home, Crippen was
convicted of her murder and hanged.

Lloyd was not alone in cheering up the pickets on their winter
vigils. Percy Honri played his concertina outside the Paragon in the
Mile End Road, while coster comedian Gus Elen sang:

> If a fellow starts to fight for his freedom and for right,
> I'm going to back him up d'ye see? ...
> For it makes no odds to me
> What the dividends will be
> Give the strikers their just claims is what I say ...
> That's a' argyment what's sensible and sound;
> Get yer stars back – pay your bandsmen –
> Treat your staff a bit more handsome –
> Or your dividends will never come round.

The police read the public mood far better than the theatre-
owners. When the popular Marie Kendall was arrested for 'obstruc-
tion' on the picket line, she was swiftly released, and returned to the
line to thunderous applause. At the height of the strike Marie Lloyd
sent a provocative telegram to the Tivoli Theatre, saying she could
not appear that night as she was 'busy putting a few flounces on my

dress'. Little Tich, her co-star, sent a similarly cheeky note that he was 'learning a new cornet solo. Cannot tear myself away.' Marie Lloyd explained her support: 'We [the stars] can dictate our own terms. We are fighting not for ourselves, but for the poorer members of the profession, earning thirty shillings to £3 a week. For this they have to do double turns, and now matinées have been added as well. These poor things' – she never minced her words, even when speaking of her friends – 'have been compelled to submit to unfair terms of employment, and I mean to back up the Federation in whatever steps are taken.'

These were noble sentiments, but Lloyd was a political innocent whose impulsive and ill-considered words were often contradictory. She wrote to the *Era*, which leaned towards the managers in the strike: 'I have been credited with many mis-statements during the [strike]' – which was true. 'What we are fighting for are better terms and conditions ... I should like a speedy settlement.' And so she did, because although her generous heart was with the underdog, she was aware that she was angering many influential figures. Oswald Stoll was one: 'Her utterances were so grossly exaggerated that it is to be hoped they are due to an innate partiality for dramatic effect rather than to the truth.' For a man as taciturn as Stoll, this was a heartfelt denunciation.

The VAF tried to enlist public support by declaring the dispute a 'music hall war', and hired the Scala Theatre to stage a 'Night with the Stars' to raise funds. In the event, no big stars appeared – perhaps advisedly, since they had been threatened with legal action if they did. Marie Lloyd and Alec Hurley applauded the show from a box, but the disapproving *Daily Telegraph* dubbed it 'A Night Without Stars'.

The music hall-owners, shocked that their supremacy was being challenged, misread the strike from the outset. They tried to engage lesser-known acts to fill the gaps left by strikers, but failed: Salvation Army bands were among those who refused their entreaties. Managers were obliged to entice acts out of retirement, one of whom, Ethel Earle – now Mrs George Adney Payne – appeared at the Oxford to sing 'The Holy City' and 'Dear Heart' in a simple white evening dress. The *Era* applauded her loyalty to her husband, but she was one of very few substitutes of quality: the really popular performers were simply irreplaceable.

As the strike continued, the big stars, worried by threats of legal action, began to look for compromise, although none wished to face the opprobrium suffered by poor 'Datas'. Stoll met Arthur Roberts, Marie Lloyd and Joe Elvin privately, but on 4 February 1907 news of the meeting leaked to the press. This was potentially very embarrassing to the stars, and strong denials of a backstairs agreement were issued: even if these denials were true, it is more than likely that the meeting hastened a settlement.

The dispute was financially punishing to both sides: no pay for the performers, and no box-office receipts for the managers. Sir George Askwith, a King's Counsel, was appointed by the Board of Trade to find a resolution, and on 13 February 1907, after twenty-four days, the strike ended, amid much relief all around. After hearings throughout April and May, an agreement was reached on 14 June. It introduced an agreed national code of practice, a model contract and a system for settling disputes. The performers won more money for matinées, a minimum wage and a maximum working week for musicians. The hated barring clauses, which in the most extreme cases banned artists from working for a year in a given locality, were modified: in future, only the highest earners would be subject to such restrictions. The strikers' victory was not complete. Managers retained control of timing and billing, and could still demand additional performances, albeit with pay. Inevitably, they dragged their feet, and the agreed changes only came into force after constant lobbying by the Artists' Federation.

The following year, Joe Elvin, who had been so active in setting up the Emergency Relief Fund, looked for a more permanent way to support artistes who had fallen on hard times. He set up the Variety Artistes' Benevolent Fund, and a property, Brinsworth House in Twickenham, was purchased as a twilight home – in which my half-brother Tom F. Moss would live for many years.

Slowly but surely, the music hall industry was catching up with social trends. It would never be an easy or a comfortable profession, but it was learning to take care of its own.

And by now my father had become one of its own. He began performing in 1901, and his experiences, handed down to me half a century later, shed light on a very different age.

21

Tom and Kitty

'It's a rotten old country we live in,
And our troubles we very well nurse,
But we're living, and that's saying something,
There's others a jolly sight worse.'

KITTY MAJOR (1874–1928)

Music hall artistes, by their very nature, were nomadic: they had to follow the bookings, and near-perpetual travel was the outcome. The more successful owned homes, some of them luxurious, but while their families might have been more or less permanently in residence, the performers moved from hotel to hotel or, more likely, theatrical digs. Many of the digs were insalubrious, and in some cases appalling, but at least they had a roof and washing facilities – and they were cheap.

Years later, I would see at first hand how performers adapted to their circumstances. After my father lost his savings and our home in his early seventies, we moved from a modest but comfortable bungalow into two rooms on the top floor of a Victorian house in Brixton. I was surprised by how easily he made himself at home in our meagre new surroundings. 'Digs,' explained my mother, smiling. 'Theatrical digs.' We shared an ancient cooker on the small landing with an eccentric neighbour whose manner of announcing himself was to poke his head around our door and pull weird faces. My parents, well used to such peculiarities, were unfazed. It was in those Brixton rooms that I acquired a tolerance for odd behaviour.

Born in 1879, my father was sixty-four when I was born. I loved him dearly, but never really knew him. He was Victorian to the core: loving but remote, the master of his own domain, with all the virtues and vices of the age into which he was born. During my childhood and teens I sat with him as his health deteriorated, but I only ever learned about a fraction of his life.

He had spent nearly thirty years, from 1901, on the road as a music hall artiste, for much of that time as proprietor of his own touring show. But beyond these bare bones his life was a mystery. In the last years of his own life, my elder brother Terry managed to fill in many of the details of those missing years, which appear to be typical of the lives of many music hall performers.

My father's life was peripatetic, and had been since he was a child. His parents, Abraham and Sarah Ball, were living in Pittsburgh, where Abraham, a master builder, was helping to construct the blast furnaces of the Carnegie Steel Works. When Sarah became pregnant she sailed home to the family roots to give birth to a son, Tom, in Bloxwich, near Birmingham, in 1879, then rejoined her husband in America with the baby. My father's youth is largely hidden, but glimpses of it came to light in the tales he told as an old man. Some I have been able to verify. Others must be taken on trust, although nothing he ever said that has been possible to check has proved to be untrue – or even, to my surprise, exaggerated.

It is not clear how long my father lived in America. Family stories suggest that he joined a fife-and-drum band and learned to swing a baton, performing before President Grover Cleveland. This is likely to be true, as he certainly was proficient in baton-swinging, which he used in his music hall act and taught my mother many years later. He also taught himself acrobatics, and at the age of eight was the top man in a four-man pyramid. He told us he had performed on the trapeze and, when we moved from our home in

Worcester Park to Brixton, some old trapeze outfits were found festering in ancient trunks. He talked also of working with the travelling booths of the boxers John L. Sullivan and 'Gentleman' Jim Corbett, and helping to draw the crowds to the cure-all medicine sellers that accompanied them.

Until my brother's researches proved otherwise, I thought my father had remained in the United States without interruption until the turn of the century. But my grandfather, Abraham Ball, is shown as the occupier of houses in Church Street, Bloxwich, in the census of 1881, and is in the 1884 Electoral Register. He disappears from the register in 1885, which may indicate that the family had returned to America. It is likely they were there for a decade, and returned to the West Midlands in 1895 or 1896. I know this only because my father was a keen swimmer all his life, and the records of the flourishing Walsall Swimming Club, and press reports of their activities, show that Tom Ball, with his adopted half-brother Alfred, was an active member from 1896 to 1899. He won races, played water polo and gave exhibitions of lifesaving. His penchant for showmanship was evident during swimming galas. In 1897 he won prizes dressed as a 'ballet girl', and two months later as a 'new woman with bloomers'. He was young, fit, energetic and gregarious, and it sounds as though he had a lot of fun. This was not a man fashioned for a life of routine.

Tom left home at the turn of the century, aged about twenty, to strike out on his own. He remained in touch with his parents. Many years later they moved into a house he owned in Prees, Shropshire, where they lived until they died: grandmother Sarah in April 1919 and grandfather Abraham in August 1931. My father spoke of them rarely, but always with affection.

How and where my father began his show business career remains a mystery. To my regret, as a child I never asked him when I had the opportunity to do so. Shortly before he died, an interview he gave to our local vicar in Brixton for the parish magazine suggests he started out by working in circuses and travelling galas organised by firms such as Wilders, the fireworks manufacturers. By 1902 he was appearing regularly on music hall bills, and it was during that year he met Kitty Grant, a singer and dancer, and they soon began to work together. In the early years their act was a combination of circus-style acrobatics, baton-twirling, patter, comic duets and comedy sketches. In August 1902 they appeared at the Grand Theatre, Stockton-on-Tees, as 'Drum + Major', presumably because their act included baton-swinging. In any event, 'Major' became his common-law name, and forty years later it would be the name on my birth certificate. Tom and Kitty married in 1910, following the death of Kitty's husband: my father was thirty-one, and Kitty five years older. It was a partnership that would last until Kitty died.

By 1903 Tom and Kitty were constantly in work. Their bookings, usually for a week at a time, took them around the country, generally earning positive reviews: to the Camberwell Palace in January; the Grand, Bolton, in February – 'Drum + Major, a capital comedy duo, go great'; the Metropole, Manchester – 'an amusing couple'; and in March at the Argyle, Birkenhead – 'all round entertainers ... considerable ability as dancers and duettists'; and the Palace, Plymouth – 'an excellent exhibition of baton wielding ... [they] cause no little amusement with their witty repartee'. In April and May they were in Stockton-on-Tees, Wolverhampton and Northampton, where an intriguing review suggests they may have been together as early as 1901, by reporting that 'they repeat the great success of their former visit'. In the years that followed Tom and Kitty, like many others, were constantly on the move, and enjoyed every moment of it.

In July 1904 they sailed for South America, returning the following April. Only uncorroborated stories survive from that visit, but my father always spoke warmly of Brazil, telling my brother stories of working in Argentina and Uruguay. In between engagements he told us he spent time as a gaucho and working in a 'millionaires' club' supervising card tables. But the pull of the halls soon called him home.

From May 1905 Tom and Kitty were back on the road: in Coventry, while June saw them in Poplar, and then in Manchester for a booking that lasted throughout July. In August they began at Warrington, where the *Stage* reported they 'scored a success', before moving on to Belfast and Blackpool. September was spent in Barrow-in-Furness, and October saw them in Bury and Waltham Green, London. By the beginning of December they were in Portsmouth, before opening in a brand-new venture: pantomime, at the Opera House, Cheltenham on Boxing Day. The *Stage* reported of the production, *Robinson Crusoe*, that 'Mr. Tom Drum' (sic) got 'plenty of fun out of the part, Billy Crusoe, and [introduced] a clever speciality with the drum-major's staff, which he handles with remarkable dexterity and swiftness'. Kitty earned plaudits as 'a sprightly comedienne and vocalist'.

The following years adopted a similar pattern, and were equally busy. My father told me of incessant travelling during which he and Kitty made – and spent – considerable sums of money. Over the years they appeared on the same bill as Marie Lloyd, Hetty King, Fred Karno, Nellie Wallace, Lupino Lane, Gertie Gitana, Florrie Forde, Joe O'Gorman, Alexander's Rag-time Band, Harry Champion and many others. They never hit the heights, but they were versatile and dependable, and always in work. Mostly they toured the regions, and from time to time were top of the bill.

They attended the famous meeting at the Vaudeville Club on 18 February 1906, when Wal Pink proposed, and Albert Schafer seconded, the formation of the Variety Artists' Federation. The first register lists the inaugural one hundred members, who include some of the great names of music hall: Joe O'Gorman, Eugene Stratton, Fred Karno, Joe Elvin and Harry Tich. That evening Tom and Kitty Major became members numbers 97 and 98.

From 1910 their act expanded to include sketches that were well received and were repeated in tours around the country: the first appears to be 'The Broker's Men'. None of the scripts survive, but 'After the Overture' (1913), which amusingly depicted the reality of show-business life backstage, and 'First Turn Again' were successful in the immediate pre-war years. In February 1915 they topped the bill at the City Varieties, Leeds, and in the same year my father appeared in the revue *Charlie Chaplin Mad*. The great clown was not in the revue, he was making films. When that ended, my father's revue *Stop Press* began its initial tour. It was still running (or, more likely, was revived) in September 1917, when because of the war my father was the only male member in the cast. At the end of the war Tom and Kitty disappear from the records of British venues – they were probably touring overseas.

In August 1919 they reappear in England, launching their revue *Ginger*, followed two years later by *A Fantasy*, later repackaged as *Special Edition*. Between December 1922 and August 1923 they disappear again – probably, yet again, overseas – before reopening *A Special Edition*, which toured successfully until June 1926.* During the 1920s my father's stage appearances dwindled, and it is unclear whether he kept his company together. Just before Christmas 1927 he appeared in the revue *On the Go*, covering for the leading comedian Johnny Mackay, but there is no indication that Kitty was in the show.

My father was never a pen-and-ink man, so I suspect the scripts of the sketches and revues were written largely by Kitty. It is likely that his contributions originated as ad-libbed witticisms during rehearsals, for the man I knew was quick-witted, and far too restless to sit down in front of a blank sheet of paper. Whatever the division of labour, between them they wrote the patter, the monologues, the songs and the music for all their shows.

I have only second-hand information about what my father and Kitty were like onstage, and not much of that. In 1990, when I was Chancellor of the Exchequer, and there had been a burst of publicity about my parents, I received a letter from a Mrs Hilda Sayers, then well into her eighties, who remembered seeing one of their shows (she couldn't remember its name) when she was about fifteen. At the time she was a member of a dancing act, 'the Four Danvers', and she visited the theatre not only to perform, but to cut up some

---

* These revues were resurrected with variations year after year, as were monologues such as 'Fair Play' and sketches like 'First Turn Again', 'The Broker's Man' and 'After the Overture'.

unwanted pamphlets to make snowflakes which featured in my father's act. She remembers a 'country scene' in which my father and Kitty sang 'romantic songs' in a sentimental manner before the final snowflake scene, in which my father appeared dressed as an old man, in shabby clothes and carrying a case with a bundle tied to it. Mrs Sayers described the act, which opened with him singing:

> Old pal, old gal, you've left me all alone,
> Old pal, old gal, I'm just a rolling stone,
> Shadows of the evening, steal across the sky,
> Always find me kneeling, in the candle-light.

He then continued in a monologue:

> Old pal, old gal, why did you leave me?
> I'm so alone, no one to guide me ...

It may sound too sentimental to the modern ear, but it was, according to Mrs Sayers, 'very moving': '[I] remember clearly there were a few handkerchiefs being used in the audience as he ended his act by laying down on the stage.' 'The Four Danvers' followed this scene with a dance in front of the curtains while the snow was cleared.

I don't recall my father ever singing that particular song to me when I was a boy, but it is certainly the sort of tear-jerker he liked. 'A good cry,' he once said to me, 'is good for the soul – and the box office!' I have always remembered that remark, because alluding to box-office takings was entirely out of character for him. My father was neither wise about money, nor especially interested in it. When he had it, it soon slipped through his hands, and when he did not he was phlegmatic about it.

The show Mrs Sayers saw is quite likely to have been Tom and Kitty's revue *A Fantasy*, in the early 1920s, which included the Denver Quartette of acrobatic dancers. The *Encore* reported on the show at the Hippodrome, Bury, in November 1921:

This duo of clever comedians are nothing if not enterprising, either in the quality of their farcical 'stunts' or in their endeavour to present a first-class production, and this is what they succeeded in doing, at least, so must the audience have thought on Monday, judging from their repeated demonstrations of approval. In the enjoyable character of the songs, the vocal efforts of the chorus, the painstaking orchestration and last, but not least, in the comedianship of Mr. and Mrs. Major, the production evinced evidence of careful training, and a refusal to neglect any expense to make the effort successful. Mr. and Mrs. Major are the central stars ... the pretty costumes and scenery ... considerably increase the artistic value of a production which should command the approval of those desirous of booking an easy winner.

Mrs Sayers was not the only correspondent to write to me about Tom and Kitty. I also received a delightful letter from Lisa Dean, then aged ten, in March 1991. She told me that her grandmother, when aged four or five, had been taken to the Elite Theatre, Birmingham, to see her aunt perform:

Aunty Kate was on stage with her husband in a troop called Kitty Major, they were a comedy act. Nan remembers that Aunty Kate had holes in her stockings on stage and she said the line: 'Bad girls get fur coats but good girls only get boxes of chocolates!' Nan was upset about the holey stockings because Aunty Kate would never normally dress like that. Aunty Kate died, she had no children and we were all wondering whether this Kitty Major troop had anything to do with your family background.

Beyond doubt, this must have been Tom Major's Kitty.

Among the few papers of my father's that have survived the years is a battered postcard signed 'T.E.G., Press Representative for ...' – the name has faded, but T.E.G.'s comments have not:

Black-face minstrel Eugene Stratton (1861–1918) was billed as 'the Whistling Coon'. Minstrel shows and 'coon singers' were phenomenally popular with British audiences, who saw nothing racist in their portrayal of black people. To most, they were simply superbly performed, family-friendly entertainment. Stratton's hit song 'Little Dolly Daydream' still resonates today.

Oh Alith! Oh!
Now where can Alice be?
I've brought a lovely sheepshead
home for tea!

G.H. Chirgwin (1854–1922), the multi-instrumentalist black-face comedian, in typically eccentric stage attire. Audiences would plead for him to sing 'My Fiddle is My Sweetheart' and 'The Blind Boy', and wouldn't let him leave the stage until he did. Surviving recordings do not capture the undoubted appeal of his performance.

Vesta Victoria (1873–1951) built a very successful career out of playing the superficially innocent girl next door. 'Daddy Wouldn't Buy Me a Bow-Wow', composed and written by Joseph Tabrar in 1892, was a big hit for her on both sides of the Atlantic. My father told me that she endowed the song with layers of innuendo that delighted her audience.

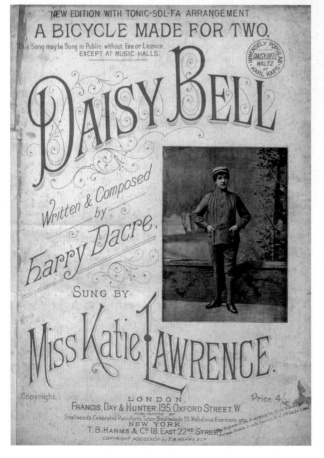

This 1893 programme for the Oxford shows a quality of execution and design not to be found in most music hall promotional material.

The song 'Daisy Bell', made famous by Katie Lawrence (1868–1913), is a good illustration of how music hall tracked real life and emerging trends. Cycling was a novel, modern pastime to which most of the audience could aspire.

Oswald Stoll (1866–1942), impresario and co-founder of the Stoll Moss theatre empire. A powerful and influential figure in music hall, he relentlessly gentrified the genre to make it as family friendly – and profitable – as possible.

Noctes Ambrosianae by Walter Sickert (1860–1942). The celebrated English impressionist was the most eminent contemporary artist to leave a visual record of the heyday of music hall. He painted several pictures of the gallery of the 'Old Mo' – the Middlesex Music Hall in Drury Lane – around 1900, and regarded this version as one of his finest works. It brings to life the spellbound mêlée 'up in the gallery'.

Sickert's controversial *Katie Lawrence, Gatti's Hungerford Palace of Varieties* (1903) is a later version of another, now lost, picture. One critic described it as the embodiment of 'the aggressive squalor which pervades to a greater or lesser extent the whole of modern existence'.

Music Hall War.

Mr. GIBBONS—ANOTHER UNTRUTH.

Mr. Gibbons says he has paid, and is paying, the Trade Union rate asked for by the National Association of Theatrical (Stage) Employees.

THIS STATEMENT IS UNTRUE.

Mr. Gibbons, prior to the agreement with the Alliance, paid less than **2¼d.** per hour to some of the Staff, others were paid **11s. per week less** than the Union rate on the Evening of the Saturday last, after Mr. Gibbons had again repeated it, and broken his word of honour.

Support the Artistes and Workers in their struggle for fair terms and conditions.

Printed by the Co-operative Printing Society Ltd., Tudor Street, E.C., and Published by J. B. Williams, 9, Great Newport Street, W.C.

The 'music hall war' of 1907 pitted overworked and exploited performers against acquisitive owners and managers in a flamboyant battle of wills. Both sides deployed very modern spin tactics on picket lines and in the press to influence public opinion.

Australian-born Florrie Forde (1875–1940) was famous for her songs and rousing choruses. Audiences loved to participate in the shared experience – especially the First World War favourites 'It's a Long Way to Tipperary' and 'Pack Up Your Troubles in Your Old Kit Bag'.

'Mr Memory' (Wylie Watson) in Alfred Hitchcock's 1935 film *The Thirty-Nine Steps*. The character was based on the music hall artiste John Bottle (1876–1956), otherwise known as 'Datas', who could commit vast amounts of information to memory. 'Is that right, sir?' he would ask after answering an enquiry from the audience. The scenes in the film faithfully reproduce his act, as well as the look and feel of an authentic music hall.

Leeds City Varieties, from which the BBC televised *The Good Old Days* for thirty-two years from 1953. Originally Thornton's Music Hall, the City Varieties kept faith with the music hall tradition while other theatres turned to cinema. My father topped the bill there in 1913 and 1915.

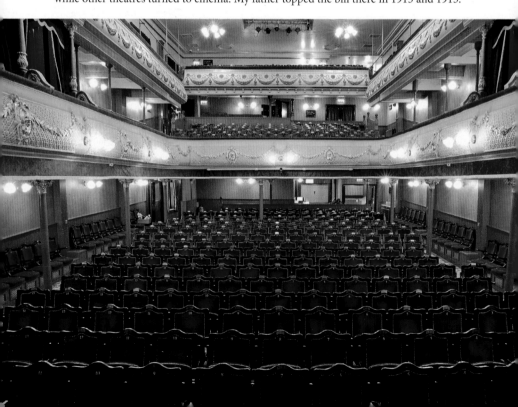

Thanks for a very good show, richly varied and superbly staged.
The music is bright and catchy … vocalists good … comic
element very decent … and the acrobatic dancers the goods …
the Apache dance being the star turn of the evening: a silent
drama well performed by the two young ladies. Your first night
was a success in front of an intensely critical audience.

My father rarely lavished praise on others, but I hope he showed
this note to 'the acrobatic dancers', Glade and Glen. Of Glade I
know nothing, but 'Glen' was eighteen-year-old Gwen Coates, a
Lincolnshire girl whose determination to dance and enter show
business was frowned upon by her upright Victorian father. Gwen
had seen Tom and Kitty's show as a schoolgirl, and asked for an
audition. She danced well, and they were prepared to accept her,
but she was a minor and needed parental approval. She persuaded
Tom and Kitty to see her parents, to reassure them that she would
be safe and well cared for. Before this meeting took place, poor Mr
and Mrs Coates were subjected to the full range of Gwen's wiles: her
smiles, hugs, pleas were constant and, worn down (or persuaded),
they gave their permission and she got her way. She usually did.
Some years later, following Kitty's death, she married Tom. She was
my mother.

Monologues appear to have been a speciality of Tom and Kitty's.
'Fair Play', written and performed by Kitty during the First World
War, is typical. It begins:

> We're living in dark days and hard ones,
> And the world seems all going wrong;
> But do you think we are being quite British?
> Don't you think we are making a song?
>
> We hear it at every street corner,
> They're the worst days we've lived in; they're not;
> That 'England's a rotten old country'
> You're just talking twaddle and rot.

The speaker then turns to the hardships of war, before concluding:

> It's a rotten old country we live in,
> And our troubles we very well nurse,
> But we're living, and that's saying something,
> There's others a jolly sight worse.

> There's a lot to be said for old England,
> A lot for, and against, you can bet:
> But if you know of a better old country,
> Why the Hell don't you find it and get?

Although the words seem dated now, the sentiments are bang up-to-date. In the midst of the war they evoked an enthusiastic roar of applause – or so said my father, moist-eyed with memory.

While writing this book I received, quite unexpectedly, a letter from Mark Jones, who was researching the history of the Royal Hippodrome Theatre, Eastbourne. He had come across some information about Tom and Kitty, who had performed their review *Stop Press* there in May 1916. With his permission I quote from the draft of his book:

> The only two characters with names, 'Peaceful Henry' and 'Virginia Creeper', were played by Tom and Kitty Major, whose 'untiring efforts to amuse' plainly succeeded, not least with Tom's 'man of the road' song 'When I Left the World Behind'. Three years later in *Ginger*, 'the girl who made all America laugh and cry'* proved herself 'a clever actress as well as a comedienne' in a melodramatic scene. Miss Kitty Major plays the title role with considerable enthusiasm and makes a big hit with her song 'Who's She?'. The principal fun manufacturer is Mr Tom Major, a practised hand in this line of entertainment, he keeps the show moving merrily onwards.

* Tom and Kitty toured America in the spring and summer of 1919.

Mr Jones goes on to write that Tom and Kitty returned to Eastbourne in July 1923 with *Special Edition*, in which Tom was content to allow Bert Brierley – 'a dashing leading man' – to have much of the limelight. The two sang 'We'll Make You Turn Round', in which they boasted they could make the majority of the audience do just that; and, aided and abetted by the chorus, which appeared at the back of the theatre, they succeeded. It was a trick, but obviously an effective one. The *Eastbourne Gazette* clearly enjoyed the show:

It is not often one finds such an enthusiastic audience as that which assembled at the Royal Hippodrome on Monday to welcome the return of Tom and Kitty Major. This delightful couple have always been held in high esteem locally and their reception was full of appreciation. Like all revues, it is a conglomeration of mirth and melody, but Tom and Kitty with their cross talk, witty gags and songs lifted it out of the ordinary rut. They worked strenuously throughout. The audience are kept in constant merriment when either is on the stage, and when they appear together the comedy is extremely good.

The *Gravesend and Dartford Reporter* reviewed the show in February 1924, and its critic was also impressed:

There is no doubt about the excellence of the musical revue, *Special Edition*, which Tom Major is presenting at the Grand Theatre, Gravesend, this week. From start to finish the show is in every way enjoyable, and there should be crowded houses for the remainder of the week.

Tom Major is a comedian of much experience and ability, and he has spared no effort to make the production a great success. He is the principal fun-maker, and with his songs, patter and clever comedy scenes, his audiences are splendidly entertained. The efforts of Kitty Major are also particularly pleasing, and whether in an individual turn, comedy interlude, or sketch, this artiste proves a firm favourite. Her monologue, 'Fair Play', which was written by herself, is especially good. Last, but by no means least, must be mentioned the acrobatic dance by Glade and Glen. The dance is entitled 'Tarzan's Wooing', in which two graceful young ladies exhibit much originality and skill. Tom Major, who was responsible for the training of these artistes, is to be congratulated.

A reporter from the same newspaper spent some time with the company, and wrote an article that featured stories of life in the theatre. Many of them became familiar to me decades later, when my father told them to me. In one, my father was appearing at a theatre in a seaport colliery district in the north of England where the manager, in an attempt to attract a wider cross-section of the local population, advertised the 'refinement' of the show. Unfortunately, the colliers and dock workers who attended were not particularly refined, and, unimpressed by the performance, they made their feelings clear. The manager stalked to the middle of the stage to reassure the audience: 'Ladies and gentlemen, this is a place of refinement, and if those noisy b—rs don't shut up, I'll chuck them into the b—y street!' In another tale, my father's partner in an aerial act fell to the stage and was badly shaken, but the audience, believing it to be intentional, cheered loudly. The next evening there was no such hitch, and the manager demanded to know why the 'box-office' fall had been omitted.

In the spring of 1928, a freak accident brought a sudden and tragic end to Tom and Kitty's long and happy partnership. A steel girder from the safety curtain came loose and fell, striking Kitty on the head and seriously injuring her. She lingered on, brain damaged, but died in June. Without Kitty my father was bereft, and his little company broke up. Later that year he appeared in a touring show, *Hot and Strong*, with Gwen Coates, by now twenty-five, also in the cast – whether by chance or arrangement I shall never know.

But I do know that, when Kitty lay dying, she had asked Gwen to 'look after Tom'. One year later they were married, and a new life began. Their marriage lasted thirty-one years, until my father's death in 1960. After marrying, my father appeared in a few more shows, making his final performance in 1930, with the revue *Ask Billy*, in which he sang 'I'll Always be Dreaming of Mary'. By that time hundreds of theatres were closing, as the public demand moved from music hall and variety to cinema and the new stars of radio. But I believe the catalyst for my father's retirement was the death of Kitty. Without her, he simply didn't have the heart to go on.

My father never forgot his many years on the boards, or the people he had known and the songs they sang. These were the years, and the memories, he treasured above all others. My mother shared the last six or seven years with him, and sometimes, as if in a conspiracy, they would sit beside one another and retreat into the past to talk of them. Upon these shared memories, no one else could intrude. They loved the theatre so much – it was their passion, and it remained so for every day of their lives.

22

The Seeds of Decline

'Every generation laughs at the old fashions, but
follows religiously the new.'

HENRY THOREAU, *WALDEN* (1854)

The great years of music hall were between 1890 and 1905, but even
at its zenith, when vast auditoriums were packed nightly and its
performers were the highest-paid celebrities in the land, new attractions were beginning to threaten the dominance of music hall.

The first of these was musical theatre – that is, a stage entertainment that combines dialogue and song and dance to carry forward
the plot. Gilbert and Sullivan's breakthrough came with *HMS
Pinafore* (1878), a massive hit in London, followed by *The Pirates of
Penzance* (1879) and *Patience* (1881), which was staged in the newly
built Savoy Theatre in The Strand. From then on their operettas
were called Savoy operas: they would include *Iolanthe* (1882), *The
Mikado* (1885), *The Yeomen of the Guard* (1888) and *The Gondoliers*
(1889). They were to be an important element in the development
of musical theatre, which would have serious implications for
music hall.

George Edwardes, in his pre-Empire days as manager of the
Gaiety Theatre in Aldwych, saw an opportunity for a more

accessible, family-friendly version of burlesque, and the colossally successful 'Gaiety Girls' musicals were born. Between 1892 and 1898 the basic plot of poor girl meets and marries wealthy aristocrat was revived time and again in productions like *In Town*, *The Shop Girl*, *My Girl* and *The Circus Girl*. These musicals were distinct from Gilbert and Sullivan, in that they were emphatically modern, with smart, aspirational, fashionably dressed young people doing fashionable things like bicycling and shopping. Music hall performers like Arthur Roberts (*In Town*) and George Robey (*The Bing Boys are Here*) embraced the new genre with enthusiasm.

Farce was another perennial favourite with the public, *Box and Cox* (1847), *Our Boys* (1875) and *Charley's Aunt* (1892) being among the best-remembered examples. The formula was a simple one. Mr Ordinary is faced with a simple problem, which fate and coincidence spin out of control. Plots that skated around adultery were popular, the imagined adulterer usually being entirely innocent. Helpfully, such innocence would not arouse the attention of the Lord Chamberlain.

Even as early as 1860, audiences of 'legitimate' theatre were much more subdued than those of music hall. One contemporary observer remarked that they 'sit, for the most part, in silent admiration'. There were no drunken outbursts, lewd comments or riotous interplay with the artistes onstage, and this gentility was enhanced by practical measures to encourage theatre-goers to focus on the stage. In the 1860s house lights were dimmed during performances, and dress circles were introduced, with their more formal dress code and physical separation from the pit. In the two decades after 1870 there was a wave of building to accommodate the fashion for drama, prompting Henry James to remark acidly that although London was awash with theatres, they were 'a social luxury not an artistic necessity'. The popularity of playwrights like Oscar Wilde and George Bernard Shaw, and of actors including Sir Henry Irving, Ellen Terry, Sir Herbert Beerbohm Tree, Sarah Bernhardt, Sir Charles Wyndham, Mrs Patrick Campbell, Lillie Langtry and many others, meant that the competition for music hall was growing.

New technologies would play a decisive role: in 1888 the gramophone disc was patented in America, and further enemies, in the form of cinema and radio, were lying in wait.

Cinema was born in the dimmed artificial lights of the Grande Café, avenue des Capucines, Paris, on 28 December 1895, when the brothers Auguste and Louis Lumière gave a public screening of ten short films. On 20 February 1896 a French music hall artist, the illusionist Felicien Trewey, British agent for the Lumière brothers, demonstrated the new technology to a handful of members of the press at the Marlborough Hall in Regent Street. Britain's first cinema performance before a paying public took place the next day, and shortly afterwards Trewey was engaged by Oswald Stoll to give picture shows at the Empire Theatre, Leicester Square. Within a month innovative hall-owners were spicing up their programmes with short visual presentations, unwittingly feeding the beast that would destroy them.

The public flocked to see the new art form, and Monsieur Trewey was still wowing audiences at the Empire nearly a year later. The *Era* called the show 'most engaging'. The 'great favourites' were films of trains on Brooklyn Bridge, traffic at Hyde Park Corner and gondolas on Venice's Grand Canal. Sights the public would never have expected to see were suddenly on show locally at modest cost. The first screen kiss, a chaste affair between May Irwin and John Rice, was seen by shocked audiences in New York on 15 June 1896, prompting swift calls for censorship to end such debauchery.

In 1899 Robert Paul built the first British film studio in Sydney Road, New Southgate. He had already been making films for four years. They featured sporting events such as the Oxford and Cambridge Boat Race, the Derby and boxing matches, as well as the first drama filmed in Britain, *Arrest of a Pickpocket*, and more general entertainment such as *Dancing Girls*, *Comic Shoe Black* and *Boxing Kangaroo*. By 1900 the length of a film had stretched to ten minutes, and hand-tinted coloured film became available. Although many of cinema's early pioneers, such as Léon Gaumont and the

Pathé brothers, were French, America, with its huge market, soon came to dominate film-making. Westerns were already popular, and newsreels screened footage of the Russo–Japanese war.

Films were still appearing regularly on music hall bills, but soon they would have their own venues. In February 1907 a former magic lantern showman, Joshua Duckworth, opened one of the first purpose-built cinemas in Colne, Lancashire. A year later he opened a larger house, the Gem in Great Yarmouth, with 1,200 seats. The death knell of music hall and variety venues could dimly be heard.

As technological innovation steamed ahead, new stars such as Mary Pickford and Douglas Fairbanks lit up the screens. In 1912 Mack Sennett began shooting the Keystone Kop comedies, and brought fame to Roscoe 'Fatty' Arbuckle. Classic books such as *Oliver Twist* and *David Copperfield*, and plays including *Hamlet*, were filmed. In 1913 Charlie Chaplin signed a cinema contract and abandoned music hall for ever. Other music hall stars, notably George Robey, also took to the screen.

Oswald Stoll was quick to spot the medium's importance, turning over his new acquisition, the London Opera House in Holborn, to films in 1917, and changing its name to the Stoll Picture House. Stoll was one of Britain's first film moguls through his distribution company, founded in 1918, followed two years later by Stoll Picture Productions. Stoll had spent a lifetime successfully catering to public taste. To such a man film was an opportunity he could not ignore, but it is not clear whether he realised it would become a worldwide phenomenon, or that it would accelerate the death of music hall.

Musical theatre and cinema were not the only enemy of music hall. Some claim it was variety that killed it, although others argue that the two were in fact the same thing. In fact, the old stager Chance Newton was surely right when he explained: 'Music hall is variety, but variety is not music hall.' Everyone attending a show instinctively knew the difference. Variety was grander and broader than music hall. It made more use of melodramatic sketches, ballets, classical music, one-act plays and bioscope movies, and was more polished, especially at venues like the Coliseum or the Alhambra in London, which had become variety theatres rather than music halls. It is true that variety was not structurally different from music hall: artists were still billed separately, and nothing linked one act to the next. But the really big theatres, built for the comfort of the audience and for staging spectacular displays, had none of the intimacy of traditional music hall. One artiste complained that appearing at the Coliseum was like 'spitting into a canyon'.

While variety was a close relation of music hall, it was followed by another theatrical style that really was different. The term 'revue' became widely used around 1910. It was a natural progression from the musical comedy shows George Edwardes had staged at the Gaiety Theatre in the 1890s. It took the form of a 'boy meets girl' sketch, with witty songs and dialogue, inserted into variety bills in the big London halls. The Empire featured George Grossmith's *Hullo! London* in 1910, and followed it up in 1911 with *By George!* Their success was so great that 'revue' expanded to occupy the whole show, and impresarios such as C.B. Cochran and Albert de Courville hired the big theatres, including the Hippodrome, the Pavilion, the Palladium and even the Oxford Music Hall, to stage revues like *Hullo Ragtime*, which opened just before Christmas 1912 to rave reviews. The *Stage* commented: 'Nowhere is to be found a more brilliant or more enjoyable entertainment.' The public agreed: the poet Rupert Brooke apparently saw the show ten times.

The stars of music hall recognised the danger. In 1915 Marie Lloyd sang 'Revue', written by Sam Mayo:

> Where are the ladies?
> Where are the ladies?
> The Lizzies and Lisas and Lous?
> Where have they gone to?
> You know they want to
> All go in revues ...

Marie, being a free spirit, did not like the prepared scripts, the stage
direction, the discipline of revue, all of which were alien to her
performance:

> You've got to do this, got to do that
> To get on in revue
> The Maudies and Bessies
> Must wear pretty dresses
> And a dainty stocking and shoe …
> Have a smile on your face
> And wear plenty of lace
> If you want to get on in revue …
> Manager told me one thing that I had to do
> Was whatever you don,
> Don't put too much on
> If you want to get on in revue …

The sting is in the tail of the song:

> The night may be parky
> Some nice man in khaki
> Says 'Come in my motor pray do'
> Should he be sporty
> Look a bit naughty
> I say 'I'll ride home with you.
> But discreet I must be
> And bring mother with me
> 'Cause I want to get on in revue.'

By the time Mayo wrote this song he and Marie knew of many
girls from revue who had had affairs or married upwards. George
Edwardes must have wondered if he was running a marriage agency.
May Gates married a Norwegian aristocrat, Baron Van Ditton.
Sylvia Storey married Earl Poulett. Gertie Millar became the
Countess of Dudley (but only after the King had prevailed on the

Duke of Westminster not to divorce his wife to marry her). Denise Orme did a double, marrying Lord Churston in 1907, and later moving even higher up the social scale to become the Duchess of Leinster.

The success of the long-running wartime revues *The Bing Boys are Here* and *Chu Chin Chow*, and of post-war hits like *Joy Bells* (1919), which starred George Robey, confirmed that the new format was bankable. Financial considerations played an important role in the rise of revue. Hall-owners were able to charge theatre prices for admission – up to three times the price of music hall entrance – and they only had to book one revue for a run of several weeks, which was far more efficient than booking individual music hall artistes every week. Moreover, apart from the big stars, salaries for the vast majority of artistes plummeted as their individual pulling power became less important than the totality of the 'revue' package. This boosted the bottom line, and was very attractive to hall-owners.

One essential element of revue, which helped to make it feel so modern, was a new form of music. From the turn of the century minstrel acts began to feature an American import: 'ragtime', a new style of 'syncopated' foot-tapping music based largely on John Philip Sousa's marching tunes and popularised by Scott Joplin. The genre was so new that producer Albert De Courville had to bring American musicians over to play it. He recalled later: 'Syncopated music had to be played in a certain way ... I used to insist on the American melodies I had brought over being played with the proper sense of rhythm and syncopation. I met with all sorts of protests to achieve this object. They told me it was not music. To keep the balance I had brought over a trap drummer and a cornet-and-trombone player from America. Jones [the orchestra leader] told me that their playing was something quite new and against all principles of music, but nonetheless he agreed with me that the syncopated rhythm was effective.'

Ragtime's popularity was short-lived – possibly because it came before sophisticated recording technology – but its importance to music hall is that it gave birth to something altogether more power-ful: jazz.

Amidst all this innovation, however, genuine music hall stars were still emerging. One notable performer, who drew upon classic music hall devices, was Harry Tate. Born Ronald Hutchison in 1872, he began his career as an impersonator, but had little success. His fortunes changed in 1895, when – according to legend – Marie Lloyd told him that if he adopted a better name she would get him an audition at the Oxford. He took her advice, and she kept her prom-ise. His rise was meteoric. Within weeks of his debut as 'Harry Tate' he was playing not only the Oxford, but the Tivoli, the Canterbury and the Pavilion alongside Dan Leno, George Robey, Maurice Chevalier and Lloyd. Reviews confirm his 'astonishing' gift for impersonation. According to the *Era*, 'He assumes the manner, the voice and the facial expression of those he imitates with marvellous fidelity.' Tate went to great lengths to develop his act: he even mimicked Cissie Loftus mimicking Jenny Lind, which the *Echo* called 'almost too cruel'. In March 1899 he appeared at a benefit for Joe Elvin in a sketch with Marie Lloyd, in which he appeared as – Joe Elvin. The *Era* commented that Tate 'mimics Elvin's peculiar-ities so closely that his appearance should be an interesting one'.

In 1903 his sketch 'Motoring' became an enduring favourite with the public, and he followed it up with similar sketches based on other popular pastimes such as billiards, flying, golf and fishing. The humour revolved around the windy, pompous but endearing Tate dressed in gaudy checks and coloured waistcoats, with the huge 'Kitchener' moustache that became his trademark, desperately trying to keep things together while his 'son', played by Tommy Tweedly, and a small cast of other characters, made unhelpful comments. Tweedly was replaced by Tate's real son, Ronnie ('Harry Tate Jr'), in 1917. Recordings of his act suggest he was heavily influ-enced by the pompous 'Mr Interlocutor' character from the minstrel shows. These sketches were so successful that he dropped impersonation from his act, and never revived it.

Tate was a naturally versatile performer, and like Robey he was quick to see the future of revue. Shows like *Business as Usual* (1914), *Push and Go* (1915), *Razzle Dazzle* (1916) and *Box o' Tricks* (1918) kept him at the top of the bill. *Razzle Dazzle*, wrote *The Times* in Robey's obituary a quarter of a century later, was 'one of the joys of the dreary years of the war'. A measure of his popularity and impact was the plethora of catchphrases, some of which have entered the language, that peppered his act: 'Good-bye-eee' (which apparently inspired the wartime song), 'How's your father?' and the sarcastic 'I don't think.'

Always free of vulgarity, Tate's act was a perfect example of the way the wind was blowing. Film and revue were the future, and Tate and Robey knew it. Quite simply, people's perception of entertainment had changed. Film, revue and ragtime all had the compelling excitement of the new about them. But music hall still clung on to its audience, and at the start of the First World War in 1914 there were very few outward indications that it was losing its appeal: halls were still doing good business and the band played on. The conflict would even produce songs that many (wrongly) associate with the heyday of music hall. 'For Me and My Gal', 'A Little of What You Fancy Does You Good', 'When I Wore a Tulip and You Wore a Red Red Rose', 'If You Were the Only Girl in the World' and 'K-K-K-Katy' were all wildly popular during the Great War. Soon the beloved choruses would resound less and less loudly, with smaller audiences and in ever decreasing numbers of halls. After the war, the illusion of a secure future would soon be shattered.

23

World War I

'I could not help thinking of all the dear lads I
came to know and whom I should never see again
... I felt more like crying than singing.'

GEORGE ROBEY (1869–1954)

To the casual eye, the night of 4 August 1914 was like any other:
George Robey was at the Stratford Empire, Little Tich was at the
London Palladium and Marie Lloyd was top of the bill at the
Pavilion. Ella Shields was at the Holborn Empire and Harry
Champion at the Golders Green Hippodrome. Vesta Tilley was on
holiday, as was George Edwardes – uncomfortably for him, in
Germany. Eugene Stratton was at the Ardwick Empire, George
Formby at the Bolton Grand, G.H. Elliot at the Empire, Newcastle,
and Bransby Williams at the Theatre Royal, Dublin. As that day
turned into the morning of 5 August, England's ultimatum to
Germany to quit Belgium ran out. Four years later, many millions
were dead, and life for the survivors, civilians as well as combatants,
was transformed forever.

In August 1914 the British Army had about 700,000 men in
uniform, and estimated a need for a further 500,000. In the absence
of conscription, which did not begin until March 1916, enlistment
was voluntary, and the government placed a huge priority on

advertising to herd young men into uniform. Some of the posters are familiar even today: the iconic image of Lord Kitchener accompanied by the words 'Your Country Needs You'; a man being asked by his young daughter, 'Daddy, what did *you* do in the Great War?'; a battle-hardened Highland soldier pointing at an idyllic British scene with the words, 'Isn't this worth fighting for? ENLIST NOW.' By the end of September over 750,000 men had enlisted; by January 1915, one million. 'Where are the Lads of the Village Tonight?' sang one of the last lions comiques, George Lashwood. They were joining up.

Music hall, bred on Empire and patriotism, was at first slow to see the role it could play in ensuring that they continued to do so. After hostilities began, the first edition of the trade paper the *Era* acknowledged the changed circumstances, but reassured its readers that crowds were still visiting theatres. It then quickly moved on to coverage of the Goodwood races. This blinkered attitude soon changed: early in the war the *Era* reported that a full house at the Devonport Hippodrome was interrupted by a message from the navy's commander-in-chief, who instructed all naval personnel to report immediately to their stations. The house emptied in a matter of minutes.

At the beginning of the war the biggest problem for the profession was in the provinces, where theatrical companies that had embarked on summer tours found themselves stranded when trains were requisitioned for the transport of troops. Even worse, their ticket concessions for any other available transport were suspended.

It did not take long for music hall to recognise that war was an implacable enemy to its prosperity. What was going to be the impact on audiences? Were there likely to be theatre closures? And what did it mean for salaries? Everyone agreed that halls should stay open, to keep up morale, but downward pressure on salaries was acknowledged. The executive committee of the Variety Artists' Federation voted to suspend the right of artistes to claim compensation for lost bookings if a hall had to close because of the war. Given the wave of patriotism sweeping the country, no artiste could risk being labelled self-serving at a time of national crisis. Wartime regulations also meant that sales of tobacco and refreshments, including alcohol, were restricted, as was the use of paper for circulars and posters. Performances had to open and close early so as to use less precious coal for lighting.

But despite these privations, the growing threat of cinema and the fact that large numbers of their audiences were enlisting in the armed forces, music hall 'houses' in London and the provinces held up well throughout the war, and most theatres remained open. Amid widespread public fear of aerial bombing, managers vied with one another to talk up the safety of their houses: the Criterion was safe as it was partly underground (a myth debunked in graphic terms when a huge crater was left in Piccadilly by a fifty-pound bomb); and the Palace Theatre was safe because it had a large amount of water stored under its roof.

Anti-German feeling ran deep, and there were unforeseen consequences for performers who had chosen glamorous, foreign-sounding stage names – even the Royal Family changed its name from Saxe-Coburg to Windsor. On the music hall stage, Karl Hertz declared his American origins, and George Mozart let it be known that his real name was George Grilling, and he had been born in Great Yarmouth. Even greasepaint was not immune. The German brand Leichner was thought to be the best, but it was banned from dressing rooms across the country. Theatrical supplier Willy Clarkson of Wardour Street seized the opportunity to run full-page advertisements promoting 'Goulding's *British* Grease Paint'. To emphasise the point, they were signed 'Willy Clarkson – Patriot'.

During the first week of the war, Oswald Stoll was very uncomfortable with the bill at his flagship venue the Coliseum. As a perfect example of a variety bill, it was an early indication of how traditional music hall was fading: a snake dancer; Charles Hawtrey in a sketch called 'The Complete Angler'; G.P. Huntley in another sketch, 'A Burlington Arcadian'; a Russian ballerina; and – most embarrassing of all – Limpinski's Dogs depicting 'Everyday Life in a German Town'. Stoll immediately ordered something more patriotic, including the hurried replacement of planned performances of extracts from operas, especially Wagner's *Tannhäuser*. In four days the revised show was ready. A huge Union Jack formed the backcloth as Lily Elsie sang 'Your King and Country Need You', the Tiller girls were put into uniform and Vesta Tilley, as usual impeccably dressed as Tommy Atkins, sang 'The Army of Today's All Right'. Military sketches were performed, and the programme carried messages from eminent figures urging men to join up and warning girls not to go out with men who failed to do so. Limpinski's act survived, but was renamed 'Day at Dogville'.

Music hall performers rose to the crisis with vigour. From the very outset of the war the *Era* printed a list of artists who had enlisted. Sketches such as 'The Slacker' and 'The Coward' heaped pressure on the able-bodied to join up, and male performers went to great lengths to make sure their entries on the bill made clear that they were either over military age or had been invalided out.

The forty-five-year-old George Robey tried to join the regular army, but even after offering to 'swear I am twenty-five and run around the parade ground at speed' he was turned down. This may have been a publicity stunt, but there is no doubt that Robey genuinely wanted to help the war effort. He volunteered to become a Special Constable, and after his evening performance would report for duty for a 2 a.m. to 6 a.m. shift searching for and extinguishing visible lights – much as my father would do as an air raid warden in the later conflict. Robey also joined the Volunteer Motor Transport Corps, and personally transported the wounded around the capital. He also used his fame and talent to lift the spirits of returning soldiers and to console mothers, wives and sweethearts as they said goodbye to their loved ones leaving for the front, and was an active fund-raiser. When the buffet at Waterloo station was in danger of running out of money, Robey was one of the leading figures who promised to raise the colossal sum of £5,000. He persuaded Oswald Stoll to loan him the Coliseum for a week, and an auction was held each evening at the end of the show. As an auctioneer Robey was peerless, and the target of £5,000 was easily passed. He auctioned

HMS *Iron Duke*'s bulldog mascot time and again, due to its being repeatedly returned by patriotic bidders.

When the armistice came, Robey's joy was muted: 'I could not help thinking of all the dear lads I had come to know and whom I should never see again, and, upon my honour, I felt more like crying than singing. Nor could I help thinking of the millions of people who, at that moment, behind windows closed and curtained, were thinking of the Dead.' After the war he continued to raise money for service charities, visit hospitals and convalescent homes, and perform in fund-raising shows such as Bransby Williams' 'Warrior's Night' at the Hippodrome in 1919, where he shared the bill with Harry Lauder, Lupino Lane and Harry Tate.

In August 1914, less than a month after the opening of hostilities, Alfred Dove, musical director of the Coliseum, was searching for material to beef up a lacklustre bill and show support for the troops. A new part of the theatre's show was billed as 'A Grand Patriotic Chorus of 1,000 Voices' and featured stirring renditions of 'Hearts of Oak', 'Rule Britannia' and other patriotic songs. Among them was a new song, written in 1912, that had been brought to Dove's notice by the *Daily Mail*, which had reported it being sung by an Irish regiment, the Connaught Rangers, as they embarked for the front. Its publishers, Messrs Feldman & Co., told Dove he could have it, but warned that they didn't have high hopes for its success. It had been sung several years earlier by Florrie Forde, but the music had not been orchestrated, so Dove would have to do that himself. He did so, and 'It's a Long Way to Tipperary' became the defining anthem of the Great War. It was recorded by the Irish tenor John McCormack, and Feldman & Co. reported two million sales of the sheet music in three months.

Alongside the nostalgia and reverie of songs like 'Tipperary', 'Pack Up Your Troubles in Your Old Kit Bag' and 'If You Were the Only Girl in the World', other wartime music hall songs sought to motivate audiences in more active ways, like 'Your King and Country Want You (We Don't Want to Lose You But We Think You Ought to Go)' and Vesta Tilley's 'The Army of Today's All Right' (both 1914), and Marie Lloyd's 'Now You've Got Yer Khaki On' (1915), which, typically for Lloyd, stressed the sexual attractions of a man in uniform.

In 1917 J.P. Long and M. Scott wrote the song 'Oh! It's a Lovely War', which gently poked fun at army life and became a great favourite with the troops when sung by Ella Shields. It has different connotations to our modern ear because of its use in the 1963 musical play *Oh, What a Lovely War!*, filmed in 1969, a scathing critique of the conflict, but to the troops at the time it was amusing.

> Up to your waist in water
> Up to your eyes in slush
> Using the kind of language
> That makes the sergeant blush
> Who wouldn't join the army?
> That's what we all enquire
> Don't we pity the poor civilians
> Sitting beside the fire.
>
> CHORUS:
> Oh! Oh! Oh, it's a lovely war ...

Wartime regulations introduced new levels of censorship. Performers were not allowed to say, or do, anything that could be interpreted as undermining the war effort. Moreover, at the behest of the Propaganda Bureau, specially commissioned patriotic plays were inserted into music hall and variety bills to boost morale and recruitment, and to stiffen the resolve of those keeping the home fires burning. Managers who attempted to resist this rather lumbering material were reminded in no uncertain terms of their patriotic duties. 'Pro Patria' (perversely pre-echoing Wilfred Owen's 'Dulce et Decorum est', a withering attack on the idea that dying for your country is a sacred act) included German soldiers raping French women, and 'The Bells of St. Valois' featured valiant Frenchmen overpowering vicious German soldiers in hand-to-hand combat.

The Metropolitan presented a dramatic sketch, 'The Spy Peril', in which a dashing secret agent thwarts the plans of undercover German spymaster 'Professor Blackhurst', and also rescues the evil professor's 'ward', Emily Blackhurst, from several fates worse than death. While such sketches may have stiffened audiences' resolve, they were a further step away from traditional music hall fare, where the bill was made up of individual acts.

'England Expects' (September 1914), written by and starring musical comedy pioneer Seymour Hicks, typified a particular kind of recruiting sketch. A group of feckless toffs are shamed into joining up after their girlfriends hear of German atrocities perpetrated in Belgium. In a telling example of the patronising mindset of upper-class Edwardians, a flock of lower-class costers, waiters and tramps willingly follow Algy, Tommy, Reggie and Guy to the recruiting station, and they all go off to the front together, with patriotic songs and much flag-waving.

Not everyone supported the war, but dissenting voices such as George Bernard Shaw, D.H. Lawrence and Bertrand Russell were shouted down and derided in the popular press. Siegfried Sassoon bitterly attacked the pro-war music halls in 'Blighters', which he wrote after a visit to the Liverpool Hippodrome in 1917:

> The house is crammed: tier beyond tier they grin
> And cackle at the Show, while prancing ranks
> Of harlots shrill the chorus, drunk with din;
> 'We're sure the Kaiser loves our dear old Tanks!'
>
> I'd like to see a Tank come down the stalls,
> Lurching to rag-time tunes, or 'Home, sweet Home',
> And there'd be no more jokes in Music-halls
> To mock the riddled corpses round Bapaume.

In his Preface to *Heartbreak House* (1919), George Bernard Shaw noted that what the public really wanted in time of war was escape: 'The best music-hall comedians ransacked their memories for the oldest quips and the most childish antics to avoid carrying the military spectators out of their depth.' Audiences, he said, thirsted for 'silly jokes, dances and brainlessly sensuous exhibitions of pretty girls. The author of some of the most grimly serious plays of our time told me that after enduring the trenches for months without a glimpse of the female ... it gave him an entirely innocent but delightful pleasure merely to see a flapper.' Two wartime shows delivered 'flappers' aplenty: *The Bing Boys are Here* and *Chu Chin Chow*.

Oscar Asche's *Chu Chin Chow* opened at Her Majesty's Theatre on 3 August 1916, and the statistics of its success are truly amazing: it ran for five years, its 2,238 performances being seen by more than two million people (a record that was not broken until *Salad Days* in 1954). The plot is that of 'Ali Baba and the Forty Thieves' – Chu Chin Chow being one of the thieves – and the show resembled an adult pantomime. Its appeal rested on the light-hearted escapism of the subject and the chorus of attractive, scantily clad young women. Soldiers returning from the front were wildly appreciative of both.

Effective fund-raising by the music hall aristocracy needed the support of the owners and managers, and generally received it. Oswald Stoll and his colleagues were generous in providing venues for benefits – aid for Belgium and the French Red Cross, funds for concerts at the front, and famously for the Star and Garter Home for Dis-Abled Soldiers in Richmond. A performance of J.M. Barrie's *The Admirable Crichton* at the Coliseum in June 1916 raised £8,000 for the Star and Garter, and featured as fine a theatrical cast as ever assembled on a London stage, with music hall star Vesta Tilley being joined by some of the biggest names in legitimate theatre: Charles Hawtrey, Nina Boucicault, Gladys Cooper, Lady Tree, Gerald du Maurier, Sir George Alexander and the seventy-year-old Ellen Terry.

Marie Lloyd, like many of her fellow stars, was tireless in her efforts to raise money and morale. She supported prisoner of war funds and the Ulster Volunteer Force Hospital, among many other causes, but unlike that of her peers her work was not officially recognised after the war. This neglect reflected Edwardian attitudes. Lloyd's personal life was even more chaotic than usual during the war years, and she featured in the headlines as much for her marital problems as for her performing and fund-raising. Her case was not helped when her husband, the drunk ex-jockey Bernard Dillon, went absent without leave from his regiment, unfairly making her seem guilty of being unpatriotic by association.

For one giant of the halls, the Great War brought personal tragedy. On New Year's Eve 1916 Harry Lauder was staying in a hotel in Bloomsbury when he heard that his son John, a captain in the Argyll and Sutherland Highlanders – who had accompanied him on his first tour to America – had been killed in action three days earlier at Poiziers. Lauder left immediately for Scotland to be with his wife. His show *Three Cheers* was postponed, but he returned to London to complete the engagement a few days later, and after a rapturous welcome from the audience, who were aware of his loss, had to sing one of his most popular hits of the day, 'The Laddies Who Fought and Won'. This must have been heartbreaking for Lauder, since the song included the lines

> When we all gather round the old fireside
> And the fond mother kisses her son ...

Like other stars, Lauder was very active in supporting the troops and visiting the wounded, but after the loss of his son he wished to do more. He tried to join up but, at forty-six, was politely declined, so he offered to go to the front as an entertainer. The War Office agreed, and he made his first visit in May 1917. Others followed, with Lauder playing in a farmyard to a handful of men, or in a natural field amphitheatre to thousands of wildly applauding soldiers. At one concert at Arras, planes flew above to deter any German aerial assault.

The servicemen loved nostalgic, warm-hearted songs that reminded them of their homes, and families, and idolised Lauder for risking his life to entertain them. But he still had a further contribution to make. In 1917 he founded the Harry Lauder Million Pound Fund for Maimed Men, Scottish Soldiers and Sailors, which became one of the most profitable campaigns of the war. He dedicated one of his tours of North America to raising money for the cause, and the large expatriate Scots population of America and Canada generously opened their hearts and their wallets to him.

A final word should go to Oswald Stoll, who was a keen supporter of good causes throughout the war. In 1915 he set up the War Seal Foundation to build flats for injured servicemen to live in with their families while they received treatment. It was largely in recognition of his work on this project that he was given a knighthood in 1919, along with Lauder and Walter de Frece – whose wife, Vesta Tilley, thus became Lady de Frece. Although the great days of music hall were beginning to fade, its royalty had, at last, become part of the establishment.

24

Aftermath

'Cherishing the jewels of the past and actively
supporting the interests of the future.'

THE BRITISH MUSIC HALL SOCIETY
(FOUNDED 1963)

At the end of the Great War music hall was facing the competing attractions of cinema, variety, revue and new forms of music. Marie Lloyd, George Robey, Vesta Tilley, Harry Champion and many others were still appearing before large audiences, although in some cases no longer exclusively in music hall. Public taste was changing. The young were seeking new forms of pleasure, and one of them, in its infancy pre-war, now came of age: jazz.

In 1917 the publishers Francis, Day & Hunter, kings of the minstrel genre, had published several 'jazz' songs, including 'When I Hear that Jazz Band Play' and 'Stick Around for the New Jazz Band'. The Jazz Age proper, however, came to Britain on a showery night in April 1919, in the form of five white men from New Orleans playing a form of music, 'jass' (sic), which originated in the multi-cultural quarters of that city.

The leading exponent of this improvised and exuberant new style was the trumpeter Nick La Rocca, an Italian immigrant to America whose Original Dixieland Jass Band were a hit in New Orleans. The band's new sound travelled far, and they soon gravitated to Chicago, playing – and improving – as they went. Once there, fame came quickly and easily. Having heard them perform, Al Jolson recommended them to New York theatrical agent Max Hart. By 1917 they were delighting audiences at New York's uptown Paradise Ballroom and Reisenweber's Restaurant, and were billed in the *New York Times* as a 'Jazz Band – An Overnight Furore – The Fad of the Hour'. They released a two-track recording, 'Livery Stable Blues' and 'Dixieland One Step', that sold a million copies on its first pressing – far outstripping other contemporary artistes including the great tenor Enrico Caruso.

The new music enthralled and appalled in equal measure. It was described as 'wild', 'savage', 'barbarous', 'out of control', 'dangerous', and even 'of the jungle'. To some it was anathema, to others wonderful and innovative. Louis Armstrong recalled in his autobiography: 'Four years before I learned to play the trumpet a great Jazz orchestra was formed [by La Rocca] … He had instrumentation different from anything before – an instrumentation that made old songs sound new … His fame will last a long long time, as long, I think, as American music lives.'

The Original Dixieland Jazz Band made its debut at London's Hippodrome on 7 April 1919 as part of George Robey's *Joy Bells* revue, and was met with an ecstatic response from the audience, many of whom were American servicemen already familiar with the band. The public had discovered something new, and everything that came before suddenly seemed tired and old.

Events helped: jazz emerged just as the recorded music industry was undergoing a massive expansion. But unlike jazz musicians, music hall stars like Robey, Leno and Lloyd were unable to replicate their genius in the recording studio. Unsurprisingly, when Britain's first periodical devoted to recorded music, the *Melody Maker*, appeared in early 1926, it was filled with news about jazz – not music hall artists.

Another technological development would soon carry 'live' entertainment directly into the family home. The British government issued radio test transmission licences in 1920, and in June that year Dame Nellie Melba was paid £1,000 by the *Daily Mail* to participate in a broadcast from Guglielmo Marconi's factory in Chelmsford. Using a microphone created from a telephone mouthpiece and some wood from a cigar box, she opened her recital at 7 p.m. on 15 June by singing an aria from *La Bohème* and other popular favourites, closing with the National Anthem. Her voice, carried from an aerial with towering masts, was heard as far away as Iran and Newfoundland, and it has been suggested that the signal was received so strongly at the Eiffel Tower in Paris that gramophone records were made from it. The *Mail* reported that at the conclusion of the transmission Melba said she had 'enjoyed it most tremendously. It is perfectly marvellous. The microphone seems a very small thing to sing to the world through, and wireless seems to me a sort of wizardry.'

Full broadcast licences were awarded from February 1922, and in a scenario straight out of an Ealing comedy, the history of British broadcasting began in a converted army hut in a field near Writtle in Essex. On 18 October the British Broadcasting Company Ltd was set up to exploit the new technology. Its first newscast was presented by Arthur Burrows, a Marconi employee, at 6 p.m. on 14 November 1922, and broadcast from Marconi House, The Strand. Its first radio drama, *The Truth About Father Christmas*, was aired at 5 p.m. on Christmas Eve. These advances posed an acute dilemma for music hall: should it embrace the new technology, with its vast reach, or steer clear and stay in the halls?

The BBC was eager for ready-made content, and some early broadcasts did come from music halls, despite managers and agents warning the artistes about the implications for their careers. In May 1923 the Variety Artists' Federation formed a committee to protect music hall from the BBC onslaught, and two years later an agreement was reached permitting brief stage broadcasts, but not on Friday or Saturday nights, or during evening performance times. By the end of December 1926 two and a quarter million radio licences had been sold, and on 1 January 1927 the British Broadcasting Company changed its name to the British Broadcasting Corporation.

The threat posed by radio to the already struggling music halls was deadly. It was not just that it kept people at home – although it did. The real problem was radio's insatiable hunger for material. Once it had been heard on radio, a routine's drawing power was drastically undermined. Moreover, radio soon developed a rapport with its audience that undermined music hall's greatest strength: the face-to-face intimacy between the artiste and the public.

Marie Lloyd and Dan Leno had mastered their craft in halls that held 1,500 people. They were (just) able to hold their own when the halls doubled in size: the audience could still see the winks, sense the inflections, taste the mood, but the connection between performer and public had stretched to breaking point. Radio, with its disembodied voices and ubiquitous presence, cut the cord completely. There was no visual intimacy. It was a lesser relationship. The marriage of artiste and audience was over.

Radio created new stars, some of whom were little-known music hall artistes like the singer Bertha Wilmot, who had a wartime hit with 'Just Like the Ivy', and the comedian and raconteur Norman Long, with his trademark 'A song, a smile and a piano'. They were among a handful of performers who found national fame in the early days of radio, but only one lasted – Tommy Handley, who went on to star in the Second World War phenomenon *ITMA*. The other early stars faded away as new – and better – performers appeared on the new medium.

Within ten years of the end of the Great War, the British entertainment scene had changed completely. Revue was dominating the large halls of the cities, jazz music was driving record sales and dance hall admissions, and cinemas were full to bursting from Inverness to Penzance. Those wishing to remain at home could now be entertained in their armchairs, listening to the 'wireless'. By the time talking pictures arrived with *The Jazz Singer* at the Piccadilly Theatre in 1928, most of the public had moved on from music hall. Ironically, the central character of the film, a minstrel played by Al Jolson, came straight out of the halls.

Music hall's great stars were departing the scene: George Formby Sr died in 1921, Marie Lloyd and G.H. Chirgwin in 1922, Albert Chevalier in 1923, Harry Houdini in 1926, and the last of the giants, Little Tich, in 1928. Small halls, especially in London, were closing with alarming speed, although a few limped on with a mixture of variety and film. Most were converted to cinemas. The decline was similar, but slower, in the provinces, where traditional bills lasted beyond the 1950s in holiday resorts like Blackpool and Morecambe, but even there the 'street corner' hall was long, long gone.

In the long run the dominance of cinema and the birth of television were irreversible. A few impresarios attempted to foster a mood of nostalgia to give music hall the kiss of life, but they enjoyed only mixed success. In 1936 Leonard Sachs and Peter Ridgeway founded the Players' Theatre Club on the top floor of the house in King Street, Covent Garden, that had once been Evans' Late Joy's, and recreated a show as it might have been seen in the 1840s. They called it Ridgeway's Late Joys, and its immediate impact encouraged them to promote the music hall genre more widely. Alec Clunes, Patricia Hayes and Megs Jenkins were among those who appeared, and Peter Ustinov made his professional debut there in 1938. The threat of bombs during the Second World War caused the Players' Theatre to be transferred to a basement in Albemarle Street, and later relocated to the relative security of Charing Cross Station, in what had once been Gatti's-under-the-Arches.

Following the war, Don Ross, widely acknowledged as the last music hall impresario, revived the genre with his show *Thanks for the Memory* in 1947. It featured many veterans of music hall, some of whom were coaxed out of retirement. But age had not mellowed them, and Ross had to overcome serious issues of temperament among his dream line-up of Gertie Gitana (his wife), together with Nellie Wallace, Hetty King and Talbot O'Farrell. The show opened at the Empress, Brixton, and toured widely. It was so successful that, following a two-week run at the Palladium, it formed part of the 1948 Royal Variety Show.

Other entrepreneurs, notably Freddie Butterworth and Harry Buxton, had begun to return some of their cinemas – predominantly in the provinces – to live entertainment from the mid-1930s. Butterworth was as significant a figure on the 'Number Two' variety circuit as Oswald Stoll and Edward Moss had been in more prestigious theatres. The 'Number Two' circuit may have been the second rank of music halls, but Norman Wisdom, Morecambe and Wise, and Frankie Howerd were among many future stars who honed their craft in Butterworth's theatres. On offer was a combination of traditional music hall, musical comedy, repertory theatre, nude revue and *tableaux vivants*. 'Wee Georgie Wood', a music hall and pantomime star, summed up Butterworth's achievement with 'gratitude for his keeping variety alive'.

Music hall had come full circle. Such was its short-term success that Moss Empires toured the show *The Good Old Days* to variety theatres around the country, and in 1953 the BBC began screening it. Broadcast from Leeds City Varieties, it ran each week for thirty-two years, with Leonard Sachs at the chairman's table. Built in 1865 as Thornton's Music Hall, and described in the *Era* as 'one of the handsomest and most commodious in the provinces', the City Varieties had kept faith with the music hall tradition while other theatres had succumbed to cinema. *The Good Old Days* was a pastiche of early music hall, with songs and sketches characteristic of the era. The audience, dressed in period costume, became a part of the show, but there was no drinking or heckling, and any innuendo was sanitised: it was a far cry from the raucous days of Thornton's, ninety years earlier. But it did capture the rapport between artiste and audience, especially in the rousing singalong moments made famous by the show's weekly closing chorus of 'Down at the Old Bull and Bush'. Many celebrated names appeared both there and at the Players' Theatre, including Roy Hudd, Arthur Askey, Tessie O'Shea, Roy Castle, Les Dawson, Larry Grayson and Bernard Cribbins.

Throughout the 1950s and '60s, retailers – mostly the acquisitive new supermarkets – coveted music hall locations, and many ended their lives under the wrecking ball of the developer. By then the halls were largely obsolete. The onset of rock and roll offered a brief respite for managers looking to keep their doors open, but there were too few Tommy Steeles and Cliff Richards to fill the halls. Even worse, the flood of teenagers made the halls less family-friendly, as, in a different fashion, did Paul Raymond's nude revues. In 1932 Vivian van Damm had created *Revudeville* at the Windmill Theatre, off Shaftesbury Avenue, with singers, dancers, showgirls and speciality numbers. But it only became a commercial success when he introduced nude *tableaux vivants*. Inspired by the success of the Windmill, Paul Raymond (himself a failed variety performer) called his shows 'revues' and opened his flagship, Raymond's Revuebar, in Soho in 1951. The idea was copied by managers across the country, and a flurry of similar shows resulted. Apart from more and more nudity, much of the fare on offer was pure music hall, featuring speciality acts, comedians, dancers and a few sketches.

There was no theme to the programme, just a succession of acts leading up to a finale. Fifty years previously the bill at the same hall would have been of much higher quality, and the finale might have been a Dan Leno, Marie Lloyd or George Robey. Now the entertainment had reverted to the *poses plastiques* of the mid-nineteenth century, but without the flesh-coloured covering.

Much later, in 1962, the writer and broadcaster Daniel Farson leased the derelict Waterman's Arms in the Isle of Dogs, to run it as a music hall–pub. He decorated it with theatre bills, song sheets and other evocative memorabilia, and salvaged architectural *objets* from the demolition of the Metropolitan in Edgware Road. The Waterman's Arms, in all its restored glory, featured in a programme Farson made for television about pub entertainment in London, *Time Gentlemen Please*, and it was so successful in recreating the old music hall magic that it inspired a series for Independent Television – *Stars and Garters*. People came in droves to the Waterman's Arms, including eminent stars such as Claudette Colbert, Groucho Marx, Tony Bennett and Sarah Vaughan; but its success was artistic, not commercial, and the show made no money. Its life was short. The final curtain came down in 1964, with one of the world's most iconic stars, Judy Garland, singing 'Come Rain or Shine' to the accompaniment of the pub piano.

Another throwback to classic music hall was the fashion for 'Continental' style halls. Apparently invented in 1958 by Harold Clark, the owner of the Palace Theatre, Hull, the idea was for a 'theatre restaurant' which he called the Continental Palace. The idea was successful for a period, and was copied by the Hippodrome in London, renamed the Talk of the Town. Though most of these did not last, the Talk of the Town survived until 1982. In the north, however, the 'Continental' gave rise to the 'club' circuits so beloved of a new generation of performers. This was music hall coming home. In varying levels of luxury the northern clubs, and the more sophisticated Talk of the Town, offered a varied bill of family entertainment where people could eat and drink in comfort. Charles Morton, or the patrons of Evans' Late Joy's, the Coal Hole, the Canterbury or the Tivoli, would have felt very much at home in them.

Even as music hall was dying, the halls still managed to create new stars who became successful by mastering an entertainment scene now dominated by recorded music, cinema, radio and television. Artistes such as Gracie Fields, Max Miller, George Formby Jr, the Crazy Gang (which featured stars Flanagan and Allen and 'Monsewer' Eddie Gray), Tommy Trinder, Max Wall and Vera Lynn all came straight out of the music hall tradition, but were able to tailor their act for new formats and successfully hold their audiences – just as Lloyd and Leno had done so long before them.

Max Miller, 'the Cheeky Chappie', was typical of this crossover. His act was pure music hall, but he enjoyed massive success not only onstage but as a recording artist and actor. His intimate rapport with the audience, including his exasperated mock appeals to them to behave decorously in the face of his lewd innuendo, were straight out of the halls. Just like Robey and Leno, he would wait in the wings for several seconds after his cue, approach the centre of the stage and simply stand there, allowing the audience simply to laugh at his presence. His garish suits and jaunty hats made him both instantly recognisable and highly visible in a huge auditorium. Most importantly for his recording career, the 'smile' in his voice carried across onto disc: many British households in the 1940s and '50s would have had one or more Max Miller records.

Later performers would follow. Norman Wisdom, Frankie Howerd, Ken Dodd, Shirley Bassey and Bruce Forsyth are perfect examples of the reinvented music hall tradition. Just like Miller, they all embraced new formats, but used techniques with live audiences that would be entirely familiar to Dan Leno, George Robey, Marie Lloyd or Bessie Bellwood. Howerd's self-deprecation, his exaggerated language and open-ended denials – 'Titter ye not!' and 'No, Missus. Don't. You'll get me into trouble' – are pure Robey. Ken Dodd 'works' his audience, addressing hypothetical individuals and explaining parts of the joke to any section that doesn't respond to his routine – pure Leno. The suggestive lyrics and sassy self-confidence of Shirley Bassey's 2006 hit 'Let's Get the Party Started', with lines like 'I can go for miles, if you know what I mean,' would be familiar to anyone who had heard Marie Lloyd or Bessie Bellwood. Even on a Saturday night in 2012, Bruce Forsyth will intimately confer with a studio audience of several hundred, and a television audience of fifteen million, and enchant them all with terrible jokes. It is stagecraft learned over decades of performing in front of an audience, and a talent the old-time stars would have completely understood.

In writing this book, I have come to realise why my parents had such an enduring love of music hall. For, whatever the deprivations – and for those who were not top of the bill there was often serious deprivation – it was a world full of life, with each performance a kaleidoscope of colour and contradiction: the beautiful and the bizarre; the glamorous and the grotesque; the romantic and the raffish; the comedic and the crude.

Whether artistes achieved the great heights and wealth of Marie Lloyd, Vesta Tilley, Dan Leno and Harry Lauder, or simply bobbed along at the bottom of the bill, they all loved to perform – and the audiences loved them for it. They were masters of their craft who, with a nod and a wink, could make an innocent word seem salacious; with a shrug or a glance could tell a life story; and with a physical or emotional stumble could take a humdrum song to the heights of artistic flight. 'A little of what you fancy does you good,' sang Marie Lloyd – and so it did, for nearly a hundred years.

I have also learned so much more about my parents' earlier life, and that of Kitty. Their peripatetic existence; the hardships they endured; the friends they made – and kept; their passion for performing; and the sheer exhilaration they experienced when their words or acts made audiences laugh or cry. They may well not have been rich in any material sense, but as lovers of life they were richer than most.

In 1913 and 1915 my father and Kitty topped the bill at the Leeds City Varieties with their sketch 'After the Overture'. That theatre has now been beautifully restored, yet behind the plush red velvet curtains the ghosts from music hall's past still linger, their spirits still alive, indomitable, full of hope – and of dreams that have yet to be realised.

That is why, as my father's life drew to a close that early spring day in 1962, I was so sure of where he wished to be. The ball was over, but his old friends were waiting in the wings to greet him as the song in his heart led on to a new dawn:

> After the ball is over
> After the break of morn
> After the dancers' leaving
> After the stars are gone
> Many a heart is aching
> If you could read them all
> Many the hopes that have vanished
> After the ball.

Index of Songs

General Index

Vivian, Charles, 166
Voltaire, 7, 29

Wagner, Richard, 322
Wakes Weeks, 236
Wall, Harry, 98
Wall, Max, 208, 336
Wallace, Nellie, 8, 157, 206, 210, 299, 333
Walmisley, Miss, 65
Ward, Tom, 135
Ware, George, 118, 181, 197, 242
Warner & Co., 197
Warren, Edmund, 19
Washington Music Hall, Battersea, 110
water spouters, 223–4
Waterloo, Battle of, 16
Waterman's Arms, the, 335
Webb, George, & Co., 197
Wedmore, Frederick, 244
Weldon, Thomas, 41
Wellington, Duke of, 16, 36
Wells, Charles, 80
Wells, Joe, 25, 31
Wesner, Ella, 166, 168
West, Mae, 283
Westgate, Sam, 220–1
Westminster Abbey, 38
Weston, Edward, 63–4
Weston's Music Hall, 64–5, 70
'wet money', 37
Whales Pleasure Gardens, 14
Whistler, James McNeill, 240

White Conduit House, 15
Wilde, Oscar, 240, 261, 310
William IV, King, 38
William and Walker, 281
Williams, Bransby, 198, 206, 211–12, 283–4, 319, 323
Williams, Fred, 65
Wilmot, Bertha, 332
Wilson, Woodrow, 162
Wilson and Montague's Minstrels, 181
Wilton, John, 69
Wilton's Music Hall, 69–70
Windmill Theatre, 335
Windsor, Duke of, 162
'wines and spirits', 203
Wisdom, Norman, 337
Wolverhampton, 196, 298
Wood, Wee Georgie, 334
Wood, Sir Henry, 200
Wood, Hickory, 137
Woolf, Virginia, 131
Wordsworth, William, 17
Wright, Sarah ('Wiry Sal'), 222–3
Wyndham, Sir Charles, 310

Yeats, W.B., 251
Yorkshire Stingo, the, 38, 44
Youdan, Thomas, 66

Zaeo and Lulu, 152
Zig Zag, 156
Zukor, Adolf, 282